53 265

D1093328

INTERIORS OF EMPIRE

MANCHESTER
1824

Manchester University Press

STUDIES IN DESIGN

GENERAL EDITOR:
Christopher Breward

FOUNDING EDITOR:
Paul Greenhalgh

also available in the series

Interiors of empire

OBJECTS, SPACE AND IDENTITY
WITHIN THE
INDIAN SUBCONTINENT,
c. 1800–1947

Robin D. Jones

Manchester University Press

Manchester and New York

distributed exclusively in the USA by Palgrave

Copyright © Robin D. Jones 2007

The right of Robin D. Jones to be identified as the author of this work has been asserted by him in accordance with the Copyright, Designs and Patents Act 1988.

Published by Manchester University Press
Oxford Road, Manchester M13 9NR, UK
and Room 400, 175 Fifth Avenue, New York, NY 10010, USA

www.manchesteruniversitypress.co.uk

Distributed exclusively in the USA by
Palgrave, 175 Fifth Avenue, New York, NY 10010, USA

Distributed exclusively in Canada by
UBC Press, University of British Columbia, 2029 West Mall, Vancouver, BC, Canada V6T 1Z2

British Library Cataloguing-in-Publication Data
A catalogue record for this book is available from the British Library

Library of Congress Cataloging-in-Publication Data applied for

ISBN   978 0 7190 6942 0 *hardback*

First published 2007

16 15 14 13 12 11 10 09 08 07   10 9 8 7 6 5 4 3 2 1

Typeset
by Carnegie Book Production, Lancaster
Printed in Great Britain
by Antony Rowe Ltd, Chippenham, Wiltshire

For Alison and for my mother and brother,
and in memory of my father,
Douglas Arthur Jones

Contents

Figures

Acknowledgements

I acknowledge with thanks the assistance, advice or support of the following in the research and writing of this book: Mala Weerasekera; Ismeth Raheem; Kumari and Lal Jayawardena; Professor Kingsley de Silva; Mohan Daniels; Professor Pat Kirkham; Anne Massey; Sarah Sherrill; Anisha Bhandary; Penny Bingham; Paddy Bowring; Adam Hardy; Maurice Owen; Sarah Hand; Peter O'Keefe; Sue Malvern, staff and students in the MA research seminar, Art History Department, University of Reading; Marius Kwint; staff and students in the MA research seminar, Department of History of Arts and Visual Studies, University of Oxford; Gretchen Buggeln and participants at the conference 'Rethinking the Decorative Arts', Winterthur Museum, Garden and Library, Delaware, USA. I also wish to thank the anonymous reviewers of the typescript of this book for their incisive and constructive comments. Many thanks also to Alison Welsby and staff at Manchester University Press for their professionalism, guidance and support.

I would also like to express my thanks to the many librarians and archivists who have assisted with this work, including: Jennifer Howes, Helen George and the staff of the Oriental and India Office Collections at the British Library, London; Kevin Greenbank and staff of the Centre of South Asian Studies, University of Cambridge; staff in the Bodleian Library, Oxford, including the Indian Institute Library; Jenny Grant; Andy Forbes; Kerry Martin; Richard Lee and staff in the Mountbatten Library, Southampton Solent University.

I acknowledge with thanks the financial assistance received from: the Society for South Asian Studies (the British Academy); the Tom Ingram Memorial Fund; the Nehru Trust for the Indian Collections at the Victoria and Albert Museum; the British Academy (Overseas Conference Travel Grant); the Centre for Advanced Scholarship in Art and Design, Southampton Solent University.

Chapter 3 is an edited and much expanded version of a paper first published in *South Asian Studies*, 20 (2004). The author is grateful to the Editor of this journal for permission to reproduce this material.

The author and publishers would like to thank the following for permission to use the illustrations: University of Oxford, Bodleian Library, figures 4, 11 and 27; London, British Library, figures 2, 3, 7, 8, 9, 10, 19, 25, 28, 33 and

36; London, National Archives, figure 5; University of Cambridge, Centre of South Asian Studies, figures 13 and 16; the Syndics of Cambridge University Library, figure 21; the Indian Institute of Architects, Mumbai and House of Fraser, London, figures 17 and 18; National Army Museum, London, figure 23.

Quotation from Hari Kunzru, *The Impressionist*, reproduced by permission of Penguin Books Ltd.

Glossary

Almirah	Wardrobe or cupboard
Anglo-Indian	Before the 1911 census, any British person in India; after 1911, any person of mixed Indian and British origin
Argand lamp	Oil lamp with tubular wick, more efficient burn and therefore brighter light, invented by Swiss Ami Argand
Babu/baboo	Polite local form of address for a man; later, a derogatory term, used by British, for a Bengali man, who had some English education
Bamtee	Cup
Banku/bankuva	Ceylonese term for low seat or stool
Black town	British designation of part of Indian town inhabited mostly by local population
Burgher	Inhabitant of Ceylon of local and Dutch parentage
Cambay/comboy	Long, wrapped cloth of white calico used as a skirt
Chabootara	Raised platform along street frontage of local, urban house
Chadar/chudder/ chaudur	Large sheet worn as a shawl or head-covering by Indian women
Chajja	Overhanging canopy or eave
Chambers	Accommodation in a club for long-term residents or transient visitors
Charpoy	Light-weight Indian bedstead
Chowk	Open space or courtyard within the centre of the plan of local house
Chunam	Prepared lime used as finishing surface for walls
Cobees	Popular local ballads

Collector	Chief British official of a district
Dak bungalow	House for travellers
Dalaan	Main social space within local house
Dane	Almsgiving
Divan	Smoking room
Divankhanu	Upper chamber adjoining street frontage in local house and used for the reception of guests
Dubash	Local factotum or agent in Madras; one who speaks two languages
Dungaree	Coarse local calico
Dupia	Bottle box
Factory	European merchant company's foreign trading station, equipped with warehousing and living accommodation
Gali	Lane or narrow street in local part of town or city
Godown	Store-room, warehouse
Goyigama	Traditional, hereditary landowning local elite in Ceylon
Half-door	Cloth-covered or louvred wooden screen drawn across open interior doorway to allow for some privacy
Haveli	Substantial local house, the plan of which is centred on a courtyard, usually located within an urban setting
Hookah	Indian smoking-pipe with flexible tube and water-filled vase
Jaggery	Coarse palm sugar
Jattras	Traditional local representations or stories
Jauntee	Nutcracker
Jharockha/jharoka	Balcony
Karava	Descendants of Kauravar race of South India, supposedly of Kshatriya stock, inhabiting Southern coastal regions of Ceylon
Khadki	Room adjoining street in local house
Khitmagar/ Kitmutgar/ Khidmatgar	Chief servant, butler or head waiter
Kincob	Brocaded silk with gold or silver thread
KusKus	Fragrant grass used in the manufacture of **tats/tatties**

Maidan	Anglo-Indian term for open space in a town; parade ground
Mal lalla	Ceylonese term for floral fretwork panel
Moderne	Style of architecture and interior decoration influenced by the Paris international exhibition of 1925
Mofussil	Rural localities as opposed to main settlements
Moracka/muraqqa	Indo-Islamic album of drawings with richly decorated borders
Morah	Indian reed or cane stool of waisted, cylindrical form
Mudaliyar	Chief headman of district in British-controlled Ceylon
Ordos	Room or rooms set away from the street front in local house
Otlo	Verandah around courtyard to the centre of local house
Parsal	Room or space located in close proximity to central courtyard in local house
Parsi/Parsee	Member of Zoroastrian sect originally from Persia; significant merchant class in Bombay
Pettah	Locally inhabited part of town situated adjacent to but separate from the European fort
Pila	Built-in platform at front of local Ceylonese house for sitting or sleeping
Pirit	Chanting of a Buddhist sacred text to ward off evil spirits
Pucka	Substantial, permanent; Anglo-Indian term indicating masonry or brick-built
Punkah	Rectangular, cloth-framed swinging fan suspended from ceiling
Purali	Seat
Purdah	Curtain fixed over doorway to allow privacy but not impede draughts of air; state of segregation of women within local house
Pyjamah	Loose silk or cotton trousers tied around the waist
Rakaub	Plate
Rukada	Ceylonese puppet show
Rumal/roomaul	Literally, handkerchief; fine local cloth made in a single loom length

Satringhee/ settringhee/ suttrenjee	Light-weight, flat-woven local carpet
Station	European civil and or military settlement in India
Stoepe	Dutch term for verandah
Tamasha	Reception or celebration
Tats/tatties	Flexible blinds made from **kuskus** or fragrant grass, which, when wetted, cooled and perfumed the interior
Taubiz	Bracelet
Teapoy	Occasional table or stand, usually with central support and three legs
Thermantidote	Mechanical device to generate a breeze within the domestic interior
Tucktapore/ tucktaposh	Raised platform for sitting or sleeping in local house
Venetians	Shutters or doors fitted with louvred slats, usually painted green
Wall shade	Glass wall-mounted candle arm(s) with glass shades
Zamindar	Landowner
Zenana	Space set aside for women in Muslim house

Introduction

T HE colonial domestic interior within India and Ceylon (Sri Lanka) sometimes amused, or amazed, but more frequently dismayed contemporary commentators. British domestic spaces within the Indian Subcontinent were represented in numerous accounts as odd, uncomfortable, barn-like environments, furnished with a motley collection of, often, second-hand furniture and lacking the basic niceties of homes within Britain, such as patterned curtains, wallpaper and softening textiles. In 1872, Edward Braddon wrote of the Anglo-Indian domestic interior:

> no costly papering drapes the walls; rarely is there any pretension to decorative effect; rich mouldings, cornices, beadings & c. are conspicuous by their absence; and very seldom does the upholsterer do more for these Eastern interiors than supply the simple furniture which is indispensable … as to any one particular item of furniture harmonizing with any other, there is rarely any thought given.[1]

In 1904, Herbert Compton asserted that

> The Anglo-Indian's bungalow is as different from an English house in its external appearance and internal arrangement as a temple from a church … the doors are ill-fitting and clumsy, the windows small and often unable to open … [and] every room has direct access to a verandah.[2]

He continued by complaining about the inconvenience of the bungalow's multiple door openings, the lack of internal passageways, the 'solid, ugly' furniture and absence of curtains or blinds. In this peculiar and unsettling environment, inclusion of comforting connections to the homeland was an important aspect of the colonists' attempt to feel 'at home' in the empire. In this regard, Compton recommended the inclusion of photographs of family and the landscapes of England – 'it is the link with home'. Slightly more problematic to acquire and maintain, but located nonetheless in a surprisingly large number of Anglo-Indian interiors, was the piano which apparently brought one 'face to face with Western civilization'.

If British homes within the Indian Subcontinent during the colonial era were characterized as peculiar and disconcerting environments, then so also were the homes of the local elite. Numerous contemporary accounts highlighted the unusual and noteworthy manner in which Western ways had been partially and, from a Western perspective, idiosyncratically absorbed into the local domestic sphere. For example, in 1850, Henry Moses described the house of a local notable, Sir Jamsetjee Jeejeebhoy, in Rampart Row, Bombay. The interiors of this imposing dwelling reflected the owner's non-local trading contacts in an almost literal manner. Moses began by describing the hall with its polished *chunam* or prepared lime floor, the walls 'hung around with portraits of some celebrated Mandarins ... by Chinese artists'. He continued:

> The first room [on the first floor] which we entered was one fitted up in English style, all the furniture having been manufactured in London. The walls were richly coloured (no paper). Here were portraits of some branches of Sir Jamsetjee's family, painted in oil by an artist, who had come out to Bombay on speculation. The second drawing room, as we were informed, was furnished in the French style and if lofty pier glasses, statuary, vases of artificial flowers, musical clocks, elegant chandeliers, marble brackets with groups of alabaster figures on them, Bohemian glass, gilt couches and chairs are in good favour with our Continental friends, this room afforded no doubt of a good specimen of their domestic decoration. The next and most interesting apartment to us was the Chinese drawing room. We were delighted with everything we saw, as it contained so many beautiful articles brought from China. The whole of the furniture appeared to be made out of papier-mache, ivory and mother o' pearl ... lounging chairs, sofas and queer little couches were distributed about in great profusion.[3]

This book both describes and explains such interiors. It discusses how, during the nineteenth and early twentieth centuries, the European home within the Indian Subcontinent was represented in contemporary discourse as a significant space intended both to constitute and to express the culture of an imperial power. This work also examines why this intention was seldom realized in actuality and discusses the effect of the gap between representation and reality on the usual relationship which white, middle-class Britons experienced with regard to the contents of their homes in the West. Creation of a familiar 'home culture' within the Subcontinent, and the place of domestic objects in self-fashioning and the affirmation of identity, it is argued here, were problematized by a range of local factors. In addition, this work discusses the effect of increasing Anglicization within the local middle-class home, how members of this group negotiated this process and its place within the formation of colonial culture. Finally, the significance of colonial public space beyond the home within object–subject relations will also be examined.

A number of contemporary commentators highlighted the changes that were occurring within the domestic sphere in India as a result of over a century of colonial contact. In 1884, Charles Buckland wrote that 'over the whole length and breadth of India there is now a large and growing colony of English families, who endeavour to maintain their old home feelings and to keep all those old surroundings, which remind them of the land of their birth'.[4] However, this attempt to 'maintain their old home feelings' was unsettled by the local domestic environment; as a later commentator noted 'the Indian house, in construction and in every possible arrangement, is an entirely different thing from anything to which we are accustomed here at home [i.e. in England]'.[5]

The homes of the local middle class were also recorded as sites where related changes were taking place, caused by prolonged colonial contact. In 1880, Sir George Birdwood opined that 'the wealthy native gentlemen have their houses furnished in European style, but only the reception rooms, from which they themselves live quite apart'.[6] Furthermore, the life-style, in a broader sense, of the local elite also underwent a number of changes during the colonial period. Both home life and cultural life beyond the home reflected the penetration of Westernized social practices and cultural activities into the daily lives of this elite. In 1881, Shib Chunder Bose recorded this relatively new phenomenon when he observed 'thus we see in almost every phase of life at home or outside, the Bengalee Baboo [Hindu gentleman] is Europeanized'.[7]

The first two quotations above bring into focus the tensions and contradictions that existed in the domestic lives of many Britons who were resident in India and Ceylon during the nineteenth and early twentieth centuries. There was a desire or intention among the British in the Subcontinent to recreate Western home life, but this was continually undermined by local conditions and local practices. The last two quotations above indicate that the everyday domestic arrangements of the local social elite within the Subcontinent were also inflected by colonial contact.

Published advice concerning the creation and maintenance of a home in India was widely available to British residents. The majority of nineteenth-century household-management advice literature, written specifically for the British within the Subcontinent, discussed a range of stratagems for survival in the tropical climate of South Asia; in addition to this vital intelligence, advice was also offered on how to organize the interior of the bungalow, house or flat, how to furnish it and how best to run it as a functioning living space (without recourse to the usual paraphernalia of an English 'home'), in ways that addressed both the physical, as well as the psychological, needs of the inhabitants. However, although by the early decades of the nineteenth century the domestic sphere and domesticity in the West had become concepts central to social self-creation, for the British, being 'at home' in the colonies was a more problematic proposition. In fact, attempts to establish a colonial domesticity challenged expression of that very awareness of individual interiority which had developed in the West since the late eighteenth century.[8]

This book discusses the development and significance of imperial domesticity, in relation both to British middle-class residents within the Subcontinent and to socially elevated but middling sections of the local population, between 1800 and 1947.[9] In this work, the role played by private domestic environments and more public interiors of empire will be assessed in relation to the formation of individual and group identity and a number of questions are posed: How did the British conceptualize home within India and Ceylon? What role did home play in the affirmation of individual and group identity (national and cultural)? How was the Western concept of home reconfigured within the Subcontinent and adapted to the different circumstances, physical, social and cultural, of South Asia? In addition, in what ways did members of the local population adapt their domestic arrangements and life-styles to the colonial context? Finally, what part did the Anglicization of local elite domestic interiors play in the constitution of colonial culture?

In this book will be described and explained a number of previously illustrated, but little discussed, types of colonial interior space found throughout India and Ceylon (Sri Lanka) – both domestic and public – during the long nineteenth century, and there will be an assessment of the significance of such spaces in the construction of cultural identity within the Subcontinent. Since the 1980s, there has been increasing academic interest in cultural relations between Britain and its former colonial possessions in South Asia. This broad field of study has been examined from a wide variety of perspectives, using a range of different approaches, including post-colonial discourse theory;[10] the anthropology of colonialism or 'colonialism's culture';[11] the study of imperialism as a cultural phenomenon in relation to popular culture, the natural world and medicine;[12] analysis of the social production of the colonial built environment;[13] and decorative-arts history studies of artefacts produced in South Asia under European patronage.[14]

Much has also been written about local traditions of architecture within the Subcontinent, both secular and religious, as well as those structures built by the British.[15] However, these texts invariably discuss the exterior of built structures in terms of their form, style, iconography, materials and symbolic meaning. Core interior spaces of the colonial era where colonial culture was constituted – interiors of empire, both domestic and public, within the bungalow, upper-roomed house, club, hotel and department store, together with their furnishings – have only been treated briefly in the literature or have been discussed using a limited range of sources. To date, there has been no book-length, scholarly assessment which addresses the significance of these interiors (and their fixtures and furnishings), how they may have functioned within the globalizing reach of empire, their role in the development of a colonial culture and as the locus for countless private, domestic negotiations between Britain and India. On the few occasions when such interiors have been discussed as part of a broader work, they have often been described rather than analyzed or have been adopted, in a passive sense, to illustrate a particular point about the quaint or idiosyncratic life-styles of Europeans resident in South Asia. This work will offer a new approach to the study of colonial interior spaces and objects in South Asia during transition from the era of the East India Company to the high Raj and Indian Independence.

Brief definitions are necessary of three terms that will be used in this book. First, despite having another meaning, the term 'Anglo-Indian' will refer here to British nationals resident in India.[16] Secondly, although the term 'bungalow' will be used throughout this work, it is not intended to imply that Britons in India inhabited only single-storey dwellings with capacious, hipped-roofs, the main elevation of which was fronted by a verandah, the whole structure set within spacious grounds (see figure 1).[17] Within metropolitan centres of the Subcontinent, as well as in bungalows they lived in a range of buildings including garden houses, lower-roomed houses, upper-roomed houses, club chambers, hotels and, from the 1920s, flats or apartments.

Thirdly, a central concept addressed within this work is that of domesticity. John Tosh has offered a plausible and nuanced definition of this concept within Victorian Britain as an 'essentially … nineteenth century invention' which 'denotes not just a pattern of residence or a web of obligations, but a profound attachment: a state of mind as well as a physical orientation. Its defining attributes are privacy and comfort, separation from the work place and the merging of domestic space and family members into a single commanding concept (in English "home")'.[18]

Much information regarding material aspects of the domestic interior in British India and Ceylon has already been published. What, then, does the present work contribute to the subject? First, it draws together previous discussion of such space found within a range of literatures. In addition, this book builds on previous work which discusses the cultural impact of colonialism on both the colonizers and colonized by taking as its focus the domestic sphere and public space within the Subcontinent. However, while acknowledging key approaches deployed within the cultural analysis of colonialism, the present work also adopts methods from design history

1 A typical Anglo-Indian bungalow and typical Anglo-Indian poses. 'Magai Bungalow, Terhoot' [Champaran district, N. India] *c.* 1880.

and material culture to investigate this phenomenon. It assesses the spaces, furnishings and social practices of the colonial bungalow, club and hotel as forms of cultural history. Definitions of the term 'culture' have altered since the 1960s, and a number of scholars have charted this change.[19] Prior to this period, the term had been applied to the visual arts, literature, philosophy and music, or to distinct ways of life. Influenced by the writings of cultural anthropologists, the idea of 'patterns of culture' evolved and the concept of culture widened to encompass shared meanings informing the practices of everyday life.

A further definition of culture developed within the field of cultural studies, with particular emphasis being placed on the significance of meaning to the definition of culture. As the historian Catherine Hall has suggested 'culture is [now] associated primarily with the production and exchange of meanings, how we make sense of the world. But it is not simply about ideas in the head, it is also about how those ideas organize and regulate social and institutional worlds'.[20] A key concept within post-colonial studies is representation, or the process of putting into concrete forms an abstract ideological concept.[21] Within a large part of the academy, language has been privileged as the means by which meaning is constructed, and language operates through representation. Language uses signs and symbols to stand for concepts in ways that allow others to interpret them.[22] Semiotics or semiology – the study of the social production of meaning from sign systems – has been an important mode of analysis deployed within cultural studies. Language has also been central to the work of theorists such as Michel Foucault and to his understanding of discourse and discursive formations. Gillian Rose has defined discourse as 'groups of statements which structure the way a thing is thought and the way we act on the basis of that thinking'.[23] Although building on the methods of linguistics, as Stuart Hall notes, Foucault's work was 'more historically grounded, more attentive to historical specificities, than the semiotic approach', although despite this historicization and the widespread influence of his publications, his work has still been criticized from a number of viewpoints.[24]

Many recent studies of colonialism as a cultural phenomenon have deployed the concept of discourse or discursive practices as a central mode of enquiry.[25] While the present work acknowledges the significance of this approach and the insights such an analysis offers, it also uses research methods and approaches from design history and material culture with the intention of producing a more finely grained and historically grounded analysis. By deploying these methods this book aims to investigate the role of colonial artefacts and space in self-affirmation and the construction of national and cultural identity within the domestic and public spheres of the Subcontinent. The rationale behind the use of these methods has been to steer a course between the overarching and occasionally doctrinaire nature of post-colonial and other critical theory and the overly descriptive or anecdotal approaches found in some writing about artefacts and the domestic interior.[26] The combination of these methods is intended to problematize interpretation of the domestic and other interiors of the British and local middle class within the Subcontinent. Thus the present work is cross-disciplinary in nature and sets discussion of colonial interior space within a conceptual framework informed by a range of discipline areas, including material culture, design history, furniture history, architectural history and consumption studies.

A concept which has influenced the development of the theoretical framework underpinning this book is that of embodiment. Judy Attfield has discussed embodiment as 'how culture is incorporated into the body, to become naturalized in the form of taste, demeanor and appearance'.[27] As she notes, Pierre Bourdieu's definition of embodiment as 'the unselfconscious discriminatory system that operates in the context of the everyday', describes it as forming part of the cultural practice – 'the habitus'.[28] Bourdieu has noted how embodiment is a deeply-rooted process within the habitus and how:

> nothing seems more ineffable, more incommunicable, more inimitable and, therefore, more precious, than the values given body ... by the transubstantiation achieved by the hidden persuasion of an implicit pedagogy, capable of instilling a whole cosmology ... a metaphysic, a political philosophy through injunctions as insignificant as 'stand up straight'.[29]

Bourdieu has also discussed how influential architectural space is in the process of embodiment as he notes 'property appropriates its owner, embodying itself in the form of a structure generating practices perfectly conforming with its logic and its demands'.[30]

In recent decades, artefacts have been discussed from a number of different perspectives. One influential and widely applied analytical framework deployed in the examination of objects derives from the study of language. The methods of linguistics applied in the study of artefacts emphasize the concepts of representation and signifying systems. A linguistic approach encourages interpretation of objects as if they were texts and characterizes both language and objects as 'communication systems' or 'system of signs'.[31] The study of objects using such methods has as its goal interpretation of encoded symbolic propositions presumed immanent within the objects themselves. This approach has been subjected to critique by scholars within the fields of design history and especially material culture. These scholars have taken issue, when linguistic methods are adopted, with the dematerialization of the object or reduction in significance of its physical properties and the consequent priority given to meaning over matter.[32]

Unlike those who have applied a semiotic approach to object analysis, scholars who deploy a material culture approach in the study of artefacts acknowledge the physicality of things and architectural structures. Daniel Miller has suggested that the significance of the object in the construction of culture may lie in its concrete material qualities.[33] In fact, he has argued that the physicality of the object acts as a bridge 'not only between the mental and physical worlds, but also between consciousness and the unconscious'.[34] A material-culture approach emphasizes how objects mediate the social process and cultural production, as well as providing frameworks to help us comprehend the context in which we are located.[35]

A key concept within the study of object–subject relations is objectification, which has been described as 'the process by which all expression, conscious or unconscious, social or individual, takes specific form. It is only through the giving of form that something can be conceived of'.[36] It has been suggested that human 'subjectivity is a contradictory mix of confirming and contending "identities"'.[37] Things have the function of stabilizing human life: individuals can retrieve or maintain their 'sameness' or identity by confronting their subjectivity against the objectivity of things and, for example, through the everyday use of domestic objects.[38] A material-culture approach to the study of objects self-evidently assesses material as culture, not simply because, for example in the present instance, domestic interiors in India and Ceylon during the nineteenth and early twentieth centuries were filled with a wide range of objects, but because those objects were 'an integral part of that process of objectification' by which Anglo-Indians and the local elite created themselves as discrete groups, with individual identities, social affiliations and lived everyday practices.[39] One significant theme within discussions about object–subject relations has been the role of memory.

Pierre Nora has written that 'memory takes root in the concrete, in spaces, gestures, images and objects'.[40] He characterizes a number of different types of memory, including, as he defines it, 'duty-memory'. Although not explicitly discussed in these terms, this description has applicability within the colonial context. The historical roots of the present-day phenomenon of globalization lie in the expansion of the British empire (as well as other European empires). The development of this power bloc played a significant role in promoting increasingly complex exchanges, relationships and interconnections between different territories, peoples and parts of the world. One result of this nascent globalization was that members of the colonial culture and the local elite experienced disruption of their own general cultural memories. In turn, as Nora suggests 'when memory is no longer everywhere, it will not be anywhere unless one takes responsibility to recapture it through individual means'.[41] A significant location where this recapturing of memory could take place was the domestic sphere. In fact, it has been suggested that furnished domestic space 'serves as a model of the psyche, a concrete personality and is the environment which the memory tends most powerfully to reconstruct'.[42]

The explanatory framework adopted in this study deploys the methods of design history and material culture to offer an interpretation of how and in what ways the British in South Asia, as well as the local social elite, made sense of their world through objects and the interior spaces of home as well as other parts of the colonial built environment – in fact, how these artefacts, spaces and the behaviour that they engendered objectified the social relations of the colonial period. Grant McCracken has argued for the significance of material culture within analysis of the symbolic or non-functional role of our surroundings. He suggests that 'material culture has a powerful and various instrumental function' and 'this instrumental ability, this capacity to serve in the construction of the self and the world, makes material culture indispensable to culture'.[43] The methods of material culture also offer a strategy for investigating the mediatory role of artefacts in the social process.[44] Such methods frame an enquiry as to how these objects (and their surroundings more generally) were appropriated (by the British and the local elite), transformed into the substance of everyday life thereby aiding the affirmation of individual identity and, more broadly, cultural production within colonial society.[45] It will be argued here that the artefacts and spaces discussed in this book had a significant but hitherto overlooked effect in these processes.

It is arguable that any assessment of interior spaces created during the European colonial period in South Asia necessarily builds upon related assessments of the domestic interior in Europe. In fact, a number of approaches have been taken to this subject, ranging from visual analyses of images as a primary source to quantitative assessments of selected house contents obtained from probate inventories. Due to the colonial bungalow's inclusion as a significant subject in a range of secondary sources, the following paragraphs review relevant literature at some length in order to more precisely situate the present research and differentiate it from previous scholarship.

Since the 1980s, discussion of domestic interiors in Britain and continental Europe in the modern period has owed much to the writings of Peter Thornton, formerly curator at the Victoria and Albert Museum, London. He has deployed historical images as a form of evidence and assessed these in order to make statements about the furnishings and arrangement of domestic interiors in previous eras.[46] One of Thornton's approaches to research into the decorative arts (which has been followed in a number of studies of the European domestic interior produced since the 1980s[47]) has been to visually assess images of interiors, ranging in date from the seventeenth to the early twentieth centuries. Such images have been treated as evidence and are 'read' for visual clues in terms of what they depict, as well as what they may symbolize in a particular historical period. In addition, images are used to corroborate (or cast new light on) other forms of evidence derived from documentary sources. This approach was adopted to reveal what Thornton described as a 'period eye'.

This approach relies on an informed knowledge and understanding of historical materials, techniques, forms and spatial arrangements that, in turn, are dependent on familiarity with archival sources. The main concerns of this technique have been to authenticate and accurately locate an image or feature within an image. These assessments have then been worked into a general interpretation of a larger group of interiors over a longer time-frame. While influential, there are some problems with Thornton's approach. For instance, his research is unintentionally skewed toward depictions of elite European domestic interiors, which have survived in the archive, first because the owners of these interiors had the wherewithal to commission representations of their homes, and secondly because they possessed a self-awareness of their place in the world as represented through their domestic material culture.

Other scholars, such as the historian Lorna Weatherill, have deployed a different form of historical evidence, probate inventories, to interpret the arrangement and contents of early modern European domestic space.[48] She adopts a quantitative approach to her data and has drawn conclusions about the material lives and consumption habits of selected groups within the population and the population more broadly. There are, however, problems with this approach. In adopting a quantitative approach to the interpretation of inventories, methods used to select the sample need to take account of biases in selection or survival.[49] In addition, other scholars have suggested that probate inventories can also be legitimately assessed using qualitative methods in order to 'gain an idea of how individuals organized their homes as mediations of prevailing ideals of the period'.[50]

Since the 1980s, research on the European domestic interior has adopted a variety of methods and assessed a range of primary material. One rich source used to analyze such interiors has been found in historical texts such as novels, diaries, journals and, in particular, household-management advice manuals. Whereas Peter Thornton looked back in his research as far as the seventeenth century, scholars who have assessed these textual sources have tended to concentrate on nineteenth-century British (and American) domestic interiors. Researchers working within a range of disciplines, including design history, literary criticism, gender studies and social history, have used these sources. Since the 1980s, scholarly assessment of the European domestic interior has focused on a number of themes, such as the cult of domesticity; the concept of separate spheres[51] (i.e. a notional segregation of home from the work-place); the subsequent qualification of this theory to the extent that, at the present time, there is an understanding of these two spaces existing in a symbiotic relationship; and, finally, study of the ways users of interior space develop rules for operating within this space.[52]

An American historian, Katherine Grier, has made a significant contribution to discussions about the domestic interior in the West in a catalogue for an exhibition held at the Strong Museum, Rochester, USA in 1988. In this work, she offers an analysis of the development of the parlour as a culturally significant interior space in North America during the nineteenth century. She discusses the adoption of a range of furnishings within this space and the polite forms of behaviour which, she argues, were engendered in such a setting. She also suggests 'a refinement of the notion of separate spheres' by discussing the seemingly opposed but linked concepts of culture and comfort within the domestic interior.[53] As she proposes, the home had to provide for 'family-centred private use, but also for the social obligations of the householder', hence the growing importance placed on the main living room or drawing room within the middle-class home.[54] This work was later issued as a book entitled *Culture and Comfort: parlor making and middle-class identity*.[55]

Grier and subsequent scholars have also argued that the home was imagined in nineteenth-century debates about domesticity as an influential space for the development of character and identity.[56] This approach has been pursued by a number of scholars and is exemplified in a collection of interdisciplinary essays edited by Inga Bryden and Janet Floyd.[57] More recently, Thad Logan, a lecturer in English and humanities, has followed similar lines of enquiry to those of Grier and has applied critical theory and object analysis to her assessment of a significant space within the nineteenth-century British domestic interior.[58] Logan sets out the objectives of her study 'as a contribution to work in various disciplines that centres on domestic experience, as a contextualizing of nineteenth century discourse on decoration and design, [and] as an intervention in studies of consumption and commodities'.[59]

A number of scholars associated with the material-culture courses at the University of London have also discussed the contemporary domestic interior, its furnishings and the social practices there engendered.[60] The literature reviewed so far deals exclusively with the domestic experience in Europe and America; what of the secondary literature relating to the domestic interior in South Asia during the colonial era?

One incisive, entertaining and far-ranging work which addresses some aspects of the colonial domestic sphere and the more public spaces of empire within the Subcontinent is Jan Morris's *Stones of Empire*, first published in 1983.[61] This book covers some of the ground addressed in the present work, with chapters entitled 'Domestic', 'Public' and 'Civic'. The Anglo-Indian domestic interior is addressed, as well as imperial public spaces, including hotels and cinemas. However, the range of the book curtailed all but a brief discussion of these spaces. There is a small but growing literature that addresses the interior spaces of empire, as well as the material culture of home and identity.[62] Much of this literature, produced between the 1930s and the 1980s, insofar as it relates to furniture and domestic life in India has been summarized and reviewed by Amin Jaffer, a curator at the Victoria and Albert Museum, London.[63] He suggests that previous literature in this area fails to relate interior spaces to Anglo-Indian furniture; nor does it, he contends, concern itself with analysis of such furniture. He discusses furnishings and the domestic interior within the Subcontinent as well as local consumption of Western-style furniture using a wide range of primary and secondary sources.

His approach is admirably thorough and rigorous, and sets new standards in the history of colonial artefacts. However, due to his curatorial role within a museum of applied arts, his research outputs are mainly object-centred (although he does address the domestic sphere in opening contextual essays). In addition, many of the items that are the focus of the study tend to be those rare and bespoke ones that have survived in museum collections (rather than the much larger number of mundane, everyday and often second-hand objects which circulated within the Subcontinent). Furthermore, his researches mostly concentrate on the objects and interiors of the British imperial and Indian princely elite (rather than those of lower down the social scale) and the main focus of his studies relates to the period 1750 to 1830, with less attention devoted to the remainder of the nineteenth and early twentieth centuries.[64] Other scholars, however, working within a range of disciplines including the sociology of the built environment, history, architectural history, the history of the body and cultural geography have produced more critically informed interpretations of the Anglo-Indian domestic interior that, significantly, extend into the late nineteenth and early twentieth centuries, the heyday of the Raj.

In any study of the built environment and domestic spaces of empire, the work of Anthony King requires consideration.[65] His research interests are located in the sociology of the built environment and the cultural use of space. Some of his research has focused on development of the bungalow as a form of housing in India and elsewhere. For example, he has discussed such concepts as the bungalow and its compound as 'a culturally constituted behavioural environment'. He has also analyzed factors in the use of colonial space both in and around this structure, and the role of the bungalow within more general patterns of colonial urbanization. His writings have contributed in a broad sense to an understanding of the built environment of colonial culture.

While he has made occasional forays into the interior spaces of the bungalow, for instance, offering a brief critical appraisal of the use of space on the verandah and within the drawing room, his main focus lies outside these zones.[66] Moreover, as a sociologist, he is concerned with the more generalized, institutional characteristics of society rather than with specific networks of relationships, which operated in interactive settings such as the drawing rooms, clubs and hotels of British India and Ceylon.[67] His work has also been critiqued by scholars working within the field of post-colonial studies, who have discussed the vulnerability of the imperial project and the manner in which, as Jane Jacobs has suggested, cultures of power continually regrouped, reinvented and reinscribed their authority against the 'challenge of anti-colonial formations and against their own internal instability'.[68] Jacobs has also noted that although King is aware of the culture of urbanization and its links to imperialism, his analysis is located within a 'world-system account of the history of globalizing capital'. She contends that world-system theories of urbanization are problematic analytic tools as they 'deactivate [colonial] space by seeing the [South Asian] city as the uncontested imposition of imperial territorial arrangements'.[69]

Since 1999, other scholars have dealt in more detail, and from a range of critically informed standpoints (particularly discourse analysis), with aspects of the Anglo-Indian domestic interior.[70] These works have highlighted a number of themes, including the merger of public and private spheres within the Anglo-Indian home; the structural arrangement of interior space and renegotiation of demarcations within the home; the hybrid nature of Anglo-Indian domestic culture; the lack of privacy and sparseness of furnishings; redefinition of the meaning of domestic material culture in the Anglo-Indian home; and discussion of the effect of the presence of Indian servants within the heart of the home. These factors, it has been variously argued, contributed to the problematic nature of home-making in India and the emergence of distinctive patterns of behaviour among the British in India as well as among the local social elite.

Most of the relevant literature to date briefly discusses the Anglo-Indian domestic interior, and hardly addresses the subject of furnishings within this space or the role of such spaces and the reproduction of Western forms of behaviour. In most cases, historical evidence is limited to the writings of contemporary commentators, either in the form of published household-advice manuals or diaries/journals. Little or no use has been made of other forms of historical evidence such as inventories, photographs (and other types of image), house plans, plans of the arrangement of furniture within interiors and extant examples of artefacts which were found in Anglo-Indian houses. Few works deal with the whole of the nineteenth and early twentieth centuries – either 1830 is the terminal date or studies commence in the 1880s.[71] The present study will assess a range of primary sources and examine a wider chronology, in order to allow for discussion of changes within the Indian domestic interior over time. The interior spaces of the middling sort will also be the main focus of this book, rather than those of the British or Indian elite. In addition, the broader date range allows for discussion of the Ceylonese domestic interior (the island became a British crown colony in 1804).

As noted above, recent literature which discusses the domestic interior within the Subcontinent has addressed a number of themes. There is a tendency in some works, for instance, to emphasize the role of the bungalow as an instrument of imperial control and to adopt an over-deterministic viewpoint with regard to interpretation of the open living plan of the Anglo-Indian dwelling. In fact, prior scholarship has 'read' in its structure an imperial design to rule by being seen, rather than being a considered response to the more practical imperatives of climate and the fact that such buildings were erected mostly by Indian craftsmen who had different frames of cultural reference to those of the British occupants.[72] In addition, analysis of household-management guides and advice manuals produced for an Anglo-Indian audience has been central to discussions in many recent secondary works. These nineteenth- and early twentieth-century publications have been trawled for quotations to support a range of views regarding the differentiated and idiosyncratic life-styles of Britons living in the Subcontinent and have been used to represent an abstract or idealized version of colonial domesticity within the public sphere.

However, little discussion of the limitations of or problems with this source has taken place in otherwise scholarly texts: no acknowledgement has been made, for example, of their limited date range (the majority date between 1880 and 1920), or their neglect of the role of men within the Indian domestic environment or their emphasis on very specific concerns such as the maintenance of health within the Anglo-Indian dwelling or keeping within a limited housekeeping budget in order to avoid financial embarrassment. Of most significance, however, is that little or no consideration has been given to the individual's negotiation of the ideals and mores promoted in these texts, nor the differences that existed according to social status and lived experience: the advice literature is presented as an over-arching narrative that explains the domestic behaviour of the majority of Britons living in the Subcontinent. In addition, discussion of non-domestic interior spaces of empire, such as clubs, hotels, shops or photographic studios, is scant. Furthermore, within the relevant literature few attempts have been made to problematize interpretation of the range of interiors within the Subcontinent during the nineteenth century or to explore the possible social and cultural meanings they conveyed.

The present work deploys a range of historical evidence to establish the physical aspects of domestic interiors in the Subcontinent created by the British, and assesses – within the limits of evidence and methods of analysis – how they mediated prevailing ideals to create individual interior spaces that suited their requirements.[73] This work will also discuss the domestic and more public interiors of the Subcontinent (both British and local) from 1800 to 1947 as significant sites in the affirmation of individual and group identity. It will be argued that, despite the best endeavours of British residents to maintain core aspects of the life-style of home, local factors intervened, disrupted this process and inflected their behaviour. In addition, the domestic interiors of socially elevated members of the local population became sites of negotiation between local traditional cultural forms and the production of Westernized life-styles.

For the British, these disruptions to the signifying and material practices of the homeland and the issue of colonial power relations with regard to the local population led to renegotiation of conventional meanings attached to domestic material culture within the Subcontinent. Material indicators of taste and social status that were familiar within middle-class drawing rooms of Britain (opulent furniture and rich textiles, refined ceramics, morally improving or patriotic paintings and prints) were only found in a limited number of British homes in India and Ceylon. In addition, within the British home in India, the gendering of space as well as responsibility for making a home was problematized. Although it has been argued that in Victorian Britain 'never before or since has domesticity been held to be so central to masculinity', it was women who were mostly responsible for the creation of the physical ambience and smooth running of the domestic sphere.[74] If men had become associated with the spiritual and public, then women embodied the material and private realms of home. Within India, however, due to the costs involved in renting, men often shared accommodation with other men; within this arrangement housekeeping and other domestic practices were gendered as masculine activities.[75] One form of male sharing of accommodation was the 'chummery', where two or more bachelors rented and shared domestic expenses; or several British male residents purchased property and lived as a group.[76] These types of domestic arrangement prevailed because the demographic profile of the British in India was also heavily weighted to the masculine.[77] For example, in 1903, Mrs Reynolds wrote that for a year she was the 'solitary lady' in the rural European settlement, where her husband was posted.[78] Although nineteenth-century household-advice manuals addressed a female audience, all British home-makers in India, both men and women, had little choice but to acknowledge, on the one hand, the redundancy of most domestic objects as meaning-bearers of status and prestige, and, on the other, attachment of exaggerated significance to the few traces of the homeland found within the domestic interior in India.

This disruption of the conventional meanings associated with domestic material culture caused the British in India, from the 1880s, to engage in exaggerated, metropolitan forms of behaviour to compensate for the absence of conventional 'markers' of home. This behaviour was intended to maintain bonds with other members of the Anglo-Indian community, but became fixed and unchanging over time and was perceived by their compatriots in the home country as anachronistic. British identity in India, after 1880, was reinforced through forms of behaviour that were less dependent on the physical surroundings of home and a notion of interiority and privacy that existed in the home country. Instead, great attention was paid on the Subcontinent to the ordering of servants and the processes of household management (numerous household-advice manuals exhorted their readers to this end) as well as maintenance of the family's health. Outdoor activities, such as field-sports, race meetings and 'camps' occupied much of the free time of the British in India. In addition, communal solidarity was enhanced by extended and repeated acts of hospitality, such as dinner parties or other forms of entertaining despite (or perhaps because of) the lack of paraphernalia of hospitality that would have been found in middle-class homes in Britain. The British within the Subcontinent assigned new meanings to home life, as the concept of the British home there was perceived as a space which was fragmented, hybrid and fraught with tensions.

In addition, modification of local elite domestic interiors within the Subcontinent was a visible but little discussed effect of the British presence. For example, furnishing choices of the majority of this group after 1850 encoded an alien value system and engendered Europeanized forms of social behaviour. In these local interiors, at least in reception rooms used for entertaining, colonial social relations were objectified. Furnishing in 'English style' allowed the local social elite to demonstrate their civility, taste and modernity, in addition to establishing common ground between them and the British. However, this process, whereby the core of the domestic interior was fitted out in a non-local manner, also created non-traditional and hybrid environments where alien cultural forms were socially produced.

Although many studies have been made of Indian art, design and architecture in the colonial period, few of these have made a comparison between practice in India and Ceylon (Sri Lanka), despite the geographic proximity and cultural similarities of the two countries. In the present work, domestic and public interiors within India and Ceylon between 1800 and 1947 will be discussed together in order to highlight differences and similarities, to localize practice and limit over-generalization. New material will be discussed for both of these regions and subjected to analysis, which is lacking in much of the literature. The main sources used in this book comprise the writings of contemporary commentators, including diaries and journals, published household-management advice manuals and medical-advice books, probate inventories, plans and elevations of domestic dwellings, advertisements, drawings and photographs, and furnishings.

A compelling reason for examining the domestic and public interiors of the Subcontinent during the nineteenth and early twentieth centuries lies in the growing British presence within the Subcontinent and, more specifically, changes that occurred to the British persona in India and Ceylon during this era. Elizabeth Collingham has argued that the Indianized British East

India Company nabob of the late eighteeenth century was transformed, during the next century, into the efficient, bureaucratic administrator of the high Raj.[79] In contrast, the British in Ceylon, during the first half of the nineteenth century and beyond, maintained a semblance of the life-style of home and rejected the more Indianized ways of their compatriots in the Presidency towns of India. A Europeanized material culture already existed on the island due to previous European colonizers, and the British in Ceylon initially worshipped in Dutch-built churches, lived in Dutch-built houses and slept in Dutch-style beds. Moreover, in the recent literature on Anglo-Indian interiors and furnishings, most emphasis has been placed on eighteenth-century rather than nineteenth-century material.[80] Previous studies of the interiors and furnishings of Ceylon have, similarly, been weighted to the period prior to the nineteenth century.

This book will concentrate on the period between 1800 and 1947 for several reasons. A time-span of a little over a century allows for examination of changes in the notion of domestic space (as well as physical aspects of this space) within India and Ceylon. This period witnessed expansion of British settlements within the Subcontinent and an increase in the number of women residing in both India and Ceylon. Different forms of private housing and public spaces for Europeans in South Asia evolved in this period, including the bungalow, the lower-roomed house, the flat, the club, the hotel, and the photographic studio and cinema – in fact, many of these interior spaces had not existed prior to 1800. The nineteenth century witnessed the expansion of a range of goods available to furnish the Anglo-Indian interior, as well as an explosion in the quantity of published advice offered to Europeans on how to survive in, as well as domesticate, the Subcontinent. In addition, during the late nineteenth century, the local social elite in the Subcontinent began to alter their consumption habits and adopt more Westernized life-styles, and their domestic interiors became important sites that both constituted and expressed this transformation. Little has been written previously on the evidence of private negotiations conducted by this group in their choices of consumer goods, how they should furnish their houses and reconcile the tensions between traditional material culture, social practices and the colonial culture.

When the domestic and public interiors of the Subcontinent have been considered at all, they have been examined as an aspect of a larger work. This will be the first book-length treatment of these spaces to draw together previous literature on the subject and offer an analysis of the construction of cultural meaning within these interiors. This more lengthy treatment will allow for a synthesis of previously published material on the interiors of empire. In addition, new evidence for the domestic and public spaces of

India and Ceylon, together with their contents, will also be described and explained.

Chapter 1 will provide a historical context to the domestic sphere and public space of the Subcontinent and discuss the secondary literature on the history of European settlement in India and Ceylon between 1780 and 1940. This chapter will assess the production of the colonial built environment insofar as it concerns domestic space, including the shift from densely populated and fortified urban settlements to scattered residential developments. New forms of housing will also be discussed, including the bungalow, the lower-roomed house, and, in the twentieth century, the flat. In addition, local environmental factors will be analysed in relation to the creation of domestic life within the Subcontinent. The physical surroundings in which the Anglo-Indian community lived continually challenged their sense of domesticity rooted in the home country.

Chapter 2 will discuss the anomalous status of British homes within the Subcontinent and the notion that, despite the endeavours of British residents to maintain elements of the life-style of home, the peripatetic existence necessitated by imperial bureaucracy and the permeation of Indian material culture into many aspects of the Anglo-Indian bungalow caused British residents in South Asia to regard their domestic interiors as troubling and hybrid spaces, which were neither entirely Western nor Asian. Assignment of new cultural meanings to the contents of the drawing rooms and halls of India and Ceylon also engendered new forms of behaviour, among the British as well as indigenous social elite. Issues which will be considered include the planning of interior spaces, the segregation of space within the home, the effect of local servants within the heart of the home and the reinscription of meaning onto the material culture of the domestic sphere.

These factors led to a modification of domestic arrangements and behaviour in the Subcontinent and caused the British in India to redefine their European domestic culture and mediate ideals expressed in contemporary household-advice literature. A central focus in this chapter will be analysis of the role of domestic and more public interiors of empire in the production of colonial culture and the formation of identity. How and in what ways did Europeans living in India deal with intrusions into their privacy by large numbers of local servants; the insinuation of public duties into the domestic interior to a greater extent than in Britain; lack of clear demarcation between male and female spaces within the home; and the phenomenon that the everyday things of the hall or drawing room signified (within Western terms) contradictory or incomplete cultural meanings?

Chapter 3 will discuss the Anglicization of local elite domestic interiors in the Subcontinent through contact with British practices. This process was a significant but previously overlooked aspect of British intervention in India and Ceylon. Cultural assimilation and the adoption of Western consumption habits by the local social elite will be examined in relation to their domestic interiors. The adoption of a 'middle course' by many of the local elite will be assessed in relation to their domestic arrangements whereby, in private, many of them followed traditional life-styles and cultural practices, as well as practicing a Westernized 'drawing-room culture'. The differences between the Indian middle class and that of Ceylon, in this regard, will be contrasted. Through their consumption of Western-style furnishings and their adoption of other non-local forms, the local elite allowed their cultural identity to be validated by British standards. Together with the adoption of Western apparel, manners and habits of consumption, the acquisition and use of Anglicized furnishings in the local domestic interior represented an influential aspect of the cultural apparatus of the West.

Westernization of the East Indian domestic interior, in terms of both furnishings and behaviour, was but one aspect of British intervention in the material culture of the Subcontinent. Chapter 4 discusses how public spaces beyond the home were also invested with meanings which were intended to reinforce a collective British identity and which became locations for the creation of a sense of national solidarity in the tropics. One of the most significant of these venues was the club. Public areas in the club replicated related spaces in the Anglo-Indian bungalow and provided spaces for the reinforcement of forms of behaviour that were specific to the British community. The club was also a site for a number of practices intended to soothe the Anglo-Indian persona and was an arena for the induction of new members into the folk-ways of this community. The local social elite also established their own versions of these, which, in the same way as the British, restricted membership to particular racial groups.

Hotels were also established in many of the larger colonial settlements. These were initially little more than large guest-houses and were the butt of adverse comment in terms of their levels of comfort and cleanliness. By the end of the nineteenth century, however, more palatial buildings had replaced these earlier hotels and became another venue for the reinforcement of colonial culture, including the rituals of socialization, such as dinner dances and the provision of spaces for the transaction of business. A number of hotels also incorporated shops which retailed both local and imported products, intended for both tourists and local inhabitants. In addition, photographic studios were also established in the Subcontinent by the middle of the nineteenth century. These studios included props in the form of chairs, davenports, desks and plant stands arranged in stylized room settings which were derived from the Western domestic interior. Both the British in India and members of the local social elite used these spaces for self-representation. Other public spaces of empire came into being during the late nineteenth and early twentieth centuries, including cinemas and department stores, and created locations where Western modernity could be experienced.

This work discusses the domestic sphere and public space of empire and their role in the construction of national and cultural identity within the Subcontinent. It has been argued elsewhere that the British in India were aware of their tenuous legitimacy as rulers and had to bolster that legitimacy through the maintenance of prestige and distance from the local population.[81] The domestic and public interiors of empire were significant locations where these aspects of British rule were played out. The domestic economy, climatic conditions and material culture of India and Ceylon, however, continually undermined British attempts to establish and maintain prestige and reinforce their cultural identity – local servants infiltrated the most private spaces of the Anglo-Indian bungalow, the tropical climate necessitated modification of European behaviour, and many of the domestic spaces of empire were impermanent or sparsely furnished by European standards.

Both the domestic and public interiors of empire evolved into hybrid spaces where the local social elite could demonstrate their taste and modernity; they were, in addition, intended as venues which constituted and expressed the colonial culture. Such interiors were influential locations where, it could be argued, the cultural apparatus of the West was paraded and where British cultural forms were socially produced. However, the concept of home for the British in India was, in actuality, fragmented, unstable and culturally porous. It was also far removed, both geographically and psychically, from the idea of home as a closed-off, secure and comfortable sanctuary which at least found currency in representations of domesticity in Britain during this period.[82]

Notes

1 Edward Braddon, *Life in India; a series of sketches showing something of the Anglo-Indian* (London, 1872), pp. 104 and 109.

2 H. Compton, *Indian Life in Town and Country* (London, 1904), pp. 157–60.

3 H. Moses, *Sketches of India; with notes on the seasons, scenery and society of Bombay, Elephanta and Salsette* (London, 1850), pp. 256–8.

4 C.T. Buckland, *Sketches of Social Life in India* (London, 1884), p. 2. In 1881, it was recorded that the European population of Bengal district comprised only 1.5% of the total population. See *Report on the Census of Bengal, 1881* (Calcutta, 1883), vol. 1.

5 W.H. Hart, *Everyday Life in Bengal and Other Indian Sketches* (London, 1906), p. 66.

6 G.C.M. Birdwood, *The Arts of India* (London, 1880), p. 199.

7 Shib Chunder Bose, *The Hindoos as They Are; a description of the manners, customs and*

inner life of Hindoo society in Bengal (London and Calcutta, 1881), p. 204.

8 J. Tosh, *A Man's Place: masculinity and the middle class home in Victorian England* (New Haven and London, 1999), p. 4.

9 This work examines the colonial material culture of white British middle-class residents within the Subcontinent. This group includes members of the Indian Civil Service, but also encompasses other Britons outside government service, such as planters, agency house partners, lawyers, bankers and merchants and is intended to distinguish these from the highest tiers of the imperial social scale. The local middle class comprised rural and urban landowners, merchants, factors, lawyers, *rentiers* and plantation owners (see Chapter 3 for a further definition of this group).

10 Homi K. Bhabha, 'The other question: difference, discrimination and the discourse of colonialism', in F. Barker et al. (eds), *The Politics of Theory* (Colchester, 1983), pp. 148–72; Ranajit Guha and Gayatri Chakravorty Spivak (eds), *Selected Subaltern Studies* (Oxford, 1988); Gyan Prakash, 'Subaltern studies as postcolonial criticism', *American Historical Review*, vol. 99 (1994), pp. 1475–90.

11 Nicholas Thomas, *Colonialism's Culture: anthropology, travel and government* (Cambridge, 1994); Bernard S. Cohn, *Colonialism and its Forms of Knowledge: the British in India* (Princeton, 1996); Nicholas Dirks (ed.), *Colonialism and Culture* (Ann Arbor, MI, 1992).

12 John MacKenzie (ed.), *Imperialism and Popular Culture* (Manchester, 1986); David Arnold, *Colonizing the Body: state medicine and epidemic disease in nineteenth-century India* (London, 1993).

13 Anthony King, *The Bungalow: the production of a global culture* (London, 1984); Swati Chattopadhyay, 'A critical history of architecture in a post-colonial world: a view from Indian history', *Architronic: the electronic journal of architecture* (May 1997).

14 Richard L. Brohier, *Furniture of the Dutch Period in Ceylon* (Colombo, 1969); Mildred Archer, Christopher Rowell and Robert Skelton (eds), *Treasures from India: the Clive collection at Powis Castle* (London, 1987); John Guy and Deborah Swallow, *Arts of India, 1500–1900* (London, 1990); Jan Veenendaal, *Furniture from Indonesia, Sri Lanka and India during the Dutch Period* (Delft, 1985); Amin Jaffer, *Furniture from British India and Ceylon: a catalogue of the collections in the Victoria and Albert Museum and the Peabody Essex Museum* (London, 2001).

15 This comprises a huge literature of which the following is but a small sample: Sten Nilsson, *European Architecture in India, 1750–1850* (London, 1968); Philip Davies, *The Penguin Guide to the Monuments of India* (London, 1989) vol. 2; George Michell, *The Islamic Heritage of Bengal* (Paris, 1984); Giles Tillotson, *The Rajput Palaces: the development of an architectural style* (New Haven and London, 1987), and as editor *Paradigms of Indian Architecture: space and time in representation and design* (Richmond, 1998); Thomas Metcalf, *An Imperial Vision: Indian architecture and Britain's Raj* (Berkeley and London, 1989); Adam Hardy, *Indian Temple Architecture: form and transformation* (New Delhi, 1994).

16 'Before the census of 1911, the term Anglo-Indian usually referred to British residents in India. Since that date it has referred to descendants of relationships between European men and Indian women'. A. Blunt, 'Imperial geographies of home: British domesticity in India, 1886–1925', *Transactions of the Institute of British Geographers*, vol. 24, no. 4 (1999), pp. 421–40.

17 Capt. Bellew, *Memoirs of a Griffin; or a cadet's first year in India* (London, 1880), pp. 172–3.

18 Tosh, *A Man's Place*, p. 4.

19 P. Burke, *History and Social Theory* (Cambridge, 1992), pp. 118–19, including the following two sentences.

20 C. Hall, 'Introduction: thinking the postcolonial, thinking the empire', in C. Hall (ed.), *Cultures of Empire: colonizers in Britain and the empire in the nineteenth and twentieth centuries* (Manchester, 2000), p. 11.

21 T. O'Sullivan, J. Hartley, D. Saunders et al., *Key Concepts in Communication and Cultural Studies* (London and New York, 1994), p. 265.

22 Hall (ed.), *Cultures of Empire*, p. 11.

23 G. Rose, *Visual Methodologies: an introduction to the interpretation of visual material* (London, Thousand Oaks and New Delhi, 2005), p. 136.

24 S. Hall (ed.), *Representation: cultural representations and signifying practices* (London, Thousand Oaks and New Delhi, 1997), p. 43.

25 One of the key early works in the analysis of colonialism as a cultural phenomenon is Edward Said's, *Orientalism: Western conceptions of the Orient* (London, 1978), in which he deploys Foucault's concept of a discourse. Foucauldian methods have also informed current writing in this area. See Hall (ed.), *Cultures of Empire*, passim.

26 Historians of empire such as John MacKenzie have articulated their concern at the application of critical theory such as discourse analysis in the study of imperialism and have emphasized the importance of interpretation of historical evidence using the methods of history. J. MacKenzie, *Orientalism: history, theory and the arts* (Manchester and New York, 1995), pp. 20–42.

27 Judy Attfield, *Wild Things: the material culture of everyday life* (Oxford and New York, 2000), p. 241

28 Attfield, *Wild Things*, p. 241.

29 Pierre Bourdieu, *Outline of a Theory of Practice* (Cambridge, 1982), p. 94, cited in Attfield, *Wild Things*, p. 242.

30 Pierre Bourdieu, *The Logic of Practice* (Cambridge, 1990), p. 57.

31 Susan Pearce, *Museums, Objects and Collections* (Leicester and London, 1992), p. 22.

32 Scholars such as Alfred Gell and Judy Attfield have each offered critiques of linguistic approaches to object interpretation. A. Gell, *Art and Agency* (Oxford, 1998) and Attfield, *Wild Things*.

33 Daniel Miller, *Material Culture and Mass Consumption* (London, 1987), pp. 98–9.

34 Miller, *Material Culture*, p. 99.

35 Pearce, *Museums*, p. 23.

36 Miller, *Material Culture*, p. 81.

37 O'Sullivan et al., *Key Concepts*, p. 310.

38 Hannah Arendt quoted in Susan Pearce, *On Collecting* (London and New York, 1999), p. 18.

39 Miller, *Material Culture*, p. 215.

40 Pierre Nora, 'Between memory and history: les lieux de mémoire', *Representations*, vol. 26 (Spring 1989), p. 9.

41 Nora, 'Between memory and history', p. 16.

42 Marius Kwint, 'Introduction', in M. Kwint, C. Breward and J. Aynsley (eds), *Material*

Memories: design and evocation (Oxford and New York, 1999), p. 11.

43 G. McCracken, *Culture and Consumption: new approaches to the symbolic character of consumer goods and activities* (Bloomington and Indianapolis, 1990), p. 70.

44 Gell, *Art and Agency*, p. 6.

45 Attfield, *Wild Things*, p. 3.

46 Peter Thornton, *Authentic Décor: the domestic interior, 1620–1920* (London, 1984).

47 Charlotte Gere, *Nineteenth Century Decoration: the art of the interior* (London, 1989); Charlotte Gere, *An Album of Nineteenth Century Interiors* (New York, 1992). See also David Dewing (ed.), *Home and Garden: paintings and drawings of English middle class urban domestic spaces, 1675–1914* (London, 2003).

48 Lorna Weatherill, *Consumer Behaviour and Material Culture in Britain, 1660–1760* (London, 1996), *passim*.

49 Margaret Ponsonby, 'Ideals, reality and meaning: homemaking in England in the first half of the nineteenth century', *Journal of Design History*, vol. 16, no. 3 (2003), p. 204.

50 Ponsonby, 'Ideals, reality and meaning', p 204.

51 Amanda Vickery, 'Golden age to separate spheres? A review of the categories and chronology of English women's history', *Historical Journal*, vol. 36, no. 2 (1993), pp. 383–414.

52 Inga Bryden and Janet Floyd (eds), *Domestic Space: reading the nineteenth-century interior* (Manchester, 1999), pp. 2–5.

53 Ponsonby, 'Ideals, reality and meaning', p. 203.

54 Ponsonby, 'Ideals, reality and meaning', p. 203.

55 Katherine Grier, *Culture and Comfort: parlor making and middle-class identity, 1850–1930* (Washington, D.C. and London, 1997).

56 Bryden and Floyd (eds), *Domestic Space*, p. 2.

57 Bryden and Floyd (eds), *Domestic Space*, p. 2.

58 Thad Logan, *The Victorian Parlour: a cultural study* (Cambridge, 2001).

59 Logan, *The Victorian Parlour*, p. xiv.

60 Daniel Miller (ed.), *Home Possessions* (London, 2000).

61 J. Morris, *Stones of Empire: the buildings of the Raj* (Oxford, 1983, reprinted 2005).

62 For example, the literature on South African interiors during the Dutch and British colonial periods. Carolyn Woodward, 'From multi-purpose parlour to drawing room: the development of the principal *voorkamer* in the fashionable Cape house, 1670–1820', *Bulletin of the South African Cultural Museum*, 4 (1983), pp. 5–19; Kathleen Wheeler, 'Interior decoration at the Cape, 1815–1835', *Bulletin of the South African Cultural History Museum*, vol. 6 (1985), pp. 5–15; Antonia Malan, 'Furniture at the Cape in the eighteenth century: an archaeological approach', in Titus Eliens (ed.), *Domestic Interiors at the Cape and in Batavia 1602–1795* (The Hague, 2002), pp. 139–59.

63 Jaffer, *Furniture*, p. 23. The following works are reviewed: Percival Spear, *The Nabobs: a study of the social life of the English in 18th century India* (London, 1932); Michael Edwardes, *The Sahibs and the Lotus* (London, 1988); Pat Barr, *The Memsahibs* (London, 1976); Margaret MacMillan, *Women of the Raj* (New York, 1988); Suresh Chandra Ghosh, *The Social Condition of the British Community in Bengal, 1757–1800* (Leiden,

1970). The author trawls these texts with a specific goal in mind, namely capturing any mention of domestic interiors and furniture.

64 In addition to the text, few (if any) photographs of interiors depicting furniture from the second half of the nineteenth century are analysed. A number of water-colours or engravings are included to illustrate the essays on British and local consumption of furniture in India.

65 A.D. King, *Colonial Urban Development: culture, social power and environment* (London and Boston, 1976); King, *The Bungalow.*

66 King, *Colonial Urban Development*, pp. 146–53.

67 Gell, *Art and Agency*, p. 8.

68 Jane Jacobs, *Edge of Empire: post-colonialism and the city* (London and New York, 1996), p. 14.

69 Jacobs, *Edge of Empire*, p. 21.

70 E.M. Collingham, *Imperial Bodies: the physical experience of the Raj, c. 1800–1947* (Cambridge, 2001), pp. 99–106; Mary Procida, *Married to the Empire: gender, politics and imperialism in India, 1883–1947* (Manchester and New York, 2002), pp. 56–77; Swati Chattopadhyay, 'Goods, chattels and sundry items: constructing 19th century Anglo-Indian domestic life', *Journal of Material Culture*, vol. 7, no. 3 (November 2002), pp. 243–71; Blunt, 'Imperial geographies of home', pp. 421–40; William Glover, '"A feeling of absence from Old England:" the colonial bungalow', *Home Cultures*, vol. 1, no. 1 (2004), pp. 61–82.

71 Jaffer, *Furniture*, while addressing furniture produced in the eighteenth and nineteenth centuries, the author mainly concentrates attention in the introductory essays on the period 1750 to 1830, the time-frame of his doctoral research. The time frame of Mary Procida's book *Married to the Empire* is between 1883 and 1947.

72 Procida, *Married to the Empire*, p. 65.

73 Ponsonby, 'Ideals, reality and meaning', p. 203.

74 Tosh, *A Man's Place*, p. 1.

75 Specific domestic advice was provided for men living in India. See, for example, Maj. L.J. Shadwell, *Notes on the Internal Economy of Chummery, Home, Mess and Club* (Bombay, 1904). The preface notes that 'when a bachelor keeps house alone or with two or three others in India … he pays twice as much as he need for his food; probably three or four times as much as he needs for oil; the sitting room is dusty and there is a general air of untidiness and discomfort everywhere', p. 5.

76 London, British Library: Bengal Wills, 1863, L/AG/34/27/170, estate of G.M. Gasper. Three male relatives of the Gasper family shared a property at 25 Garden Reach, Calcutta: G.M. Gasper, a landowner, A.M. Gasper, an attorney at law, and M.M. Gasper, a practising surgeon.

77 For example, *The Census of India, 1901*, vol. 7, part 3 (Calcutta, 1901), for the town of Calcutta recorded 6,701 residents whose birthplace was 'Countries in Europe' and of these 3,785 residents were English-born. Of these, 2,832 were male and 953 were female. There were a total of 1,253 British-born women registered in Calcutta in 1901 and 4,444 British-born men. The population for the town of Calcutta as a whole (including the local population) was 847,796.

78 Mrs H. Reynolds, *At Home in India; or Taza-be-Taza* (London, 1903), p. 52.

79 Collingham, *Imperial Bodies*, p. 3.

80 Jaffer, *Furniture, passim*.

81 Collingham, *Imperial Bodies, passim*.

82 Recent discussion of the Victorian home has, in fact, highlighted the disquieting
    nature of this space, the tensions that existed there and how, it has been argued, the
    Victorian domicile could be interpreted as an 'anxious' space.

1 ✧ Locating the East Indian home: settlement, forms of housing and the local environment

A NGLO-INDIAN domestic dwellings of the nineteenth and early twentieth centuries formed part of a distinctive pattern of settlement within the Subcontinent. Whether these dwellings were located in urban, suburban or rural settings, they constituted prominent features of the colonial built environment or landscape. They also occupied a significant place within the wider network of colonial spaces which included, for example, such venues as clubs, hotels and shops. All of these spaces, including the Anglo-Indian bungalow, were intended to provide places of refuge and protective 'routes' for the Anglo-Indian community through the colony. They were imagined as spaces to help the Europeans navigate their way through the alien environment of South Asia.

The intention of Europeans on inhabiting the colonial bungalow was, as far as possible, to reproduce a Westernized space and Western social practices. However, a combination of local factors inflected the way in which they inhabited this dwelling, and disrupted their sense of home within the empire. These factors included the plan of the bungalow, its spatial arrangement, the materials from which it was constructed and its location, as well as a range of local environmental conditions. This chapter draws on discussion of the South Asian colonial built environment within the secondary literature, and locates the East Indian home within that environment. It also describes and explains how the physical aspects of domestic space within the East Indian home unsettled the perceptions of British residents in India and disrupted both their cultural and sensory memories of the fabric and functioning of related spaces in the homeland.

Much has been written since the 1960s about the colonial built environment within the Indian Subcontinent. Scholarly output in this area can be grouped under a number of headings and each of these has been informed by approaches from different disciplines. A number of works on this topic are situated within the disciplines of art history or architectural history. For instance, in *European Architecture in India, 1750–1850*, published in 1968, Sten Nilsson discusses the impact of neoclassical architecture within the Subcontinent and examines specific structures such as government buildings, churches, and some domestic dwellings, built by the Danes, the French and the English. Nilsson also assesses how European architectural forms were modified due to the local climate and concludes that there developed in India a distinctive Euro-tropical style of architecture.[1] Other architectural historians, such as Gavin Stamp, have discussed the (re)creation of British architecture within India after 1857.[2] Giles Tillotson's writings, such as *The Tradition of Indian Architecture* (first published in 1989), chart the influence of British architecture within India and the consequent modification of Indian architectural design and taste.[3] The outputs of other scholars such as Jeremiah Losty present a narrative account of the growth of Calcutta and a topographic history of that city between the time of its foundation and 1858.[4] The majority of these works discuss such aspects as the development of colonial urban architecture and the style and form of public buildings created within the Subcontinent from the eighteenth to the twentieth centuries. The domestic dwelling, if addressed at all, is briefly described and that description is usually limited to its exterior features. Since 2000, however, other architectural historians, researching European-style buildings within South Asia, have concentrated their attention on the internal spatial arrangement of the colonial dwelling (either the urban house or the bungalow), discussing how such interiors were organized and the effect of such spaces on the European persona.[5]

Other works which address the colonial urban environment have been situated in different disciplines. The writings of Anthony King have been discussed above. King has addressed in a number of publications the colonial built environment, including the colonial bungalow, and located his assessment within a world-system framework. His work discusses the geographical, social and cultural spaces of the 'colonial culture' including the cantonment or permanent military station set close to, but apart from, local urban centres within the Subcontinent. In a similar manner, James Duncan has discussed the landscape and built environment, both pre-colonial and colonial, of the town of Kandy in the central highlands of Ceylon. A cultural geographer, he has applied structuralist methods to landscape analysis and has addressed how frameworks of power (either indigenous kingly or colonial) have been contested and mapped on the ground, so to speak, within pre-colonial and colonial South Asia.[6] In a similar manner to that in King's writings, the local environment in Duncan's publications is presented as a deactivated or inert space. It is imagined as an arena for the imposition of colonial systems of power, rather than being a permeable environment where both local and European practice and ideologies were contested and negotiated.

The secondary literature on the colonial built environment up to the present time, in general, addresses the development of European enclaves in India, the importation of European architectural styles, the creation of municipal buildings and inscription of colonial power relations in the layout and arrangement of built structures in the colonial urban setting. Rarely has attention been focused specifically on the European domestic dwelling within South Asia, the interior space of the dwelling and the problematic nature of such space in relation to cultural hybridization and the mapping of power relations. In addition, previous scholarship has largely neglected the non-functional role of objects within the colonial dwelling.

The British settled in India and Ceylon at different times. From the seventeenth century the English East India Company, trading in the raw and manufactured produce of South and East Asia, by degrees, came to control a large part of the Indian Subcontinent. 'Factories', or the fortified trading outposts of European merchant companies, were established at strategic locations around the coast of India during the seventeenth century. These outposts acted as collection and shipment points for the raw and manufactured products of the hinterlands to which they were connected. In addition to trade, over time, the English East India Company also began to play a far more prominent role in the administration and control of the regions in which it was located. In fact, as Christopher Bayly has argued, in its heyday 'the East India Company suppressed open warfare, unified the Subcontinent and introduced a new legal system'.[7]

After the Indian Mutiny of 1857, the British Crown took over the government of the English East India Company's Indian possessions and, in 1877, Queen Victoria was declared Empress of India. The history of late nineteenth-century India was dominated by growing British economic weakness and various crises, including the introduction of the Ilbert Bill, the Amritsar massacre and the quest for independence by Indian nationalists. The period after the First World War witnessed the growth of Indian nationalism and increasingly forceful demands for independence.

In contrast to the situation in India, the British were relative latecomers to Ceylon. The forces of the English East India Company expelled the Dutch from the island in 1796. Between 1796 and 1802 the latter shared political control of the island with the British Government. After 1802, Ceylon became a Crown Colony and was administered by a governor appointed by Parliament. British government forces captured the Kandyan kingdom in the centre of the island in 1815, bringing the whole country under a unified administration for the first time in its history. Apart from a rebellion in the

Kandyan Provinces in 1848, the island remained a largely quiescent and stable part of the British Empire until independence in 1948. The plantation sector and Ceylon's position on the international shipping routes across the Indian Ocean brought a large measure of prosperity to the island.

European settlement in India

Within a few decades of its creation in 1600, the English East India Company had established a series of 'factories' at Calcutta (Kolcata), Madras (Chennai), Surat, Masulipatnam, Bombay (Mumbai) and elsewhere around the coastline of the Subcontinent. In 1614, an English trading base was established at Surat, an important port on India's north-western coast and outlet for the fine textiles of the hinterland. Madras was founded in 1639 to take advantage of proximity to the products of the weaving communities in Tamil Nadu; by 1700 the city contained a population of 100,000. Job Charnock established an English trading post at Calcutta in 1690 and this presence grew in the first decades of the eighteenth century as a result of the productivity of Bengal's weavers and opportunities afforded by trade inland. In 1661, Bombay had been given to the British crown as part of the dowry of Catherine of Braganza. By the 1780s, the city had become a centre for the shipment of cotton worldwide and of opium into China, and possessed thriving commercial communities of Parsis, Gujerati merchants and Muslim traders.[8] In Ceylon, both the Portuguese and the Dutch had established a number of fortified enclaves around the coast, the most prominent being Galle and Colombo. Colombo became the capital of the crown colony of Ceylon when the British expelled the Dutch from the island.

A number of common themes run through the colonial urbanization and the domestic sphere within the Indian Subcontinent, including Ceylon. European settlements usually developed within fortified enclaves. These enclaves contained domestic accommodation, warehousing, offices and, usually, a church. Space for residential building was severely restricted within the forts. Occasional dwellings for Europeans were built beyond the walls of the fortifications but, before 1750, these were unusual. During the second half of the eighteenth and early nineteenth centuries, as the political and military situations became more settled, residential dwellings were erected in larger numbers outside the walls of the fort. These, however, still tended to be close to the fortified area of the town. Often they followed major routes from the city centre to the outskirts and beyond and were built as loose ribbon developments.

A large number of residential properties built during the late eighteenth century in India were situated within extensive grounds or compounds, with large areas of undeveloped land surrounding each property. Small clusters of European-style dwellings developed in favoured areas close to the fortified centre of Madras, Calcutta and Colombo. However, with increasing numbers of Europeans residing in the Subcontinent, as well as a growing local middle class, infilling took place whereby new properties were built in the intervening spaces between older and more spaciously planned dwellings. By the early nineteenth century, on many routes leading from the centre of the city, a continuous street frontage of boundary walls and gateways presented itself, comprising both older and more recently constructed residential dwellings.

Madras (Chennai)

S. Muttiah, the foremost present-day historian of the city, has memorably asserted that 'before the British there was no Madras'. In fact, before Madras came into being, there existed a scattered collection of villages around the mouth of the River Cooum, peopled by weavers and other craftsmen.[9] The creation of the settlement of Madras occurred in 1639 when Francis Day, a representative of the English East India Company based at a nearby trading enclave at Armagaum, received a grant of land from the local ruler to erect a trading post which was to become Fort St George. The foundation of Madras 'was the first significant settlement of the British East India Company on the Indian Subcontinent'.[10] By 1644 a small fort had been constructed, from which the city grew.[11] The trading post was established within the walls of a fortification and the leading merchant of the time, Beri Thimappa, established a settlement of weavers and other craftsmen to the north of the fort which was to become known as 'Black Town'. The structure of present-day Madras began to take shape when, in the 1670s, Governor Langhorne built a hunting lodge at Guindy. This building was to become Government House, and the thoroughfare from the Fort to Guindy evolved into one of the main arteries of the city of Madras, namely Mount Road (now Anna Salai).

Madras grew in size during the late seventeenth and eighteenth centuries through the acquisition by the English East India Company of surrounding village land, initially through leasehold agreements with the local representative of the Sultan of Golconda, who by the 1670s controlled Carnatic and Hyderabad. These villages comprised the settlements of Triplicane, Purasawalkam and Tondiarpet. The earliest reliable maps of Madras, such as that produced by Governor Thomas Pitt in 1710, reveal the extent of the settlement, which by the early eighteenth century had developed northward from the fort and inland to the west.

The decades from the 1740s to the 1790s were a time of instability and conflict in the region. The French captured Madras from the British in 1746 and destroyed much of the local or 'Black Town'. However, the British regained the settlement in 1749 at the Peace of Aix-La-Chapelle, and Madras became the seat of government for the English East India Company Presidency in 1752.[12] In 1753, with the construction of Government House on the Island immediately south-west of Fort St George, there was rapid urban growth at the north-west end of Mount Road.

During the late eighteenth century, in addition to French attacks, the British settlement was also subjected to periodic assault by the local ruler Tipu Sultan. However, with his defeat and death at the Battle of Seringapatam in 1799, there commenced a period of peace and political stability in south-east India. The years after 1800 witnessed the rapid development of George Town and the construction of North Beach Road, as well as the foundation of commercial establishments such as Binnys, Parrys and Arbuthnots, in addition to many banks and agency houses. Political, military and economic stability was ensured in 1801 with the annexation of the Carnatic by the forces of the English East India Company.

The nineteenth century witnessed the rapid growth of Madras, the construction of major civic works of architecture, the introduction of the railway and the building of many palatial private dwellings or so-called garden houses in favoured areas of the city. St George's Cathedral was consecrated in 1816, as was St Andrew's Kirk five years later. In 1832, the Madras Club, one of the earliest in the Subcontinent, was established off Mount Road in J.D. White's house. In 1840, Elphinstone Bridge was built over the Adyar River in the southern portion of the city, and South Beach Road was laid out in 1846. Ten years later, Royapuram Railway terminus was inaugurated and Madras Central Railway Station was opened in 1873. Between the 1870s and the 1890s Poonamallee High Road, which ran from west to east into the Fort, developed as a residential area as land to the north and south of the Fort had became congested. Henry Irwin's High Court was built in 1893 and in 1904 Higginbotham's Bookshop, the largest and oldest such outlet in the country, was established on Mount Road.

The essential structure of nineteenth- and early twentieth-century Madras had been established around 1800 when a map was produced entitled *Environs of Madras, Surveyed in 1814*.[13] This map reveals the most densely populated areas as those around the north, south and west of the Fort, namely Triplicane, Vepery, Egmore, Purasawalkam and Tondiarpet (the villages acquired by the East India Company in 1720). A map dated one hundred years later, *Thacker's Reduced Survey Map of India*, reveals the basic structure of the city and concentration of populations as remaining largely the same. By the turn of the twentieth century, dense urban areas around the Fort had expanded and the most heavily populated districts were 'Black Town', Royapuram, to the north of the Fort, Vepery and Purasawalkam to the west, Chintadrapet and Triplicane to the south and west and St Thomé in the southern portion of the city.

A *Guide to the City of Madras and its Suburbs*, published in 1889, highlighted the districts and types of domestic dwellings within the city where both the British and local elite made their homes.[14] Areas such as 'Teynampet' and 'Nungumbaukum' were considered fashionable localities, and the houses were mostly 'extensive and well-built containing flower gardens, tastefully laid out with rare and beautiful descriptions of plants'.[15] However, after 1850 the Adyar district was considered the most fashionable location in Madras. It was described as:

> The residence, principally of the elite of Madras society, the residents being chiefly those occupying prominent positions under Government. The locality may fairly be called the healthiest and most pleasant of all the suburbs of the town, the surrounding country being open and to some degree picturesque … The houses are well built and spacious with extensive compounds. Some of them still retain the names of former residents such as 'Brodie Castle', 'Gambier's Gardens' … and 'Elliot's Gardens'.[16]

A particular type of residential dwelling developed in Madras during the nineteenth century, which became known as the 'garden house'. This designation was due to its location in spacious grounds or gardens which were often filled with tropical fruit trees or set within wide expanses of open land (see figure 2).[17] Many of these structures were built well away from the concentration of populations in Triplicane, Vepery and elsewhere in proximity to the Fort, as well as from the commercial centre of the city around the north-west end of Mount Road and Poonamallee High Road. In 1841, Mrs Clemons described such houses in the city:

> The garden-houses, as they are named, are the chief residences of the officers and civilians [of the East India Company] … They are situated in the middle of a garden [a large open space planted with trees] and the greatest number have only a ground floor; some that are of a very superior description, have one story above. They are generally surrounded by a deep verandah, supported by pillars … The rooms are very lofty, from twenty to thirty feet high.[18]

Many of these houses were built in Mylapore and Pudupet districts between Peter's Road, Ice House Road and the Adyar River. Maps of Madras produced at the turn of the twentieth century depict some of these dwellings such as Newington House at the southernmost end of Mount Road, Leith Castle, south of St Thomé, Dunmore House, off Mowbray's Road and Doveton House, off Colonel Silver's Road and College Road in Vepery.[19] Doveton House was, in fact, one of the earliest (and largest) of the garden houses to be built (*c.* 1798), most probably as the home of Benjamin Roebuck, and

2 A spacious Anglo-Indian house set within extensive grounds. A Madras garden house, *c.* 1840.

was home to Lt-Gen John Doveton between 1837 and 1847.[20] Unusually, the house was built as a three-storey structure and was planned in the shape of a compressed letter T. The front of the building presents an imposing central portico supported by Ionic columns, which rises through two storeys. As with the majority of garden houses in Madras it is built of brick and plastered with lime. In addition, and again as found in many other Madras domestic dwellings, the roof and first floor are composed of wooden beams set at intervals and covered by a layer of bricks held in position by lime mortar (so-called Madras Terrace roofing).[21]

Calcutta (Kolcata)

The foundation of the English East India Company's settlement at Calcutta, on the Hoogly River, in Bengal dates from 1690 when Job Charnock established an initial foothold in the region. English merchants were permitted to fortify the town from 1697 and Old Fort William has its origins from this date.[22] By the first decade of the eighteenth century, the settlement possessed a hospital, barracks and a church. In the 1740s local raiders from Orissa threatened the English enclave, and this prompted the construction,

from 1757, of a new and greatly enlarged Fort William, designed by Captain
John Brohier.[23] As Philip Davies has suggested, this development

> dictated a major change in the pattern of urban development. Buildings
> were no longer concentrated inside the walls; instead, the city expanded
> beneath the protective ramparts of the most impressive European fortifi-
> cations in Asia.[24]

A large space was cleared around the fort to command an open field of fire
and, by 1780, this had developed into the Maidan and Esplanade. More
permanent classical villas built of brick and chunam covering replaced the
earlier bamboo and thatched dwellings of the merchant class.[25] These new
urban dwellings presented similar features to the street front, including
a three-bay façade with colonnaded verandahs, pedimented centrepieces
and pilastered walls, all faced with brilliant white chunam. Whole areas
of the city were developed, due to the enhanced military security, ensuing
prosperity and a speculative building boom, which reflected the growing
wealth of the settlement. Districts such as Chowringhee, Alipur and Garden
Reach offered an impressive architectural prospect and were described by
George, Viscount Valentia in 1803 as 'the finest view I ever beheld in any
city'.[26] As a result of these classicizing urban developments Calcutta earned
the assumed name of the 'city of palaces'.[27]

These classical villas denoted the evolution of a modified form of
architecture, derived from European models but significantly adapted to
the Indian context. The majority of these dwellings comprised a classically
proportioned block usually of three bays and either of two or three storeys
in height, set in a garden compound, with the inner rooms protected from
the heat by colonnaded verandahs.[28] Toward the end of the eighteenth
century, residential areas such as Chowringhee and the Esplanade acquired
a continuous street frontage of boundary walls, screens and gates. Surviving
examples of such buildings include the Royal Calcutta Turf Club, the Bishop's
Palace, the Tollygunge Club and Belvedere (now the National Library).

By 1773, Calcutta effectively had become the capital of British India,
and the English East India Company began to erect public buildings which
expressed its self-confidence and acknowledged the city's status.[29] These
buildings included Government House (1803), designed by Captain Charles
Wyatt for the Marquess of Wellesley, Governor-General from 1798 to 1805
and based on Robert Adam's Kedleston Hall, Derbyshire; the Town Hall
(1811) modelled by Colonel James Garstin; St Andrew's Kirk (1818); and the
Silver Mint (1831) by Major William Nairn Forbes. The rapid and unplanned
growth of residential areas of the city which began after 1750 continued
for the next hundred years. In fact, the building boom and consequent
speculation was a profitable source of income for East India Company

employees and members of the local population.[30] In 1777, a contemporary commentator, Mrs Kindersley, described the general arrangements within Calcutta houses:

> In all good houses the apartments are upstairs, and all on one floor; the rooms are large and very lofty; most of the houses are built with a *varendar*, which is a terrace on a level with the rooms in the front; and sometimes in the back part of the house, supported by pillars below, and a roof above, likewise supported by pillars … The *varendars* give a handsome appearance to the houses on the out-side and are of great use, keeping out the sun by day, and in the evenings are cool and pleasant to sit on.[31]

Architectural historian Swati Chattopadhyay has proposed that, although contemporary and later commentators made much of the distinctively

3 Multiple door and window openings in the rooms of the Anglo-Indian home. Plan of house, Calcutta, by Shadwell and Goss, builders, *c.* 1830.

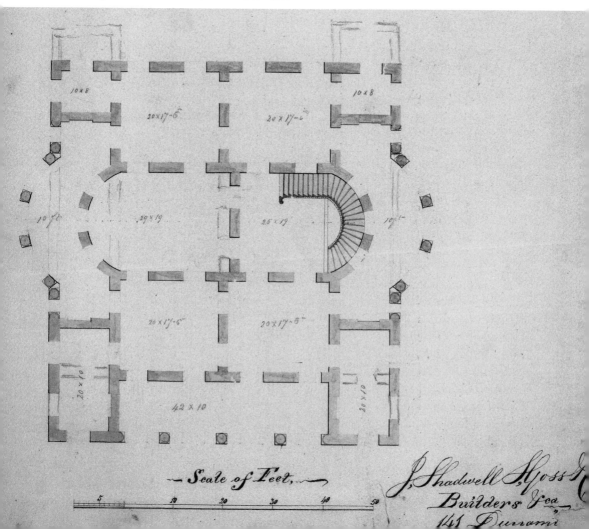

Plate 1.

4 Typical nineteenth-century Anglo-Indian urban dwelling. View of lower-roomed house in Calcutta, *c.* 1860.

classical architecture of Calcutta, in fact the plans of Calcutta houses bore little relation to the Palladian or neoclassical villas and town houses of the homeland. She characterizes the general plan of Calcutta houses during the colonial period as being arranged on a three-bay principle with 'one [set of rooms] on an axis with the carriage port and the south veranda and two sets of rooms on either side'.[32] Chattopadhyay also suggests that the design of the colonial dwelling in Calcutta can be viewed as an attempt to adapt 'the principle of the Indian house of single-loaded rooms around a courtyard within the geometry of a single-roofed entity', and that the hall in the colonial house functioned as a focal point for socialization and a point of access to other rooms 'in much the same way as a courtyard' in a traditional Indian house.[33] An example of such a three-bay house plan is found in a drawing of around 1830 by Shadwell and Goss, builders of Durrumtollah, Calcutta (see figure 3).[34]

Writing in 1862, contemporary commentator Colesworthy Grant described the two main types of European dwelling in Calcutta, namely the lower-roomed and the upper-roomed (or two-storey) house (see figure 4).[35] Entry into the lower-roomed house was effected directly from the verandah and subsequently into a large, rectangular central hall with two pairs of rooms arranged on either side of this space.[36] Grant also indicated a generally held understanding among his contemporaries concerning the polyvalence of interior space within the colonial dwelling, and erasure within the Subcontinent of the function-specific nature of individual rooms located within the homeland. As he notes, the hall in the lower-roomed house functioned either as 'parlour, dining, drawing or sitting room', although these terms, which were derived from English practice that implied specific usages of domestic space, were not generally applied in an Indian context.[37] In addition, he described a typical hall in a lower-roomed Calcutta house as measuring thirty-five feet long by twenty-five feet broad – an unusually large size for a main reception room in all but the grandest of houses in England.[38]

Bombay (Mumbai)

In 1661, Bombay became a possession of the British crown as part of the dowry of Catharine of Braganza and, in 1668, was assigned to the English East India Company on a yearly rent.[39] By 1720, the town had a population of 50,000, including around 1,000 Europeans. The centre was fortified in the late seventeenth century and, in 1736, a prominent member of the Surat Parsi community, Lavji Nasarvanji Wadia, built a dockyard adjacent to the fort.[40] Bombay's prosperity grew through its maritime trade with Arabia and south-east Asia, rather than with the Subcontinent, a situation which persisted until the defeat of the Maratha at the battle of Kirkee in 1817 and the subsequent opening up of inland routes to the Deccan. In 1803, a fire destroyed much of the town within the fort, and this event led to the construction of residential and civic buildings outside the walls. Initially, civic buildings in Bombay were constructed in the classical idiom, such as the Town Hall (1820–35) and the Mint (1824–27).[41]

Bombay's great era of prosperity resulted from the disruption to trade caused by the American Civil War and the subsequent shortage of American cotton coming into British textile mills. The civic authorities began to reclaim land in 1862 that linked the seven original islands of Bombay into a continuous peninsula and the walls of the old fort were removed two years later. Under the guidance of James Trubshawe (fl. 1860–75), a series of municipal buildings in the Gothic Revival style was erected. These included: the Secretariat (1867–74), the Public Works Office (1869–72), the Law Courts (1871–79), Crawford Markets (1871), and the Victoria Terminus (1878–87) of the Great Indian Peninsula Railway.[42]

Suburban bungalows were built from the early nineteenth century among the coconut groves of Malabar Hill, Tardeo, Byculla, and also around Chinchpoglie and Parel.[43] The greatest concentration of European residents, by 1800, was north of the fort at Mazagaon and the next 'suburb' of Byculla. Houses with names such as 'the Grove', 'Belair', 'Storm Hall', 'Claremont' and 'the Belvedere' indicate the extent of European occupation of these districts.[44] Mrs Sidney Terry, who lived in Bombay between 1844 and 1847 noted that

> substantial dwellings … are to be found either within the fort, or at Girgaum, Byculla, Chintz Poogly and other places beyond the bazaars, where European residents have erected groups of *pucka* [masonry] built and handsome houses, with excellent gardens and offices attached.[45]

Grant Road was described in 1876 as the 'northern limit of the native town proper; beyond this road is Tardeo, Byculla. Mazagaon and Parell the European element of the population is again prominent'.[46]

During the second half of the nineteenth century, Malabar Hill became the main residential area for Europeans. The *Guide to Bombay* of 1876 describes the development in this district of the city:

> Malabar Hill, thirty years ago, had only two bungalows built upon it … now a large proportion of the European population of Bombay lives there … The old fashioned bungalow, usually but one storey high, with spacious rooms, thick walls and broad verandahs and surrounded by a large garden … is indeed a place of residence delightfully suited to the needs of the climate of Bombay … Many of the new houses, however, have been built hastily, with little regard to health or comfort; and the hill is now too much built over and too thickly populated to be so pleasant a resort as it used to be.[47]

Contemporary commentators noted the types of European dwelling in the city, including both bungalows and two-storey structures. Many of the mid-nineteenth-century bungalows in Bombay possessed thatched roofs and were disparagingly compared to 'English cow-house[s]'. However, their internal arrangements met with more approval, as an anonymous commentator noted in 1852 that on entering one of these bungalows, he stepped directly

> without any intervening hall or passage, into a large and elegant drawing-room, supported upon pillars of faultless proportions, and furnished with every modern luxury that either taste could suggest or wealth command. A large screen of red silk divided this apartment from a spacious dining-room … an entire suite of apartments is appropriated to the use of each individual, consisting of a bed-room, dressing-room and bath-room, and one or all of these usually open upon the verandah which surrounds the house.[48]

During the nineteenth century, the British also resided in larger, two-storey houses and these were described as 'lofty and stately-looking mansions, with facades adorned with spacious porticos supported on pillars'.[49] The internal arrangements were described as similar to comparable houses in Britain:

> the ground-floor containing the dining and breakfast-rooms, library & c., and often one or two suites of apartments appropriated as guests' chambers … the staircases are generally wide and handsome, conducting to the reception and family rooms; and not infrequently, a charming withdrawing-room is found on the flat top of the porch by surrounding it with a balustrade.[50]

In addition, and a unique aspect of the built environment of the Subcontinent, from September to May, temporary accommodation was also available for Europeans in Bombay in the form of tented 'bungalows' erected on the Esplanade.[51] When this practice began is uncertain, but part of the Esplanade represented on a *Plan of the Fortress of Bombay, 1827* by Capt. William A. Tate, is inscribed, 'Ground appropriated during the Fair Season for Gentlemen's Bungalows with Enclosures'.[52] In 1838, Mrs Postans described these tented structures:

> During the hot season, the Esplanade is adorned with pretty, cool, temporary residences, erected near the sea; their chuppered[53] roofs and rustic porches half concealed by the flowering creepers and luxuriant shrubs, which shield them from the mid-day glare. The bungalows [i.e. tents] are situated in a line with spaces between each … the material of which they are made is simply bamboo and plaster lined with stained dungaree [coarse local calico], dyed pale straw colour … the whole is enclosed with a pretty compound, filled with fine plants.[54]

She also described the internal arrangements of these semi-permanent tents, including the advantages of such dwellings and some of the furniture usually found there:

> the smooth China matting which covers the floor; the numerous lamps shedding their equal light from the snowy ceilings; the sweet perfume of the surrounding plants and the fresh sea breeze blowing through the trellis-work verandahs, render them delightful retreats … a fine-toned piano and a good billiard table are the usual additions to varied articles of luxury and convenience.[55]

Although not an entirely a new phenomenon in Bombay, during the 1930s blocks of flats or apartments were developed on reclaimed land on what became Marine Parade (discussed further in Chapter 3).[56] These introduced another form of dwelling to colonial South Asia and, as discussed below, both expressed and constituted a fundamental change within the kinship arrangements of the local middle class.

Ceylon (Sri Lanka): Colombo

Unlike the situation within India, the British in Ceylon came to a domestic built environment largely created by the previous colonizers of the island, the Dutch. A number of small, fortified enclaves had been created by the latter at strategic points around the coast of the island, such as Matara and Galle in the south, Jaffna in the north and Colombo in the west. During the second half of the nineteenth century, Colombo, the most populated settlement in Ceylon, underwent a period of growth due to expansion of the British administration and burgeoning plantation economy. Although the Dutch (who were the previous European colonizers on the island) had built a small number of dwellings outside the fortified core of the town, the political and military situation on the island was far from secure.[57] As Sir James Emerson Tennent, a British Colonial Secretary, noted in 1859 'owing to the precarious nature of their relations with the people of Kandy, [they] were careful not to erect [the majority] of their dwellings beyond the guns of the fortress'.[58] During the nineteenth century, however, the British and local elite began to construct dwellings and reside in sufficient numbers that distinct suburbs developed beyond the Fort in districts such as Mutwal and Tanque Salgado to the north east and Colpetty (Kollupitya) to the south.[59] Bungalows, as well as substantial two-storey structures, were built in increasing numbers after 1850.

However, during the first quarter of the nineteenth century British residents inhabited a material world of Dutch making: many of them still resided in Dutch-built houses within the Fort at Colombo (the oldest Westernized part of the town). The Fort, and more especially the 'Native' Town or Pettah, which was situated to the East and divided from the Fort by clear ground, were both densely populated urban environments from which the British, as the century progressed, wished to distance themselves. Similarly at Galle, a smaller town situated in the south-west of the island, British residents inhabited compact, single-storey terraced houses built by the Dutch, and also worshipped in a Dutch-built church.

In 1803, a British commentator, Robert Percival, described the general layout of the Fort at Colombo and the type of house built by the Dutch, shortly before the British had taken control of the island:

> Columbo is built more in European style ... The interior of the Fort has also more the appearance of a regular town ... The Dutch houses are all regularly built, though few of them are above one story high ... Before each house, and connected with it, is a large open space roofed in and supported on pillars of wood. It is called a *viranda*, and is intended to afford a shade from the sun, and an opportunity of enjoying any refreshing breeze that springs up from the sea ... Most of the houses are of the same

construction and consist of the hall in the front, with a chamber at each side, and another room in the back part, equal in length to the other three, and called the back *viranda*. This apartment, owing to the sloping form of the roofs, is much lower than those in the front. Behind the back viranda are one or two ranges of smaller buildings proportioned to the size of the house ... and intended for the accommodation of the servants, for cellars and sometimes for sleeping rooms.[60]

The interior layout of the houses Percival described is shown in a plan of the Fort at the National Archives (see figure 5).[61] These dwellings, owned by a Mr Waring, Chinner and Andries faced Chatham Street. At the front ran a verandah continuous across all three properties, supported on columns; the plan of each residence presents a narrow plot set back deeply from the street front. Each house possessed an entrance hall and main reception room, which opened onto another room. Each dwelling also contained an internal courtyard flanked by a back verandah. Further rooms were arranged around or to one side of this open space. Although the proportions of the interior spaces were generous, the plan illustrates the high density of such housing in the Fort during the first half of the nineteenth century. Although window and door recesses are shown, circulation of cooling sea breezes would have been hampered by the closely packed housing. The relatively high concentration of people living in close proximity, and inadequate provision of proper sanitation, also presented health hazards.

In 1809, another visitor to the island described the appearance of houses constructed by the Dutch in Galle, a fortified town on the south-west coast.[62] The location of the majority of these houses in concentrated urban settlements, protected by fortifications, reflected the prevailing local political and military situation during the seventeenth and eighteenth centuries. As this context changed during the middle decades of the nineteenth century and group security became less of a priority, the British required different architectural spaces in which to live.

One indication of this change of attitude was manifested by the demolition of the ramparts of the old Dutch Fort in Colombo between 1868 and 1870.[63] This can be explained in different ways. It could be viewed as an act of self-confidence and symbolic expression of group security. This contrasted with the situation in the many Presidency towns and cities of post-Mutiny India where even some railway stations built after 1857 incorporated fortifications.[64] It could, however, be explained in terms of practical necessity, namely the removal of an impediment to the development of the railway. Although some British residents continued to reside in Dutch-built town houses, in Colombo and elsewhere, along the western seaboard by the 1850s and 1860s the British began to re-locate to different regions of the city to take advantage of the cooling sea breezes

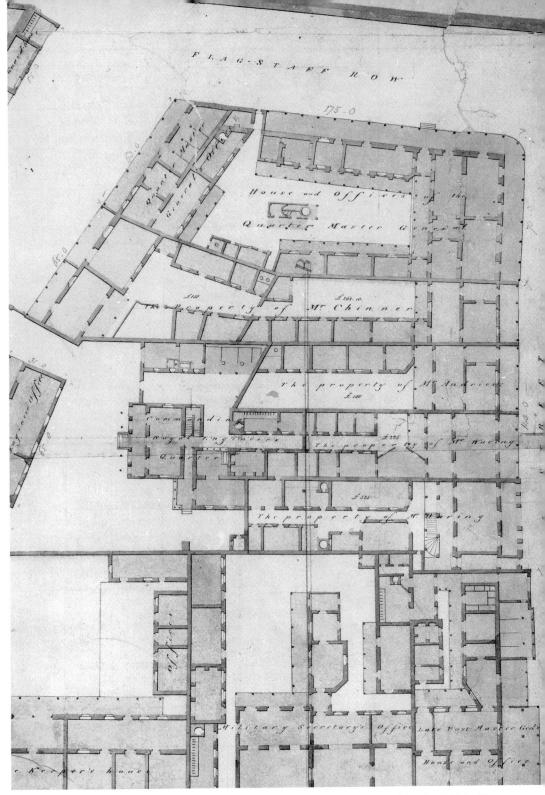

5 Densely concentrated urban dwellings of the Dutch colonial period inhabited by the British. Plan of the square in the Fort, Colombo, *c.* 1833.

and reduced risk to personal safety in living beyond the Fort. In 1841, Mrs Griffiths, a British resident on the island, described these new areas and gave an example of a particular bungalow called 'Uplands' which belonged to a Mr Carr and was most probably located in the suburb of Tanque Salgado. She noted that it lay 'beyond the Pettah [native town], on the other side [north] of Colombo'. The chief characteristics of the property were that it was 'roofed with tiles as they all are, and the outer verandah is supported by low white pillars ... it is so pretty and so cool after the house we have left ... [and] stands on an elevated piece of table land, above the sea'.[65]

Another district in Colombo, 'Colpetty' [Kollupitya], that was situated approximately one mile south of the Fort, became a very fashionable residential area during the nineteenth century. In 1892, Constance Gordon Cumming painted a word picture of this suburb:

> Just below Galle Face lies Colpetty ... one of the most delightful suburbs of Colombo ... all around the grassy shores of the beautiful lake (and indeed in every direction) are scattered the pleasant homes of the residents ... The majority of these are all of bungalow type i.e. only one storey high, built of stone or brick and with the roof very high-pitched.[66]

Contemporary prints and photographs, composed to represent an idealized view of life in the tropics, also portray these ample bungalows set in luxuriant or spacious grounds (see figure 6).[67] In 1860, Sir James Emerson Tennent summarized the situation with regard to the type of housing stock, which was built in Colombo in the middle decades of the nineteenth century:

> In the suburbs the better houses seldom rise to a second story, but the area which each of them covers is large. Their broad verandahs are supported on columns; their apartments are lofty, and cooled by Indian punkahs; their floors are tiled and the doors and windows are formed of Venetian jalousies, opening to the ground for the sake of freshness and air.[68]

Colombo possessed no cantonment in the Indian sense, although military barracks were built *en échelon* just to the south of the Fort, fronting Galle Face Green. As in many Indian towns, an area of undeveloped land separated the inhabitants of the Fort from indigenous population within the Pettah and this is clearly visible on a map of the Fort of Colombo of 1839.[69] However, during the middle decades of the nineteenth century, the inhabitants of the Pettah were mainly middle-class members of the local Burgher community (see Chapter 3), and this area was a respectable location within the city with many substantial dwellings, which contemporary commentators describe as being filled with fashionable, costly and locally made furniture.[70]

Despite contemporary rhetoric concerning a notional separation of 'white town' and 'black town', within the suburbs of Colombo, in a similar

6 A sprawling bungalow set in spacious grounds. Col. Clarke's bungalow, Colombo, *c.* 1880.

manner to the situation that prevailed in urban centres of India, there was little or no segregation of elite European and local dwellings along racial lines. In addition, although it is problematic to generalize, European ownership of property differed between Ceylon and India. In contrast to practice in India, members of the Ceylon Civil Service, the British military, or other Europeans in government employ, spent a large part of their careers on the island, often in one location. Consequently, in many cases, British residents in Ceylon purchased or built bungalows and houses (rather than simply renting them) and invested in their homes, to a greater extent than was the case within India.[71]

Members of the upper echelons of the Ceylon Civil Service, the British military and coffee planters, built substantial residential properties outside the Fort in picturesque areas around Beira Lake. One such example is the residence of Thomas Hudson, a coffee planter, which was built around 1865 at Polwatte, Colombo.[72] Plans and elevations of Hudson's house depict a large two-storey house in Italianate style, with central classical, pedimented portico and applied pilasters to the first floor below a tiled, hipped roof. The ground floor comprised an imposing rectangular space enclosed all around by a verandah. On the plans, internal divisions of the rooms have been kept to a minimum (there are no door openings as such) and the designations of 'dining', 'hall' and 'billiard' indicate how this open-planned space might have been used. Kitchen accommodation was located in a separate but connected building. Generously proportioned bedrooms, dressing rooms and bathrooms were situated on the first floor.

By 1899, when a map of the centre of Colombo was produced by the Surveyor General's Office, the densely populated areas of the city to the east and north-east of the Fort are visible, including the Pettah, St Paul's and St Sebastian's.[73] The main routes emanating from the Fort to the east and south are also depicted as having sporadic ribbon development. One of the most fashionable districts located south-east of the Fort was Cinnamon Gardens. The name derived from the original Dutch plantation of this valuable commodity, although by the early nineteenth century no traces of this remained. Clearly visible on the 1899 map in this district and in some cases designated by their names – 'Devon House', 'Horton Lodge', 'Peak View', 'Fern Lodge', 'Osborne House', 'Alexandra House', 'Rosebank', 'Ellerslie' – are the large houses set in spacious grounds that had been built by the British and wealthy locals to the east of Victoria Park in Rosmead Place, Barnes Place and Horton Place during the nineteenth century.[74]

Between 1880 and 1910, many bungalows, as well as two-storey houses, were built around the western coastal belt of the island and followed the major roads in ribbon fashion. All the major routes out of Colombo also witnessed rapid ribbon development.

In addition to urban dwellings within the port cities of colonial South Asia, the British (in lesser numbers) also inhabited bungalows situated well away from populous areas in isolated situations, usually located within plantations in the highlands, of coffee, tea and cinchona or in the lowlands, of indigo. The bungalow, as a colonial urban phenomenon, has already been treated in the literature.[75] However, prior discussion of such dwellings located beyond the colonial city in the *mofussil* [rural localities as opposed to the chief settlements] is limited.

Rural bungalows varied in scale and internal arrangement. At one end of the spectrum, those dwellings owned and occupied by the British owners of indigo factories located in the Champaran district, near Patna in north-eastern India, were often semi-palatial structures and were filled with an assortment of domestic furnishings and paraphernalia.[76] Other bungalows in outlying regions, intended for less socially elevated members of the colonial culture, were on a smaller scale and were more basic in terms of their amenities. In 1887, W.M. Reid described the rudimentary accommodation provided for the Assistant Manager of an indigo plantation in the following terms: 'the bungalow will probably contain a dining-room, bedroom, dressing and bath-rooms, with a pantry and 'godown' (or store-closet) with back and front verandahs ... Nothing, in this particular instance, is sacrificed to art. This amount of accommodation is all that is really needed for a bachelor'.[77] Evidence of other sorts, such as photographs, building plans and contemporary accounts, also provides a sense of the simplicity of domestic arrangements within plantation bungalows.[78]

The effects of local conditions on the domestic interior and European life-style

There were local constraints on the design and fitting out of house and bungalow interiors within the Subcontinent. The effects of the hot and humid climate had to be mitigated, and insect and reptile intrusion kept to a minimum. Houses and bungalows built in India or Ceylon during the nineteenth century incorporated local features and features developed through European experience of domestic life in the tropics to cope with the harsh environmental conditions. Furthermore, furnishing the colonial interior presented an entirely different set of problems to those confronted in the homeland. These factors inflected social practices which were engendered within the colonial interior, and disturbed European sensory perceptions of domestic space.

Keeping cool in the domestic interior

Keeping cool in the colonial domestic interior was effected in various ways. Many commentators noted the large size and especially the high ceilings of Anglo-Indian dwellings.[79] In many cases, the planning and building of bungalows and houses took into account the location and orientation of the dwelling in order to maximize the flow of air into the interior. In the first decades of the nineteenth century, situating new buildings to catch sea or land breezes enhanced natural ventilation; hence the popularity in Colombo of dwellings built in such areas as Mutwal and Colpetty (Kollupitya), which were located a few miles outside the walled enclave of the Fort, the former on rising ground.[80] Even inland, the positioning of new buildings was a matter of concern. An article in *The Bangalore Gazette* of 1881 noted:

> One great mistake in this country [India] is that houses are seldom built in proper position with regard to the sun. When they are so it is by chance; for the rule appears to be to place them facing and parallel to the nearest road: if this suits the sun good and well ... This is really a very important matter, for the temperature and salubrity of the house depend upon it. Another important matter, which is generally neglected is the direction of the prevailing winds.[81]

Even if they had no control over the location of their dwellings, Anglo-Indians could at least modify the ways in which they used their interior spaces to take advantage of cooling draughts of air. In April 1843, the Reverend Charles Acland noted of his bungalow in Cuttack that he had 'moved to the other side of the house in order to have our bed-room to the West; because the sea-breeze, which blows every night is a South-West wind'.[82]

The British in India had no European antecedents to offer a model of living in a tropical climate. Local traditions of building, ventilating and restricting the ingress of heat and light into the interior were adapted, with varying degrees of success, to the requirements of European residents. For example, the use of glass panes in window frames is recorded from the late eighteenth century and became more common within metropolitan centres of India from the second quarter of the nineteenth century.[83] The British in Ceylon, at least during the early years of the nineteenth century, inhabited a material world created by the Dutch, the previous Western power to occupy the island. The latter had developed forms of housing which combined local and Western features. However, the British found some aspects of Dutch dwellings on the island far from satisfactory, especially with regard to the manner in which the circulation of air was restricted. A number of contemporary commentators noted the closed-in aspect of many Dutch dwellings and the way in which they excluded breezes. In 1803, Robert Percival noted that many of the Dutch-built houses in the Fort at Colombo were fitted with 'glass-panes after the European manner' and how the Dutch on the island preferred to keep their 'houses close shut both in the hot and cold seasons'.[84] Reiterating these comments, in 1859, Sir James Emerson Tennent recorded that 'on arrival of the English, in 1796, they found the Dutch houses at Colombo suffocatingly hot, in consequence of the windows being closed with *glass*'.[85]

The planning of the Anglo-Indian interior, especially in relation to the number and size of door and window openings, was also intended to improve ventilation. A plan of Lieutenant Colonel Gilbert's bungalow at Hazaribagh, Bihar, drawn in 1825, reveals that the dining/drawing room included nine door openings (see figure 7).[86] In 1830, Shadwell and Goss, builders of Durramtollah, Calcutta, specified on their plan for a dwelling in that city three French windows and six door openings in the largest room of the house;[87] the other rooms each included at least six doorways. In a similar fashion, in 1881, an estimate for the construction of a ten-room bungalow at Bangalore, in southern India, itemized twenty-six doors and sixteen windows.[88] Similar evidence of multiple openings for doors or windows is found in plans of dwellings built by the British in Ceylon and the accounts of contemporary commentators.[89]

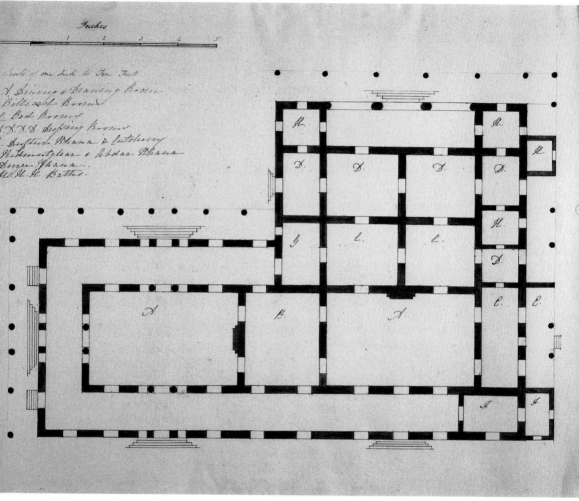

7 Numerous door and window openings to enhance ventilation within the Anglo-Indian domestic interior. Plan of Lieut. Col. Gilbert's bungalow, Hazaribagh, N.E. India, *c.* 1825.

The experience of living in dwellings which contained so many doors and windows was frequently recorded by contemporary commentators. For instance, in 1843, the Reverend Charles Acland noted of his bungalow at Cuttack:

the room I am now in has one French window opening into the verandah …, another towards the church, a door opening into the next room and another into the go-down or store-room. All these windows and doors are now open, and I am sitting as near the centre as I can, to catch what little breeze there is.[90]

So many openings in the walls of Anglo-Indian bungalows and houses also caused the occupants to feel that they were constantly on display. Until they became familiarized with this spatial arrangement, their sense of interiority was frequently unsettled, giving 'expression to estrangement and alienation'.[91] An anonymous commentator, writing in 1852 about housing in Bombay, noted that 'to promote a thorough circulation of air, the number of doors and windows is necessarily great' and 'some time must elapse before the stranger can divest himself of the idea that he is always in public ... and as he enters an Indian bedroom ... that he is to be the occupant of a magnified bird-cage'.[92] In a similar vein, in 1887, another commentator noted the open aspect of the Anglo-Indian bungalow and consequent disruption to the European sense of interiority and privacy, as well as a clear sense of an alien presence. He describes how, even when 'at home' within his bungalow, the Assistant Manager of an indigo factory could not escape the gaze of the local population. He recounts how a local stranger, seated motionless at the edge of the bungalow's garden, was able to look straight into the interior of the dwelling, and how this voyeuristic looking unsettled the Assistant Manager's tranquillity:

> In vain the aspirant for indigo honours tries to evade the steadfast eyes of the watcher – smoke as he may, read as he may, intently as he may dive his nose into the page or newspaper – his eye will slowly, gradually, but surely be dragged, line by line ... up the page to the top ... and his eye will inevitably meet the eye of the 'watcher' fixed patiently upon him ... It's no use; he KNOWS you MUST LOOK at him; he never stirs, he never speaks; he sits there, mute, asking for nothing ... Only you will have to look and MUST, eventually LOOK AT HIM; and herein lies his triumph![93]

Another integral aspect of the bungalow was the verandah, the purpose of which was to mitigate the ambient heat (by slightly cooling the air before it entered the dwelling) and prevent monsoonal rain penetrating the interior. Intended as a practical necessity due to the climate and as a notional barrier between the interior of the bungalow and the exterior, the efficacy of this space as a zone of segregation was diminished by a number of factors, such as its occupancy by household servants and as a place of negotiation with local traders.[94] The verandah also acquired a social function, often being treated as an additional room (or series of rooms) and was frequently furnished as such.[95] An account of Bombay in 1852 noted that the verandah, 'which is considered indispensable in the construction of even the poorest abode', in addition to offering protection from the sun during the day, also presented 'an agreeable family resort, when the refreshing evening breeze tempts every one to exchange the heat and light of the drawing-room for a delightful reunion in the open air'.[96] In 1892, Constance Gordon Cumming described this aspect of the built environment of Colombo as 'these cool verandahs, which generally extend round the bungalow, [which] are … furnished with comfortable lounging-chairs and light tables, [and] … become pleasant family sitting-rooms'.[97] In some cases it is most probable, especially in cities such as Calcutta, where space was at a premium, that verandahs also functioned as workspaces or additional areas for storage.[98]

Measures were also adopted in the planning and building of the Anglo-Indian dwelling to control the ingress of light and heat from the sun into the domestic interior. On grander buildings, sunshades – usually of corrugated iron sheeting or painted wooden boards – were attached to the façade above south-facing window openings.[99] Venetian blinds were also incorporated into doors and windows and were found in most Anglo-Indian dwellings. The slats of wood in these blinds could be rotated so as to exclude (or more rarely) admit sunlight. Often glazed windows had these fitted to the outer frames. In 1813, Charles Doyley noted that the south-facing windows of Indian houses were 'provided with strong outside Venetians, which serve as shutters'.[100] In 1862, Colesworthy Grant provided a fuller description of Venetians found on Anglo-Indian houses when he noted that

> the outer doors of all houses, are, if not invariably, at least very generally, Venetianed from top to bottom … Venetians form a very marked feature in Indian houses; three sides of a room … being in many instances, formed of nothing more than immovable Venetian shades.[101]

Contemporary commentators in Ceylon also recorded these fixtures.[102]

In certain rooms, such as the dining room or, in grander houses, the ballroom, large swinging fans or *punkahs*, which were suspended from the ceiling, were also deployed to mitigate the heat of the interior. These devices had been used in Anglo-Indian interiors since the late eighteenth century and many commentators noted their presence and efficacy during the nineteenth (and very early twentieth) century.[103] In 1906, for instance, William Hart described 'the long swinging fan, fringed with Holland or with strips of grass matting without which most Europeans can hardly work, eat, or live'.[104] Although familiar to British residents in India, these swinging fans appear to have been unknown to the Dutch, who lived in Ceylon during the eighteenth century; the first *punkah* had reputedly been introduced to the island around 1801 by General Macdowall ' who had been used to them in Bengal'.[105] The first record of *punkahs* being used in government houses in Ceylon occurs in 1834, when '4 *punkahs* with ropes' are itemized in the King's House, Colombo.[106] In 1841, a British resident in Ceylon was unfamiliar enough with this device to describe in detail an example, which she saw at Mr Carr's house in Colombo. She noted:

> it consists of an oblong frame of wood, covered with canvas and painted white* (* this description applies to those *punkahs* that are used in Ceylon).

It hangs about six feet from the ground, lengthways with the [dining] table, so that everyone partakes equally of the breeze it creates. Cords are attached to one side, which passing through the wall, the *punkah* is set in motion by a servant, who pulls it outside, and is invisible. They are not so generally used in Ceylon as on the [Coromandel] Coast [of India], but few houses are without one suspended over the dining room table.[107]

Punkahs were gradually superseded, in the first decades of the twentieth century, by ceiling-hung fans with rotating blades, powered by electricity.[108] Both of these devices enabled normal domestic activities to function despite the heat and humidity of the Subcontinent. The disposition of *punkahs* in dining rooms – and reception rooms, also, most probably – affected the arrangement of furniture in some interiors. In long, spacious rooms (such as the hall of a Calcutta upper-roomed house), where several *punkahs* were hung, there was a tendency to arrange items of furniture in rows parallel with the walls (or against the walls) to take maximum advantage of the cooling draughts of air from the swinging fan.[109] This created the impression of a furniture showroom, rather than a domestic interior. The consequent disruption to the usual placement of furniture found in the homeland, necessitated by the need to circulate cooling draughts of air within the domestic interior, further contributed to a sense of dislocation within the Anglo-Indian home, and mildly affronted the propriety and taste of middle-class Britons living in Calcutta, Madras or Bombay.

Another aspect of their dwelling which perturbed Anglo-Indians was the exposed and unadorned ceiling. In order to disguise the exposed and unsightly ceiling beams of some bungalows and houses (left as such in order that insect attack could be quickly noticed and checked), as well as to create at least a visual impression of coolness, a tightly stretched white cloth was occasionally attached across the ceiling. In 1841, Mrs Clemons described such an arrangement in Madras houses where the occupiers 'procure strong and coarse white cloth, which is sewn together, and forms a sheet, that extends the whole length of the room; this is placed from wall to wall, and stretched and nailed across; frequently a deep frill is put round it, which forms a kind of cornice'.[110] In 1892, Constance Gordon Cumming also described such a feature in Ceylon bungalows, and noted that with the stretched cloth in place 'the whole space within the roof is a reservoir of air'.[111] Other fittings within the interior, intended to aid the circulation of air, such as door screens or 'half-doors' (which allowed doors to be left open but created some privacy for the occupiers of the room) and *purdahs* or curtains fixed to door frames for a similar purpose, were also ever present reminders to British residents that the organization of their domestic space was determined to a great extent by local environmental factors and local usage.[112]

A wide variety of other local heat-reducing devices was deployed within the Anglo-Indian home. 'Tats' or 'tatties' – flexible blinds which were made from strips of rattan, a variety of grass or palm fibres that could be rolled up when not in use – were deployed on the outside of many dwellings within the Subcontinent to mitigate the light and heat of the sun. In Ceylon, rattan was the preferred material; in India, a fragrant grass known as *kuskus* was often used.[113] When wetted, these *kuskus* 'tats' gave off a fragrant aroma and helped reduce the temperature within the house.[114] 'Tats' were hung across doorways, over windows or between the columns of verandahs. Another device developed during the nineteenth century to reduce heat within the domestic interior was the thermantidote, described in 1864 as 'a species of revolving fan in a box with tatties at the sides; they are wet and the fan is turned round with a handle, producing a current of cool air'.[115] Curtains were rarely found in the Anglo-Indian interior before 1850 (as they harboured insects and impeded the flow of air), after which date windows decked with light-diffusing drapes became a more common, although by no means universal, feature.[116] In fact, the inclusion of textiles within the Anglo-Indian home, unless this was located in the cooler climate of the hills, was an unusual occurrence before 1850. After this date, however, a greater number of European homes in India included textiles in the main reception rooms, their inhabitants setting aside advice offered in Anglo-Indian household-management advice literature.[117]

In comparison to the situation within the homeland, the absence of (or reduced usage of) textiles within the Anglo-Indian domestic interior during the nineteenth century was noted by many contemporary commentators. This contributed to the generally expressed belief among the Anglo-Indian community that their domestic spaces were 'unfurnished' and lacked comfort. Without the softening effect of textiles which was so much a feature of the domestic interior within the homeland (both physically, in the sense of smoothing away sharp angles and also metaphorically, as markers of taste and manners), domestic space in the Subcontinent presented a general appearance of bareness and also signified a want of politeness to the occupiers. It also signalled an unsettling inability, among the European community, to exercise complete control over their domestic environment. The imperatives of a hot and malarial climate militated against the inclusion of textiles within the domestic interior. Local practice reflected this, and all Anglo-Indians were in the same position, in that a key priority within the Subcontinent was the maintenance of the health of the household; however, evidence suggests that many of them ignored these concerns and endeavoured to ameliorate the bare and harsh aspects of the Anglo-Indian domestic interior through the use of a range of textiles.

Floors and floor coverings

Anglo-Indian homes also lacked the softening effect of knotted and piled carpets on the floor. Due to their resistance to attack by insects, the ground floors of bungalows and houses within the Subcontinent during the nineteenth century were formed of either brick, tile, polished-*chunam* [burnt lime] covered aggregate, stone paving or cement. In 1813, for instance, Charles Doyley noted of Anglo-Indian dwellings that 'the floors are never boarded … [and] throughout India, terrace-work [i.e. brick-work and lime mortar] is substituted for plank'.[118] In 1841, Mrs Clemons described the flooring in Madras houses and noted that they were 'of stone or brick, or a composition of lime and gravel; they are also *chunam*ed over, in black and white squares, which gives them a beautiful appearance'.[119] An account written in 1869 of the housing stock in Colombo noted that in older houses 'polished floors and pillars … were formerly produced by mixing *jaggery* (coarse palm sugar) and eggs with lime. But this expensive application is now superseded by the use of imported cements'.[120] Other commentators also noted the usage of cement or stone paving.[121] The first floor of two-storey dwellings was either constructed of 'terrace-work' or wooden boards, usually a strong, utilitarian timber such as jackwood, which could resist attack by white ants; these boards were cut to varying dimensions depending on their function. For instance, in 1831, an estimate prepared for fitting new floors in the 'sleeping apartments' at King's House, Colombo itemized a large number of jackwood planks ranging in thickness from ¾ of an inch to 2 inches.[122] Other timbers were also selected as materials for floorboards, such as teak and 'dell'.[123]

The floors of Anglo-Indian bungalows were invariably covered with joined lengths of finely woven matting. In 1813, these were described as being 'made of very hard reeds about the thickness of a crow-quill, worked in stripes of … a foot or more in breadth each' which 'gives a very remarkable neatness to the apartments'.[124] Matting was also made of a variety of long grass.[125] Matting enhanced the coolness of interiors in a climate where woollen carpeting of a European type would have been both visually as well as physically intolerable. Different regional varieties of matting were found in houses within the Subcontinent: in Madras, rattan matting was most common; in Hyderabad district, mats could be made of 'date leaves plaited together', which cost a small amount of money but required renewal each year.[126]

In Ceylon, a variety of matting was produced at Dumbara near Kandy.[127] Some matting was also imported into the Subcontinent from China. Inventories of the British government houses in Ceylon, written during the first half of the nineteenth century, record the types, cost and origin of these mats. In 1833 the King's House in Colombo was described as being fitted with a large number of 'rattan mattings' of varying cost.[128] Those designated as 'Chinese' were the most highly valued, with three 'sets Chinese [matting] @ £6.10s each'. Other mats in the government houses were described as originating from either 'Bengal' or 'Kandy'.[129] Matting was not a fixture in all houses, and British residents often had to purchase the necessary floor coverings. In 1841, Mrs Griffiths recorded the purchase of mats for her house in Colombo:

> A man came today with some mats for sale. Many of them are beautifully made, though not equal to the Madras matting, which persons, who are anxious to have their houses furnished in the handsomest style, send for, and have made to order, but these come very expensive and the Cingalese matting is exceedingly cheap. We bought a set of bedside mats today made of reed, in imitation of the Madras, for £ 1.00 and I believe we were <u>well cheated</u>.[130]

The use of matting in the Anglo-Indian interior was a near-universal phenomenon and evidenced the incorporation of another local feature into the European home in South Asia. In fact, numerous nineteenth-century inventories include, as the last item in a room, the standard form of words: 'the mat on the floor'. This adaptation of a local form of furnishing was not necessarily met with unease; in fact, most British residents were favourably impressed by the visual effect of neatness and coolness of a room entirely covered with matting. More coarsely woven coir matting (a by-product of the harvest of the coconut palm) was also used to cover the floors of verandahs, especially in Ceylon.[131] Its adoption as a furnishing material may have been based on the contemporary belief that the material deterred snakes from entering the house.[132]

If a room was not entirely fitted with matting, the inclusion of small mats on bare floors helped create a semblance of comfort as well as the maintenance of a sense of politeness and gentility within the domestic interior and, in addition, aided the creation of unified 'islands' of furniture in a room setting. In the bedroom, the bed and its individual mats were invariably associated as a furnishing group. Nineteenth-century concepts of germ theory and the importance of domestic cleanliness also encouraged the adoption of mats, although in fact dust and dirt fell through the weave of these floor coverings, the undersides of which became breeding grounds for insects.

The use of tufted carpets in the Anglo-Indian domestic interior, a rare occurrence during the eighteenth century, became more noticeable from the second quarter of the nineteenth century, although their use was still restricted to a limited number of (usually urban) interiors.[133] Most of these carpets were of Indian manufacture; however, in the last quarter of the nineteenth century, household-management advice guides recommended that, in addition to locally produced carpets, Persian ones could also add colour and interest to the bungalow interior.[134]

Lighting the domestic interior

Previous scholarship has neglected the lighting of the Anglo-Indian interior. In India and Ceylon, before the widespread adoption and use of electricity in the domestic interior (i.e., until around 1900), methods of lighting, despite some developments, relied on basic technologies. These developments did, however, have a profound effect on socialization in the home after dark, the ability to read or work and the placement of furniture within the interior. Furthermore, the provision of light after dark was not merely a practical concern. It has been argued elsewhere that, during the nineteenth century 'light became a sensory metaphor for genteel society'.[135] In fact, the requirement for bright, steady light throughout the grander houses of the Subcontinent may have been more than a simple necessity; it most probably also signified that 'light was an element in the brilliance of grand entertainments in parlours and drawing rooms' of the nineteenth century.[136]

In the early nineteenth century, wax and spermaceti candles were used widely in domestic interiors of India and Ceylon, in conjunction with local, oil-burning forms of lighting.[137] In 1813, Charles Doyley described the type of lighting found in the Anglo-Indian interior, as well as the device used to protect the flame from continual draughts (as well as insects). He noted:

> the necessity, which exists for keeping the doors and many windows open, at all times, renders it expedient to guard the candles, which are invariably of wax, from the gusts of wind that would … speedily blow out every light. Shades, made of glass, are put over such candles as stand on tables.[138]

In 1829, an inventory of the property of Joseph Dacre, a civil servant with the East India Company in Madras, recorded his ownership of nine 'old candle stands with shades'.[139]

In the same passage above, Doyley also described another standard form of light source in the Anglo-Indian interior, namely the 'wall-shade', or 'sconce branch', each of which is 'furnished with similar protections, made in the form of a deep narrow vase [of glass]'.[140] 'Wall-shades' or 'wall lights' were recorded in numerous accounts of contemporary commentators and inventories in the late eighteenth and early nineteenth centuries. They remained the most common form of light source in many, especially metropolitan interiors, well into the 1850s, when they were superseded by more effective devices.[141] In 1845, for example, the drawing room of Major Fitzgerald, Calcutta contained six pairs of 'double branch wall-lights with plated arms, carved toon wood brackets, vase shades and oil burners'.[142] Later in the nineteenth century, other forms of wall-mounted lighting were adopted in Anglo-Indian homes, such as 'Duplex wall lamps [with glass] globes and ... chimneys'.[143] In rural localities, however, more basic forms of lighting were to be found. For instance, in 1843, the Reverend Charles Acland described the manner in which his rented bungalow at Cuttack, north-east India, was lit:

> a flat candlestick [standing on a sideboard], with a glass shade, to keep the insects from the flame. The candle is wax; we cannot use tallow for two reasons: the climate ... is so hot that the candles would not remain upright, and the sheep here have very little fat upon them. On the table are two Indian table-lamps ... The lower part is like an upright candlestick, on which is placed a glass cup half filled with water, the other half with cocoa-nut oil. In the bottom is a little bit of lead with two thin cotton wicks in it, which reach ... above the surface of the oil. These are alight. Over the whole is a large inverted bell-glass.[144]

By the second quarter of the nineteenth century, a wide variety of light sources illuminated the Anglo-Indian interior. Despite having an official function, as the residence of the Governor of the colony, the reception rooms in King's House (after 1837 renamed Queen's House) in Colombo, were of a similar scale to those found in many grand private dwellings in Calcutta and Bombay. The contents of this house therefore offer representative examples of lighting which were located in many imposing British-inhabited dwellings in metropolitan centres within the Subcontinent as a whole. In 1833, an inventory of the contents of King's House itemized various forms of lighting.[145] Under the subheading 'Glassware', the inventory listed '2 Chandeliers with 8 shades @ £28.2.6 each; 2 Bronzed Hanging Lamps or Lusters @ £16.17.6 each; 1 Large centre Lantern @ £15.2.6' and a variety of 'hanging lamps' of different sizes ranging in cost from £3.15 to £1.7 each. These were most probably lit by candles as the inventory also records an oil-powered 'Lantern with 4 burners @ £11.5'. The house also contained a large quantity of 'wall shades', either 'double branched' or single, ranging in cost from £5.12.6 to 11 shillings each. By 1850, many Anglo-Indian interiors were also lit by plain glass hanging lamps with inverted cloche-shaped or spherical bowls below circular glass smoke deflectors. These lamps were ordered from Britain, as were the majority of glass lighting devices within the Subcontinent. In one letter of 1853, these devices are described as 'hanging oval lamps, with chains, oil glasses & c ... of plain glass ... neat pattern and the chains of white metal'.[146]

The tables of wealthier British residents in the Subcontinent might be furnished with imported 'plated branched candlesticks' or 'plated large table candlesticks'.[147] Table centrepieces fitted with candelabra and shades are also recorded.[148] For the highest levels of British society within India, local cabinetmakers also produced stands for lighting devices; descriptions of 'ebony candle sticks with shades' and 'ebony candle stands' are recorded in the inventories of the British government houses in Ceylon.[149] In 1855, the firm of Deschamps, one of the most prominent European cabinetmakers in Madras, provided 'a candelabra in carved rosewood' for the Governor General of the Presidency.[150]

After 1830, a major development in lighting the Anglo-Indian interior took place with the introduction to the Subcontinent of the Argand lamp. This lamp could be placed on tables, or the Argand patent device could be fitted as part of a hanging lamp, depending on the domestic situation. This lamp produced much stronger illumination than candle-powered or other oil-burning devices and allowed a greater number of people in a room to benefit from such light. This development had a marked effect on the placement and use of furniture in the Anglo-Indian interior. Peter Thornton has noted that this improved intensity of illumination 'encouraged the use of the round table about which [people] could read, sew or play cards'.[151] The disadvantages of these and other oil-burning lamps were 'the inconvenient shadow cast by their reservoirs' and the heat generated by combustion (in an environment which was already hot).[152]

Argand lamps are first recorded in the British government houses within Ceylon from 1839.[153] However, these lamps were adopted by many levels of Anglo-Indian society. For example, in 1846 William Wise, a pilot employed by the East India Company in Bombay and, as evidenced by the inventory of his estate of modest means, was recorded as possessing '1 Argand lamp' among his other furnishings.[154] These lamps are also itemized in grander houses within India. In 1859, an inventory of the contents of Robert Dunlop's house in Calcutta recorded in the drawing room 'Argand Hanging Lamps – A set of four splendid frosted and cut glass Hanging Lamps with elegant bronze mountings under dishes, domes etc'.[155] Other lamps, such as Tucker's Tent Lamps, were also available in the Subcontinent after 1850.[156] In addition to Argand lamps, other patent devices such as 'Argyle table lamps' were used in the Anglo-Indian interior.[157] Oil or kerosene lamps supplied light to the domestic interiors of India and Ceylon until the last decade of the nineteenth century, when electric lighting was gradually introduced.[158]

Rain, humidity and pests

For Anglo-Indians in their homes, as well as striving to maintain basic levels of comfort within the domestic interiors of the Subcontinent during the nineteenth century, they found their composure unsettled by other local nuisances – arising from the tropical climate – which were of an entirely different order to related nuisances encountered within the domestic context in Europe, and which disturbed Western sensory experiences in the heart of the home.

In addition to mitigating the heat and glare of the sun, domestic interiors within the Subcontinent had to withstand the effects of the violent and prolonged rainstorms of the two monsoons. In 1803, Robert Percival complained that, in his house at Colombo during the rainy season, the tiles on the roof 'admit water in such a manner, that it is difficult to find a dry spot to place ones head under'.[159] Similarly, in 1855 Sir Henry Ward, the Governor of Ceylon, while listing the repairs needed to his house in Colombo, described to the Secretary of State for the Colonies the effect of the north-east monsoon on the interiors of that dwelling:

> for five consecutive days, the rain has poured into every room in the house with as much violence, as if there were no roof at all – to the serious injury of the furniture, floors and great staircase, on parts of which the water has remained standing, in pools half an inch deep.[160]

In 1856, Thomas Machell, a planter at Coonoor in southern India, described his domestic life high in the hills and the problems caused by wet weather during the monsoon. In his journal he drew a plan of his home, the poignantly named Bonn Espoir bungalow, and noted that

> the above plan of our present house looks very well on paper but a little consideration will show that the inner rooms are dark and the outer rooms damp: in fact, the roof is so contrived that it serves only to convey the water down the walls and the tiles used here ... absorb nearly their own weight in water.[161]

Because of the heavy rainfall in most parts of the Subcontinent at certain times of the year and the associated high relative humidity, many domestic interiors were, during the monsoon seasons, perpetually damp. In 1859, Sir James Emerson Tennent mentioned that

> the chief inconvenience of a mansion in Ceylon, both on the coast and in the mountains, is the prevalence of damp, and the difficulty of protecting articles liable to injury from this source. Books, papers and manuscripts rapidly decay; especially during the south-west monsoon, when the atmosphere is laden with moisture.[162]

In a similar vein, in 1884, Lady Nora Scott described conditions inside her house in Bombay during the monsoon and how 'drenching rain and storms of wind' penetrated the living rooms. She also noted the damage done by the wet weather and the drastic remedies effected to protect fragile materials:

> this weather is very bad for books. One man ... is all day engaged in airing and drying books. He takes a *sigaree* (a pot with a little charcoal fire in it) and sets it down before a book-case and then takes the books down and

sets them upon end, partly open to let the heat in, in a circle round the fire, and then when they are dry he goes to another book-case. It looks so odd … the solemn circle of books like a little Stone Henge and the fire in the middle.[163]

As well as damaging paper, such dampness was also detrimental to textiles and soft furnishings.

Tropical insects also created different problems in relation to building and furnishing the Anglo-Indian domestic interior. Damage caused to house contents by 'white ants' (termites) was a recurring theme in contemporary accounts.[164] In 1850, Henry Charles Sirr described their destructive power in the following terms: 'this small insect [the white ant] is dreaded by both Europeans and natives, as it will undermine houses, destroy furniture, devour clothing and render provisions useless'.[165] Contemporary commentators also described the precautions necessary to prevent insect attack on items of furniture. In 1862, Colesworthy Grant noted of the domestic interiors in Calcutta that 'the feet of bed-posts and other articles of furniture, which may demand the precaution, [were rested] upon stone or metal stands, in which there is a groove … around the centre filled with water'.[166] This method of deterrence also offered some protection for the human occupants of such furniture. For example, in 1841 Mrs Griffiths wrote of the house she was renting in Grand Pass, Colombo 'we have nothing in [the bedroom] but the large bed … which stands in its bowls of water in the centre of the room, this making us as secure as possible from reptile intrusion'.[167] However, during the evening hours before bed-time, Anglo-Indians were often bothered in their homes by a variety of Asian frogs, beetles, lizards, mosquitoes and other flying insects, which were attracted to the artificial lights of the interior.[168]

The physical environment of India and Ceylon, together with local climatic conditions, which had shaped indigenous buildings, their interiors and local social practices for centuries, continued, at least throughout the nineteenth century, to modify the domestic spaces, furnishings and social practices of British residents within the Subcontinent. The material qualities of the colonial bungalow served as troubling reminders to these European residents, as Will Glover has suggested 'of the co-presence of different sensory qualities, meanings and values tied to more local histories of production and use'.[169] Although the material culture of domestic space in the homeland was by no means fixed or unchanging and required completion by the occupier, evocation by Anglo-Indians of a cultural memory of 'home' within the colonial bungalow was disrupted by the physical qualities of that space. Instead of stimulating remembering (of the domestic interior in the homeland), the material culture of the colonial bungalow continually cut across the construction of meaning and interrupted the process of evocation which the notion, as well as reality, of home promised. Anglo-Indians also had to accustom themselves to a greater relinquishing of control over their domestic environment than they were used to in the homeland. In order to cope with the harsh climate of the region, they had to follow, or at least adapt, local material-culture practices. Through these actions, they were compelled to embody and enact many of the alien practices of a subject people. This daily process presented a continual challenge to their self-perception as rulers and, as discussed in the next chapter, caused them to re-think material-culture practices normally associated with domestic space and the artefacts of home.

Notes

1 Sten Nilsson, *European Architecture in India, 1750–1850* (London, 1968). Susan Lewandowski has discussed the growth of Madras. S. Lewandowski, 'Urban growth and municipal development in the colonial city of Madras, 1860–1900', *Journal of Asian Studies*, vol. 34, no. 2 (1975), pp. 341–60.

2 Gavin Stamp, 'British architecture in India, 1857–1947', *Journal of the Royal Society of Arts*, vol. 129 (May 1981), pp. 357–79.

3 G.H.R. Tillotson, *The Tradition of Indian Architecture: continuity, controversy and change since 1850* (New Haven and London, 1989). Published in the same year, Thomas Metcalf's, *An Imperial Vision: Indian architecture and Britain's Raj* (Berkeley, 1989), among other aspects, discusses Arts and Crafts architecture in India and power relations between Britain and India within the architectural field.

4 J.P. Losty, *Calcutta: city of palaces* (London, 1990) and 'British trading settlements and trading centres', in A. Jackson and A. Jaffer (eds), *Encounters: the meeting of Asia and Europe, 1500–1800* (exhib. cat., London, 2004), pp. 144–53.

5 Swati Chattopadhyay, 'Blurring Boundaries: the limits of "white town" in colonial Calcutta', *Journal of the Society of Architectural Historians*, vol. 59, no. 2 (June 2000), pp. 154–79; Will Glover, '"A feeling of absence from Old England": the colonial bungalow', *Home Cultures*, vol. 1, no. 1 (2004), pp. 61–82.

6 James Duncan, 'The power of place in Kandy, Sri Lanka: 1780–1980', in J. Duncan and J. Agnew (eds), *The Power of Place: bringing together geographical and sociological imaginations* (Cambridge, 1989), pp. 185–201; J. Duncan, *The City as Text: the politics of landscape interpretation in the Kandyan kingdom*, (Cambridge, 1990).

7 Christopher Bayly (ed.), *The Raj: India and the British, 1600–1947* (exhib. cat., London, 1990), p. 11.

8 Bayly (ed.), *The Raj*, p. 70.

9 S. Muthiah, 'From sandy strip to metropolis', in K. Kalpana and F. Schiffer (eds), *Madras: the architectural heritage* (Chennai, 2003) p. 19.

10 Philip Davies, 'Madras: history and urban development', *Grove Dictionary of Art Online* (Oxford University Press) www.groveart.com (accessed 19 March 2005).

11 Davies, 'Madras', *Grove Dictionary of Art Online*.

12 Fort St George was reconstructed between 1755 and 1783 by a number of British military engineers including Captain John Brohier and Colonel Patrick Ross. During

the Wars of Carnatic, Madras was captured by the French under Bertrand-François Mahé de la Bourdonnais in 1746 and Thomas-Arthur de Lally in 1758.

13 Kalpana and Schiffer (eds), *Madras*, p. 18.

14 *A Guide to the City of Madras and its Suburbs* (Madras, 1889).

15 *A Guide to the City of Madras*, p. 29.

16 *A Guide to the City of Madras*, p. 31.

17 *A Visit to Madras; being a sketch of the local and characteristic peculiarities of the Presidency in the year 1811* (London, 1821), p. 10.

18 Mrs Clemons, *The Manners and Customs of Society in India* (London, 1841) pp. 10–12.

19 *Thacker's Reduced Survey Map of India* (Calcutta, 1914).

20 Kalpana and Schiffer (eds), *Madras*, p. 198.

21 Kalpana and Schiffer (eds), *Madras*, p. 341.

22 Philip Davies, 'Calcutta: urban development, 1690–1845', *Grove Dictionary of Art Online* (Oxford University Press) www.groveart.com (accessed 19 March 2005).

23 Davies, 'Calcutta', *Grove Dictionary of Art Online*.

24 Davies, 'Calcutta', *Grove Dictionary of Art Online*.

25 Chunam: 'prepared lime; also specially used for fine polished plaster', Col. H. Yule and A.C. Burnell (eds), *Hobson-Jobson; a glossary of colloquial Anglo-Indian words and phrases, and of kindred terms, etymological, historical, geographical and discursive* (London, 1886, reprinted 1994), p. 218.

26 Davies, 'Calcutta', *Grove Dictionary of Art Online*.

27 Losty, *Calcutta*, pp. 7–8.

28 Davies, 'Calcutta', *Grove Dictionary of Art Online*.

29 Davies, 'Calcutta', *Grove Dictionary of Art Online*.

30 Losty, *Calcutta*, p. 37.

31 Mrs Kindersley, *Letters from the Island of Teneriffe, Brazil, the Cape of Good Hope and the East Indies* (London, 1777) cited in Losty, *Calcutta*, p. 40.

32 Chattopadhyay, 'Blurring Boundaries', p. 159.

33 Chattopadhyay, 'Blurring Boundaries', p. 170.

34 London, British Library: Add.Or. 3204, builders' design for a two-storey house showing front elevation and ground plan, inscribed 'J. Shadwell S.Goss & Co. Builders, 141 Durumt[ola], Calc[utta]', *c.* 1830.

35 Colesworthy Grant, *Anglo-Indian Domestic Life; a letter from an artist in India to his mother in England* (Calcutta, 1862), p. 5.

36 Grant, *Anglo-Indian Domestic Life*, p. 8.

37 Grant, *Anglo-Indian Domestic Life*, p. 8.

38 Grant, *Anglo-Indian Domestic Life*, p. 8.

39 Philip Davies, 'Bombay: history and urban development: early history, before 1803', *Grove Dictionary of Art Online* (Oxford University Press) www.groveart.com (accessed 19 March 2005).

40 Davies, 'Bombay', *Grove Dictionary of Art Online*.

41 Davies, 'Bombay', *Grove Dictionary of Art Online*.

42 Davies, 'Bombay', *Grove Dictionary of Art Online*.

43 Gillian Tindall, *City of Gold: the biography of Bombay* (London, 1982), p. 167.

44 Tindall, *City of Gold*, p. 168.

45 Tindall, *City of Gold*, p. 198.

46 James Maclean, *A Guide to Bombay; historical, statistical and descriptive* (Bombay, 1876), p. 223.

47 Maclean, *A Guide to Bombay*, p. 239.

48 *Life in Bombay and the Neighbouring Out-Stations* (London, 1852), pp. 14–15.

49 *Life in Bombay*, p. 16.

50 *Life in Bombay*, pp. 16–17.

51 Sharada Dwivedi, 'Homes in the nineteenth century', in P. Pal (ed.), *Bombay to Mumbai: changing persepctives* (Mumbai, 1997), p. 165.

52 *Bombay to Mumbai*, pp. 44–5.

53 'chupra': 'a collection of straw huts'; 'chopper': 'a thatched roof', Yule and Burnell (eds), *Hobson-Jobson*, pp. 209 and 220.

54 Mrs Postans, *Western India in 1838* (London, 1839), p. 13.

55 Postans, *Western India*, p. 15.

56 In 1885, Lady Nora Scott described a visit to friends living in a flat above the Alexandra Girls' School, Bombay. University of Cambridge, Centre of South Asian Studies, Scott papers, 28 February 1885.

57 An example of this type of house, owned by Daniel Ditloff, Count van Ratzow and located two kilometres from the Fort in the direction of the Kelani River, is illustrated in M. de Bruijn and R. Raben (eds), *The World of Jan Brandes, 1743–1808: drawings of a Dutch traveller in Batavia, Ceylon and Southern Africa* (Zwolle and Amsterdam, 2004), p. 240. The house is a single-storeyed structure built in the 'Lanka-Dutch architectural style' of the eighteenth century, with sloping, tiled roof extending to form a verandah, supported by wooden columns.

58 Sir James Emerson Tennent, *Ceylon: an account of the island, physical, historical and topographical* (London, 1859) vol. 2, p. 669.

59 Ismeth Raheem, 'Colombo', *Grove Dictionary of Art Online* (Oxford University Press), www.groveart.com (accessed 19 March 2005).

60 Robert Percival, *An Account of the Island of Ceylon* (London, 1803), pp. 103–4.

61 London, National Archives: MPHH 3 (4), 'Plan of the Square within the Fort of Colombo bounded by the four streets, King Street, Chatham Street, Galle Street, Flagstaff Row', 15 November 1833.

62 Viscount Valentia, *Voyages and Travels to India, Ceylon, the Red Sea, Abyssinia and Egypt in the years 1802–1806* (London, 1809), p. 266.

63 I. Raheem and P. Colin Thomé, *Images of British Ceylon: nineteenth century photography of Sri Lanka* (Singapore, 2000), pp. 82–3.

64 However, a number of schemes emerged in India during the 1860s and 1870s to demolish the old walls of European forts in Presidency towns. In 1864 the walls of the old fort at Bombay were removed as part of the first major municipal improvements under direction of James Trubshawe, architect to the Ramparts Removal Committee.

65 University of Peradeniya, Sri Lanka: Journal of Major and Mrs J. Darby Griffiths, 4 vols, 'Ceylon during a residence in the years 1841–2', vol. 1, 12 April 1841, p. 103.

66 C. F. Gordon Cumming, *Two Happy Years in Ceylon* (Edinburgh and London, 1892), vol. 1, pp. 56–7.

67 John Deschamps, *Scenery and Reminiscences of Ceylon* (London, 1845), plate 6, 'View of Colpitty from Cinnamon Gardens'.

68 Tennent, *Ceylon*, vol. 2, p. 669. Jalousie – slatted shutter on outside of window or door.

69 London, National Archives: MR 1/522, 'Map of the Fort of Colombo exhibiting the figure of the ground appertaining to each house … Colombo', 10 July 1839.

70 Henry Charles Sirr, *Ceylon and the Cingalese* (London, 1850), vol. 1, p. 44.

71 For example, James Steuart, the Master Attendant at the Port of Colombo, owned outright land and buildings on 'both sides of the High Road leading from Colombo to the Point de Galle' as well as a dwelling house at number 13, King Street, the Fort, Colombo. Worcester, Record Office, Register of Wills, vol. 6, part 3, Steuart, James, 30 April 1870, Last Will and Testament of James Steuart. See also note 72. Thomas Hudson owned considerable amounts of land in Colombo during the 1860s.

72 University of Oxford, Rhodes House Library: Mss.Ind.Ocn.t.6, 'Plans of Coffee Estates in Ceylon and of Polwatte Mills and Coffee Store, Colombo', Colombo, 1865. These were owned outright by a planter, Thomas Hudson.

73 *Map of the Municipality of Colombo* (Colombo, 1899).

74 Further details of the nineteenth and twentieth houses of the British and local elite in Colombo can be found in Lakshman Alwis, *British Period Architecture in Sri Lanka* (Colombo, 1992).

75 A.D. King, *The Bungalow: the production of a global culture* (London, 1984).

76 A collection of photographs taken by Henry Manners in the 1870s, formerly in the Special Collection of Bath Academy of Art (ref A954), records the large-scale bungalows belonging to the British owners of indigo factories north of Patna, around Sonepur, Turkaulia and Pipra.

77 W.M. Reid, *The Culture and Manufacture of Indigo; with a description of a planter's life and resources*, (Calcutta, 1887), p. 9.

78 London, British Library: Mss.Eur. B369/5 (53), Journals of T. Machell, 'Travels in Hindoostan, the Punjab & Scinde & Kashmir, 1854–5', which includes a plan and elevation of a Bonn Espoir bungalow, 'Koonoor', S. India; London, Church Mission Society, Missionary Photographs, 'photograph of coffee planter's bungalow in Ceylon, 1874'; Cambridge University Library, Royal Commonwealth Society Archive: Y3022G (27), photograph by Charles Scowen of tea estate bungalow in Ceylon, *c.* 1870; *Life in the Mofussil; or the Civilian in Lower Bengal* (London, 1878), pp. 55–6 for description of Assistant Magistrate's bungalow in country region.

79 London, National Archives: CO 54/163, 'Plan Section's and Elevations of a Residence for the Assistant Agent and District Judge … built at Kaygalle … on the road to Kandy', Colombo, 28 April 1838. This document illustrates the scale of rooms in this dwelling, the largest of which is 24 feet by 20 feet by 16 feet high. See also Clemons, *The Manners and Customs*, p. 11; The Reverend C. Acland, *A Popular Account of the Manners and Customs of India* (London, 1847), p. 64; Grant, *Anglo-Indian Domestic Life*, p. 9; London, British Library: Bengal Wills, 1863, L/AG/34/27/170, Estate of G.M. Gasper, which records among the moveable property (and also offers a sense

of scale of the main reception room), a swinging fan or punkah, 26 feet in length.

80 Matlock, Derbyshire Record Office: Coke of Brookhill Collection, D/1881/L2. In a letter of 4 February 1810, Sir William Coke, a senior judge in Ceylon, wrote to his brother about living conditions in Colombo. He noted of his bungalow at Mutwal, a district beyond the densely-packed housing in the city centre, that although: '[during] the middle of the day … the sun is very powerful, but … with a fresh breeze from the sea it is pleasant enough' and 'my house proposes great advantages over the Fort in this regard'.

81 University of Cambridge, Centre of South Asian Studies: Thompson Papers, newspaper cuttings, *Bangalore Gazette*, 5 March 1881, 'An Architect Wanted'.

82 Acland, *A Popular Account*, p. 64.

83 Amin Jaffer, *Furniture from British India and Ceylon: a catalogue of the collections in the Victoria and Albert Museum and Peabody Essex Museum* (London, 2001), pp. 55–6.

84 Percival, *An Account of the Island*, p. 103.

85 Tennent, *Ceylon*, vol. 2, p. 669. Other commentators also recorded the closed-in aspect of Dutch houses. Describing her newly rented property in Grand Pass, Colombo, Mrs Griffiths wrote in 1841 that although it was 'large and commodious' it was 'unfortunately built in the Dutch style with glass windows'. University of Peradeniya, Sri Lanka: Griffiths, 'Ceylon during a residence', vol. 2, p. 49.

86 London, British Library: Add. Or. 2515.

87 London, British Library: Add. Or. 3204.

88 University of Cambridge, Centre of South Asian Studies: Thompson Papers, 'Estimate for house to be built at Bangalore as per plan of 17th September 1881, M.W. Thompson, Architect, Holmesdale, St John's Hill, Bangalore, 23rd November 1881'.

89 London, National Archives: CO 54/163, 'Plan Section's and Elevations of a Residence'. The two main rooms were each designed with six door openings. In 1841 Mrs Griffiths noted the large number of doorways and window openings found in a bungalow which she and her family rented in Colpetty, Colombo. University of Peradeniya, Sri Lanka: Griffiths, 'Ceylon during a residence', vol. 2, p. 104.

90 Acland, *A Popular Account*, p. 65.

91 The open, spatial arrangements within the Anglo-Indian dwelling and consequent potential for voyeuristic looking by outsiders and local servants, has led some scholars to discuss the colonial bungalow in terms of 'the architectural uncanny'. This can be defined as 'a domesticated and limited frisson of unease', whose most effective locus is the home 'made unhomely by the sense of an alien presence'. See A. Vidler, *The Architectural Uncanny: essays in the modern unhomely* (Cambridge, MA, 1992), *passim*; Glover, '"A Feeling of Absence"', pp. 76–7; Andrew Ballantyne, 'The Architectural Uncanny: essays in the modern unhomely', *British Journal of Aesthetics*, vol. 34, no. 2 (April 1994), p. 193.

92 *Life in Bombay*, p. 17.

93 Reid, *The Culture and Manufacture of Indigo*, pp. 9–10.

94 Glover, '"A Feeling of Absence"', p. 76.

95 A photograph taken in 1865 of Polwatte Bungalow, near Beira Lake, Colombo which was owned by coffee planter Thomas Hudson shows the extensive verandah of the property furnished with an assortment of easy chairs and tables. University of Oxford, Rhodes House Library: Mss.Ind.Ocn. t.6, 'Plans of Coffee Estates in Ceylon'.

96 *Life in Bombay*, p. 15.

97 Gordon Cumming, *Two Happy Years*, vol. 1, pp. 56–7.

98 The inventory of Elizabeth Johannes Sarkies (the wife of an Armenian broker), filed on 12 February 1859, recorded the items 'In the Verandah' of her house at 4 Clive's Row, Calcutta. These contents indicate that commercial activities also most probably took place in this area, as they were described as follows: 'a substantial sitsaul wood table …, a wooden chest …, a zinc-lined ice chest, a toon wood bedside stand …, a lot of planks for packing shawls, a toon wood camp table, a saul wood table, two toon wood garden chairs with rattan seats, five painted armchairs, an 8 day capital striking clock by Barraud …, a shawl platform [and other items]'. London, British Library: Bengal Wills, 1859, L/AG/34/27/163, Estate of Elizabeth J. Sarkies.

99 In 1855, while Governor of Ceylon, Sir Henry Ward complained to the Colonial Office in London of the incomplete building works at his official residence, Queen's House, Colombo and bemoaned the fact that: 'sunshades, which are indisputable in a climate like this, [had been] wholly omitted'. London, National Archives: CO 54/316. Newly-fitted corrugated iron sunshades can be seen in a photograph of Queen's House, Colombo taken in 1875 in the collection of the Royal Commonwealth Society Archive, University of Cambridge, Y303B, plate 42.

100 Charles Doyley, *The European in India* (London, 1813), n.p.

101 Grant, *Anglo Indian Domestic Life*, p. 12. Grant also illustrates a typical Venetian shutter.

102 In 1850, Henry Charles Sirr wrote that: 'the abodes of all Europeans in Ceylon bear a striking similitude to each other … every door and window alike open and the portals of distinct apartments having moveable blinds placed midway in the frame-work'. In 1859, Sir James Emerson Tennent referred to the 'Venetian jalousies' fitted to Anglo-Ceylonese houses. Sirr, *Ceylon and the Cingalese*, vol. 1, p. 65; Tennent, *Ceylon*, vol. 2, p. 669.

103 Doyley, *The European in India*, n.p.; Grant, *Anglo-Indian Domestic Life*, p. 22; William Hart, *Everyday Life in Bengal and other Indian Sketches* (London, 1906), p. 74.

104 Hart, *Everyday Life in Bengal*, p. 74. He dryly notes that, at a time of political unrest, the servant employed to pull the *punkah* was 'the most useful agitator in Bengal' and that it was his job to keep the fan swinging 'through the hot, weary hours. The motion of the air just makes life tolerable'.

105 John Penry Lewis, *Ceylon in Early British Times* (Colombo, 1913), p. 32.

106 London, National Archives: CO 54/136, 'Inventory of furniture in the King's House, Colombo', 31 December 1834.

107 University of Peradeniya, Sri Lanka: Griffiths, 'Ceylon during a Residence', vol. 1, p. 107, 2 April 1841. Other commentators, such as Henry Charles Sirr, noted the use of *punkahs* in the Anglo-Ceylonese interior; in fact, the latter describes an accident involving one. Sirr, *Ceylon and the Cingalese*, vol., 1, pp. 65–6.

108 The early models often resemble the propellers of First World War fighter bi-planes. Examples of such rotating fans can be seen in photographs of the interior of the Old Mess House, Harrington Street, Madras, *c.* 1920, University of Cambridge, Centre of South Asian Studies, Stokes Papers. In the 1920s and 1930s, Greaves Cotton and Co. supplied Crompton rotating ceiling fans to the Subcontinent, see advertisement in *Journal of the Indian Institute of Architects*, vol. 3, no. 1 (July 1936), opp. p. 172.

109 See plate 2 in Grant, *Anglo-Indian Domestic Life*, which illustrates a typical hall room in a Calcutta house.

110 Clemons, *The Manners and Customs*, p. 11.

111 Gordon Cumming, *Two Happy Years*, p. 56.

112 *The Englishwoman in India* (London, 1864), p. 36; 'in most houses there are half doors between each room … these are a sort of screen opening with hinges … but leaving a free current of air above and below'.

113 London, National Archives: CO 54/173, in December 1839 the 'Return of the Furniture in the Public Rooms of the Queen's House, Colombo' itemized '16 Ratan Tats Large'. In 1864, the author of *The Englishwoman in India* opined that 'In the hot season a house can be kept cool with *kuskus* tatties … [which] are thin screens of a sweet grass placed in a door or window on which the hot wind blows and kept constantly wet', pp. 39–40. Grant, *Anglo-Indian Domestic Life* also describes the use of '*khuskhus tattees*', p. 27.

114 Jaffer, *Furniture*, p. 56.

115 *The Englishwoman in India*, p. 40.

116 Contemporary accounts noted the lack of curtains in the Anglo-Indian domestic interior. For example, in 1844, in his novel *Peregrine Pultuney*, John Kaye describes a fashionable Calcutta drawing room through the eyes of a newcomer to India, who when examining the windows saw 'nothing like a curtain about it'. In 1861 only 'Window blinds' were recorded in the private apartments of the Governor of Ceylon in Queen's House, Colombo. In 1862 Colesworthy Grant noted the bare and un-curtained interior of a Calcutta hall room. In the last quarter of the nineteenth century, some household management advice literature suggested that lace curtains should be brought out from England to furnish the bungalow. John Kaye, *Peregrine Pultuney or Life in India* (London, 1844), vol. 2, p 64; London, National Archives: CO 54/359, 'Report by the Deputy Commissary General's Office', 28 February 1861; Grant, *Anglo-Indian Domestic Life*, p. 9; Maj. S. Leigh Hunt and Alexander Kenny, *Tropical Trials; a handbook for women in the tropics* (London, 1883), p. 56.

117 The role of textiles in Britain, in both personal adornment and interior décor, became increasingly marked during the second half of the nineteenth century. Michelle Henning has argued that after 1850 'men's dress and demeanour had become less and less ostentatious … [whereas] women's dress and the interior décor of the home had become central means by which signifiers of class were communicated (especially, though not exclusively, through the use of luxury fabrics)'. M. Henning, *Museums, Media and Cultural Theory* (Maidenhead, 2006), p. 30.

118 Doyley, *The European*, n.p.

119 Clemons, *The Manners and Customs*, pp. 11–12.

120 A.M. Ferguson, *Souvenirs of Ceylon* (London, 1869), p. 154.

121 London, National Archives: MPH 864, 'Plan, Section and Elevation of the Court House, Galle', 26 June 1834, 'floor-tiles and lime mortar'; Acland, *A Popular Account*, p. 65; Grant, *Anglo-Indian Domestic Life*, p. 13; University of Cambridge, Centre of South Asian Studies, Thompson Papers, 'Estimate for house to be built … flooring-stone paving', 1881; Lewis, *Ceylon*, p. 45.

122 Colombo, National Archives: NA 5/153, 'A Probable Estimate of the Expense Required to King's House, Colombo', 21 November 1831. In this estimate jackwood was also used for tie beams, ceiling joists, wall-plates and flooring beams. Other timbers were also itemized, including *millille* (*vitex altissima*) no English equivalent and *nadoon* (*pericopsis mooniana*) no English equivalent.

123 Dell: from the Sinhala *del* (either *artocarpus nobilis* or *altilis*). London, National

Archives: CO 54/291, 'Supplementary Estimate … for Completing Repairs & c. to the Queen's House, Colombo', 9 October 1852: 'teak plank' was specified for the floor of the ballroom and 'dell' for the verandah.

124 Doyley, *The European*, n.p.

125 Grant, *Anglo-Indian Domestic Life*, p. 13. He describes the grass as *madoor-katee*.

126 *The Englishwoman in India*, p. 36.

127 Ananda K. Coomaraswamy, *Medieval Sinhalese Art* (Broad Campden, 1908), pp. 243–4; N. Mudiyanse, 'Art and architecture of the Kandy period (16th–18th centuries)', *Spolia Zeylanica*, vol. 35, no. 1/2 (1980), p. 376.

128 London, National Archives: CO 54/127, 'List of Furniture in the King's House, Colombo', 18 January 1833, pp. 114–17.

129 London, National Archives: CO 54/156, 'Inventory of Furniture in the King's House, Colombo' and 'Inventory of Furniture in the Public Rooms of the Pavilion, Kandy', 29 September 1837, p. 92 and pp. 94–5.

130 University of Peradeniya, Sri Lanka: Griffiths, 'Ceylon during a residence', vol. 1, p. 87, 15 April 1841.

131 Cambridge University Library, Royal Commonwealth Society Archive: Y303E/104, bromide print of 'the Beckington bungalow, Colombo, 1880', with coir matting visible in the verandah; see also Raheem and Colin Thomé, *Images of British Ceylon*, p. 73, for depiction of coir matting in the verandah of Calverley House, Turret Road, Colombo, *c.* 1910, in a photograph by Mme. Del Tufo.

132 Gordon Cumming, *Two Happy Years*, p. 59.

133 London, National Archives: CO 54/173, 'Return of the Furniture in the Public Rooms in the Queen's House, Colombo', 6 December 1839, '1 Carpet Rug' is itemized in the Governor's Office and '2 Carpet Rugs' in the Council Room; London, British Library: Bengal Wills, 1845, L/AG/34/27/133, estate of Major Fitzgerald, in the Drawing Room: 'A Handsome Mirzapore carpet of flower pattern on a drab ground, 20 × 16 ft'; Bengal Wills, 1877, L/AG/34/27/184, estate of George Alexander Atkinson, Monghyr, '2 floor carpets' are itemized.

134 Hunt and Kenny, *Tropical Trials*, pp. 151–2.

135 R.L. Bushman, *The Refinement of America: persons, houses, cities* (New York, 1992), p. 126. Bushman cites W.T. O'Shea [*The Social History of Lighting* (London, 1958)], who suggests that the proliferation of light-giving devices in the late 18th and 19th centuries was 'not the result of utilitarian pressures for better lighting, but of the evolution of a way of life, whose chief objects were entertainment and display'.

136 Bushman, *The Refinement of America*, p. 126.

137 In 1810, Maria Graham described the rudimentary form of lighting in a rest house in Ambalangoda, Ceylon. In 1843, James Whitechurch Bennett noted the imports of wax and whale-oil candles into Ceylon. Maria Graham, *Journal of a Residence in India* (Edinburgh, 1813), p. 97; J.W. Bennett, *Ceylon and its Capabilities* (London, 1843), p. 36.

138 Doyley, *The European*, n.p.

139 London, British Library: Madras Wills, 1829, L/AG/34/27/261, estate of Joseph Dacre.

140 London, British Library: L/AG/34/27/261, estate of Joseph Dacre.

141 One or more pairs of 'wall-shades' are itemized in the following inventories: London,

National Archives: CO 54/127, 'List of Furniture in the King's House, Colombo', 18 January 1833; London, British Library: L/AG/34/27/261, estate of Joseph Dacre; L/AG/34/27/133, estate of Major Fitzgerald.

142 London, British Library: L/AG/34/27/133, estate of Major Fitzgerald.

143 London, British Library: Bengal Wills, 1880, L/AG/34/27/187, estate of William Smith, manager of Jogapore indigo factory, Chuprah district.

144 Acland, *A Popular Account*, p. 65.

145 London, National Archives: CO 54/127, 'List of Furniture'.

146 London, National Archives: CO 54/298, 'Lamps for the Queen's House, Colombo', 22 January 1853.

147 London, National Archives: CO 54/71, 'Schedule of the Goods, Chattels, Credit and Effects of the Honble. Sir William Coke', 6 October 1818.

148 'In the matter of the last will and testament of Charles Ambrose Lorenz of Colombo … August 1876', B.R. Blazé, *The Life of Lorenz* (Colombo, 1948), n.p.

149 London, National Archives: CO 54/101, 'Inventory of the Queen's House, Colombo', 6 December 1839.

150 *Madras Exhibition of 1855; catalogue raisonné* (Madras, 1855), number 629.

151 The Argand lamp was oil-fuelled and had a 'glass funnel to draw the air more efficiently through the vertical metal tube, which was surrounded by a tubular meshed wick'. As Thornton notes, the invention of the Argand lamp in 1783 by the Swiss, Ami Argand, had a 'profound effect on the way rooms looked at night and even the way rooms were used'. Peter Thornton, *Authentic Décor: the domestic interior, 1620–1920* (London, 1984), pp. 157, 193, 255. See also *Country House Lighting* (exhib. cat., Leeds, 1992), pp. 79–80.

152 London, National Archives: CO 54/415, 'Report on the Queen's Houses: Report on the Public Furniture', 15 October 1866. See also *Country House Lighting*, p. 80.

153 London, National Archives: CO 54/173, 'Return of the Furniture in the Public Rooms in the Queen's House, Colombo', 6 December 1839.

154 London, British Library: Bombay Wills, 1846–50, L/AG/34/27/397, estate of William Wise.

155 London, British Library: Bengal Wills, 1859, L/AG/34/27/163, estate of Robert Dunlop.

156 *The Englishwoman*, p. 24.

157 London, British Library: Bengal Wills, 1863, L/AG/34/27/170, estate of Philip Delmar, professor of music, 28 Elliott Road, Calcutta, records a range of lighting devices including: 'a set of four patent Argand hanging lamps with chains, domes [etc], a bronzed patent sideboard lamp with shade and chimney, a patent Argyle table lamp with moon and chimney, two plated pedestals with shades, a bronzed reading lamp …, a pair of plated double branched pedestals with 2 spare arms …, a plated table pedestal with 2 shades, a Bullseye lantern, two lacquered lamps with chimneys, twelve wall brackets with lacquered arms …, a bronzed mounted hanging lamp with smoke top, a plated pedestal with shade … 3 night lamps … seven oil burners'.

158 Electricity was introduced to the Pavilion at Kandy in Ceylon around 1900. Nihal Karunaratna, *From Governor's Pavilion to President's Pavilion* (Dehiwela, 1984), p. 66.

159 Percival, *An Account of the Island*, p. 104.

160 London, National Archives: CO 54/317, 'Dispatch from the Governor', 11 October 1855.

161 London, British Library: Mss.Eur. B369/5 (53), journals of Thomas Machell.

162 Tennent, *Ceylon*, vol. 2, pp. 669–70.

163 University of Cambridge, Centre of South Asian Studies, Scott Papers, 19 July 1884.

164 Rev. M. Winslow, *Memoir of Mrs Harriet L. Winslow; 13 years a member of the American mission in Ceylon* (New York, 1840), pp. 270–1. Grant, *Anglo-Indian Domestic Life*, p. 16.

165 Sirr, *Ceylon and the Cingalese*, vol. 1, p. 216.

166 Grant, *Anglo-Indian Domestic Life*, p. 19.

167 University of Peradeniya, Sri Lanka: Griffiths, 'Ceylon during a residence', vol. 2, p. 49.

168 Acland, *A Popular Account*, p. 66; University of Cambridge, Centre of South Asian Studies, Scott papers, 19 October 1884.

169 Glover, 'A Feeling of Absence', p. 73.

2 ✧ Objects, memory and identity: the Anglo-Indian domestic sphere

AT THE PRESENT TIME, one persistent and widespread perception of the British within their Indian empire is of their aloofness, their keeping themselves apart from the cut and thrust of daily life within the Subcontinent. For example, in his novel *The Impressionist*, published in 2002, Hari Kunzru narrates the thoughts of a young man of mixed English and Indian parentage coming to England for the first time during the last days of empire. He describes how this visit to the metropolitan country finally made sense to him of British behaviour he had witnessed in India:

> Everywhere [he] finds the originals of copies he has grown up with, all the absurdities of British India restored to sense in their natural environment … here thick black doors lead away from the electric streets into cluttered drawing rooms, with narrow windows to frame squares of cold watery London light. Cocooned in a leather armchair, [he] understands for the first time the English word 'cosy', the need their climate instils in them to pad their blue-veined bodies with layers of horsehair and mahogany, aspidistras and antimacassars, history, tradition and share certificates. Being British, he decides, is primarily a matter of insulation.[1]

British attempts to 'insulate' themselves from the material world of India within their bungalows and lower-roomed houses and the problems encountered in this project form part of the discussion that follows. The remainder of this chapter examines the organization of space and practices of furnishing within the Anglo-Indian dwelling, in both metropolitan centres and rural locations. It assesses the nature of that environment as material culture and discusses its place within the construction of British imperial identity. As noted above, in recent decades, much attention has been devoted to the study of Western European and American domestic interiors created during the nineteenth century. A range of books (as well as other outputs such as films and television programmes) have also focused on the home life of British residents within India during the same period. However, the majority of these outputs, dating mainly from the 1970s and 1980s, are inflected by nostalgia for empire, are anecdotal in their approach and tend to describe or romanticize, rather than seeking to explain the Anglo-Indian interior.[2]

In addition, more recent scholarly assessment of nineteenth-century British interiors within the Subcontinent, produced during and since the 1990s, while theorizing the subject, has, with few exceptions, emphasized a single source of evidence, namely contemporary published household-management advice literature aimed at an Anglo-Indian audience. Foregrounding this useful textual source in the development of their argument, a number of present-day scholars have discussed how colonial domesticity was represented within the public sphere. However, in so doing they have examined domestic experience at one remove (i.e., through its representation within a generic type of literature) and have consequently paid less attention to the evidence of things that Anglo-Indians accumulated in their homes and the practices engendered and supported through those things. Furthermore, little attention has been paid to the physical presence of colonial domestic space as materialization of cultural memory.

Due to its concentration on this household-advice literature, previous scholarship has also focused largely on the home life of the 'official' British population or civil administrators, the target audience for such literature. It is argued here that recent studies which have concentrated on this group present a partial understanding of Anglo-Indian domestic life that takes little account of the domestic experience of the wider or 'non-official' British population within India and Ceylon. Moreover, as the intended audience for such advice literature was the imperial administration, the majority of whose members spent the greater part of their careers in rural locations or *mofussil*,[3] previous studies relying on this literature have inadvertently bypassed discussion of domestic interiors within urban centres of the Subcontinent.

Using a range of archival and published material, particularly in relation to house plans, auction sale lists, inventories of estates, evidence of furnishing practices and the arrangement and design of the Anglo-Indian domestic interior, in addition to household-management advice literature, this chapter adopts a different position to that in much of the recent secondary literature. It interrogates domestic interiors in India both including and beyond those created by members of the imperial civil service. The present chapter examines the furnishing and internal arrangement of the Anglo-Indian dwelling, in both rural and metropolitan centres, and assesses as cultural forms the nature of this environment and the artefacts it contained.

In contrast to recent literature on the colonial domestic interior, the present work adopts a material-culture approach to examine this space and poses questions about how British residents within the Subcontinent endeavoured to make sense of the world through the physical objects of their immediate surroundings.[4] In addition, it seeks to explain a number of factors in relation to the Anglo-Indian home and its furnishings, including the anomalous position of the British interior within India during the high Raj, the mediatory role of artefacts and interior space in the social process, and the significance of colonial domestic space and furnishing schemes in self-affirmation and the maintenance of national and cultural identity.

During the second half of the nineteenth century, a discourse of domesticity developed in Britain, and this was reflected and reproduced in the works of contemporary commentators, such as R.W. Emerson, who wrote of 'the Englishman' in 1857:

> born in a harsh and wet climate, which keeps him indoors whenever he is at rest … he dearly loves his house. If he is rich, he buys a demesne, and builds a hall; if he is in middling condition, he spares no expense on his house. Without, it is all planted; within, it is wainscoted, carved, curtained, hung with pictures, and filled with good furniture.[5]

In Victorian Britain, home and its contents were assigned great symbolic significance. Home was conceptualized as a place of refuge from the contaminations of the outside world, especially the world of work. It was also a location where, as contemporary critics such as John Ruskin suggested, the artefacts and specifically the buildings of culture produced our identities and, to paraphrase the latter, that 'the objects we handle and the structures we inhabit significantly affect our individual subjectivities and our collective histories'.[6] Indeed, nineteenth-century household-management advice literature assigned to the domestic environment and the setting and contents of home the power to shape human character.

The historian Katherine Grier has coined the phrase 'domestic environmentalism' to describe the conflation of moral guidance offered in these publications and the appearance and layout of the house and its contents. She has argued, using a semiotic approach, that most Victorians well understood the indirect influence exerted by objects within the domestic interior and the notion that interior décor and furnishings acted as 'communicative [media] for higher ends'.[7] There is also evidence to suggest that Victorian middle-class interiors were understood to represent the moral character of the householder and his family – and, increasingly, the beneficial influence of domestic space and personal possessions within the home linked the formation of good character with 'correct' habits of consumption.[8]

Victorian domesticity did not simply remain at home, so to speak. It was imagined as an underpinning element which supported the development of the nation (i.e., England), both within its own national boundaries and beyond these overseas. In 1857, as one commentator, perhaps with some exaggeration, noted:

> Domesticity is the taproot, which enables the [British] nation to branch wide and high. The motive and end of their trade and empire is to guard the independence and privacy of their homes. Nothing so much marks their manners as the concentration of their household ties. This domesticity is carried into court and camp.[9]

Within the Indian context, the literary critic Ian Baucom has discussed how the 'subject-producing capacities of architecture' were given expression in a lecture entitled 'Architectural Art in India' delivered by T. Roger Smith to the Royal Society of Arts, London in 1878.[10] His lecture addressed public architecture within India rather than domestic dwellings. Nonetheless, Smith reiterated and relocated a Ruskinian notion that the re-creation of English architectural forms and spaces within the Subcontinent not only had the power to impress the local population but, more significantly, also ensured that 'the English collector [chief official of a district] remain[ed] British to the backbone in the heart of India'.[11]

The essence of Smith's argument was that the English edifice within India acted as a bulwark against the threat of identity loss and, as Baucom continues in his characterization of Smith's views, 'one becomes, or remains, English … by observing, handling, entering, and brushing against English objects'.[12] In his lecture, Smith also discussed how the British in India, in contrast to the lighter wearing apparel they had adopted at the beginning of the nineteenth century, had recently begun to dress in the same clothes that they wore in the homeland. Despite the high temperatures and humidity in India, they had not cast off their 'national habits, or manners, or dress' and dressed in the (stiflingly hot) broadcloth of home. However unsuited to the climate, this apparel was adopted 'because [it was] infinitely associated with Englishmen' and 'custom has decreed the retention of these things'.[13] Baucom characterizes English architecture in India (as well as English clothes) as 'mnemonic artefacts' which communicated 'a stabilizing relation with home' to the English colonists. He glosses these things as fetish objects or touchstones. However, this reading neglects to treat these things as authentic manifestations of culture which actively participated 'in a process of social self-creation in which they [were] directly constitutive of' Anglo-Indians' understanding of themselves as colonizers and of their relationship to the colonized.[14]

Home, for the Victorian middle class in Britain, was a specific physical location which signified 'ownership, possession and permanence'.[15] However, rarely could these attributes be applied to the Anglo-Indian dwelling. Within the Subcontinent, the great majority of Europeans rented their bungalows or houses rather than owning them outright; many commentators also noted the idiosyncrasies of the Indian dwelling and the impermanence or transience of European domestic arrangements in India. In 1888, for instance, Flora Annie Steel and Grace Gardiner noted that '[domestic] life in India always partakes of the nature of a campaign, where light marching order is a great desideratum'.[16] In a similar vein, writing in 1906, William Hart asserted that 'the Indian house, in construction and in every possible arrangement, is an entirely different thing from anything to which we are accustomed here at home [i.e., England]'.[17]

If the domestic environment in Britain during the nineteenth century was believed to stabilize or shape the personhood of the inhabitant of that space, and house furnishings and décor were ascribed such significance in the formation and maintenance of character, then how did British residents within the Subcontinent endeavour to affirm their individual, national and cultural identities within the strange, dislocated and idiosyncratically furnished interiors of their bungalows or houses?

That they endeavoured to do so through the contents of their homes and their everyday practices, despite the best advice in household-management literature of the day, is attested by evidence in many contemporary accounts and other archival sources, which record their often cluttered and over-filled interiors.[18] Writing in 1884 about British domestic life within the Subcontinent, Charles Buckland summarized a view generally held among Anglo-Indians when he wrote 'over the whole length and breadth of India there is now a large and growing colony of English families, who endeavour to maintain their old home feelings and to keep all those old surroundings, which remind them of the land of their birth'.[19]

However, concern was expressed in the works of some contemporary commentators that the European persona in Asia underwent a process of alteration, and that 'correct' consumption habits and modes of social behaviour appropriate to status were more difficult to maintain and police within the Subcontinent. Indeed, it has recently been argued that 'for the European-born, the Indies was transformative of cultural essence, social disposition and personhood itself'.[20] The Anglo-Indian home was envisioned as a significant location (other locations included clubs, hotels and the official architecture of the Raj) where these troubling processes might be held in check.

The Anglo-Indian home as a bulwark against India

Previous scholars of empire, such as Anthony King and Thomas Metcalf, have proposed that during the second half of the nineteenth century the British in India endeavoured to insulate themselves by various means from the local environment and local population: this is the trope of social distance.[21] During the second half of the nineteenth century, various factors reinforced the desire to implement a distancing strategy, including the Sepoy Mutiny or Insurrection of 1857, medical discourse in relation to disease, growing emphasis on racial difference between Britons and Indians, as well as changed practices in relation to the British body as an instrument of prestige and colonial authority.[22]

It has been argued that the Anglo-Indian home was a key site for insulating the British from India and of creating 'an island of Englishness' in the midst of the alien and noxious surroundings of the Subcontinent.[23] Indeed, British homes in India and their proper organization were allocated a wider and more significant place in the maintenance and protection of colonial society. However, recently it has been suggested that the colonial home was a problematic space and that 'management and knowledge of home environments [in India] ... [by] European colonials [was] based on the notion that the domestic domain harboured potential threats both to "defence of society" and to the future "security" of the (European) population and the (colonial) state'.[24]

Anglo-Indian domestic practices adopted within the bungalow have also been theorized as vital and formative components in the creation and maintenance of British authority in India. As Ann Laura Stoler has suggested, in the European colonies it was 'the domestic domain, not the public sphere, where ... essential dispositions of manliness, bourgeois morality and racial attribute could be dangerously undone or securely made'.[25] The importance of 'correct' personal behaviour and proper deportment in front of Indian servants within the home, and the cumulative effect of the individual, everyday social practices of Anglo-Indians within the governance of India (rather than government policies and public ceremonial), were indeed emphasized by contemporary commentators such as Maud Diver who wrote in 1909:

> It is a true saying ... that for the upholding of British prestige in the East, far more credit is due to the individual men and women who have carried out in their lives the loftiest conceptions of English truth and virtue, than the collective wisdom of the office [of the Prime Minister] in Downing Street.[26]

In fact, the interior of the Anglo-Indian bungalow was conceptualized – within the extensive advice literature on household management aimed at the British in India during the late nineteenth century – as a vital location for the cultivation of specific character traits and personal attributes, such as self-control and self-discipline, which enhanced British prestige and authority in the eyes of the local population and thereby underpinned British rule in India.[27] As a consequence, it has been suggested that the Anglo-Indian bungalow was viewed by its inhabitants as 'an extended form of personal space', and a 'culturally determined radius', where they were able to cultivate and protect their own culture.[28]

However, the notion of the Anglo-Indian bungalow interior as a closed-off or impermeable space was challenged by a number of factors, including the plan of the building, the scale of the rooms, the material qualities of these spaces, the range and type of furnishings they contained and the very visible presence of local servants within the heart of the home. In addition, within the Anglo-Indian context the notionally separate spheres of the public world of work and the private world of home merged within the domestic space of the bungalow, as Mary Procida has suggested: 'the home [in India] was an arena for political discussion and administrative action, and civil society itself was identified with that limited cadre of people who could appropriately be invited into the Anglo-Indian home'.[29] Despite strenuous endeavours by the inhabitants to mitigate or indeed counter these factors, India (either informally or officially) permeated every aspect of the Anglo-Indian home.

Although some material qualities of the Anglo-Indian dwelling have been outlined above, the Anglo-Indian bungalow, particularly in relation to its plan, merits examination here in more detail. Regional differences notwithstanding, the plan of most bungalows within the Subcontinent presented a rectangular structure of one storey in height, usually surrounded by a verandah, the interior comprising a standardized arrangement of rooms (whose overall proportions were, in many cases, larger than those of the home country), each opening directly into another and rarely with the inclusion of passageways (as found in houses in the homeland). In all types of dwelling inhabited by the British in India, including houses, multiple doorways and window openings were included to increase the circulation of air in the interior. There was also far less segregation of space by function in the Anglo-Indian domestic interior than in the metropolitan country. In fact, contemporary commentators and particularly appraisers preparing inventories were often compelled to categorize rooms not by their function but by their orientation – i.e., north, south, etc. In other words, the function of the room was not immediately apparent from its furnishings. In addition, unlike house plans in Britain, which usually incorporated an entry hall fitted out with coat-stand and perhaps basic seating, most Anglo-Indian dwellings did not incorporate a zone of transition from the exterior to the interior. The verandah served as a substitute intermediate zone, but entry was usually gained into Anglo-Indian drawing rooms or hall rooms directly from the outside. This had the effect of leaving the private, domestic sphere of the inhabitants open to continual and unannounced intrusions by servants and occasional visitors.

The accounts of contemporary commentators and, more rarely, surviving house plans present a reasonably consistent picture of the internal arrangements of the Anglo-Indian dwelling (see figure 8). In 1856, Thomas Machell, a planter living in the hills of Southern India near Coonoor, wrote an account of the bungalow (Bonn Espoir) in which he lived and also sketched a plan of the dwelling.[30] His bungalow comprised eight rooms, two porches, a pantry, a store and two bathrooms; the majority of these rooms were disposed in a rectangular plan, the widest sides being 52 feet, with one

8 A damp bungalow with idiosyncratic plan. Plan and elevations of the Bonn Espoir bungalow, Coonoor, S. India, *c.* 1856.

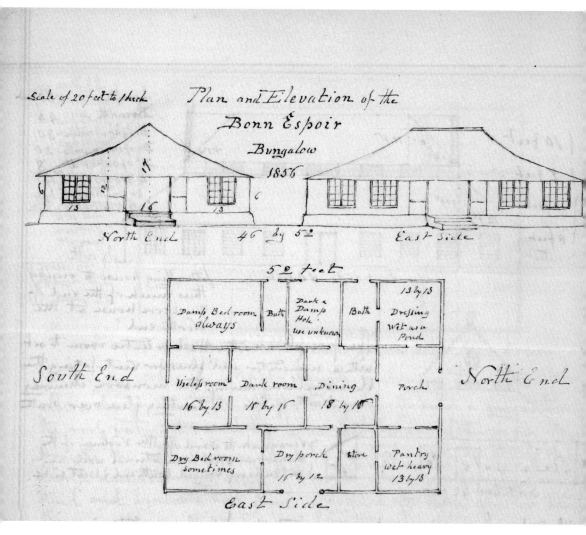

of their walls facing the exterior. However, two rooms, including the dining room, were entirely enclosed by the other rooms, with no window openings to the outside. Machell succinctly described this situation in his journal in the following terms 'the above plan of our house looks very well on paper but a little consideration will show that the inner rooms must be dark and the outer ones damp'.[31] In fact, he noted disparagingly the chief characteristics of many of the rooms, such as 'damp bedroom always', 'dark damp hole', 'dressing [room] wet as a pond', 'dry bedroom sometimes'. Writing in 1862 and in more favourable terms of the domestic situation in the metropolis of Calcutta, Colesworthy Grant noted that the internal arrangements of houses inhabited by Europeans in that city 'differed but little'. The main reception room was the hall which ran from front to back and 'answers all the purposes of parlour, dining, drawing and sitting rooms'.[32] On either side of the hall were located four rooms (two on each side, comprising bedrooms and dressing rooms) with bathrooms attached.[33]

Writing in 1906 of the domestic situation in Bengal and more particularly Calcutta, William Hart reiterated that the plan of many houses in that region comprised a central hall room with other rooms arranged around this space. He described 'the plan of the typical house' as

> an extremely simple one. A large central room runs through from front to back. An arched or pillared division will probably hint at a separation of this into dining and drawing room. From this large hall two or three rooms open out on each side, and a deep verandah runs around the whole. The kitchen and servants' quarters will be somewhere at the edge of the compound.[34]

In 1923, Kate Platt echoed the description of the plan of this dwelling, although she noted that at the time she was writing 'modern-built bungalows are often built on quite a different plan'. She described surviving nineteenth-century bungalows as follows:

> the typical old-style bungalow with high-pitched roof, single storied and surrounded by a verandah, has a main central space inside divided by a curtained or screened archway into dining- and drawing-rooms. The other rooms on either side communicate with these by doors … All the rooms are spacious and lofty, lighted by clerestory windows.[35]

In addition, an amalgam of local and European building conventions in the design and construction of the colonial bungalow had been standardized and codified into a type of dwelling plan, which was vigorously promoted by the Public Works Department throughout India after 1850.[36] This had the effect of embedding imperfections of plan and construction within an imperial schema for the production of the colonial bungalow which could be applied to the erection of such a dwelling in any location throughout the Subcontinent. Furthermore, specific social practices and customary domestic arrangements adopted within the Anglo-Indian bungalow also differed from those of the homeland. For example, contemporary commentators noted that young children of the household (under five or six years of age before being sent to England for their education) were allowed to run freely and noisily throughout the bungalow and were not restricted to the nursery as they were in the home country. In addition, the manner in which local servants inhabited the British home within the Subcontinent also unsettled the composure of the colonizers in a location which was intended to soothe and insulate them.

Recent scholarship has emphasized the significant presence of Indian servants within the Anglo-Indian domestic interior. If the British in India attempted, in the siting or selection of their dwellings, to distance themselves (however unsuccessfully) in a physical sense from the local urban settlement or 'Black Town', then they negated that policy by allowing their private, domestic space to be peopled by members of the local population in the role of house servants. For various reasons, such as caste restrictions regarding the performance of particular tasks, cheapness and availability of local labour and a perception (fostered by both the British and local population) that the socio-political status of the English Sahib required the attendance of numerous servants, many British homes in India contained considerably more servants than comparable households in the homeland.

In the Victorian middle-class home in Britain, servants were largely an unseen presence. A small number waited directly on their masters, but the work of many servants was conducted when a room was unoccupied by the owners of the house. The plan of the nineteenth-century British middle-class house also included features – such as hallways and back stairs – which were intended to separate masters from servants in their daily routes through the building. Although members of the middle class in Britain were certainly aware of the tensions caused by living in close proximity with their working-class servants and, indeed, recorded the problems they experienced with them, in the home country the work of maintaining, cleaning and heating the house could be carried out with minimum contact between servants and the served.

By contrast, Anglo-Indians lived in close proximity to their Indian servants within the colonial bungalow. The issue of local servants was a major, if not dominant, theme within all genres dealing with Anglo-Indian life, and a discourse emerged in this literature on how best to control and organize this local group within the heart of the home. Discussion of local servants featured consistently in the accounts of contemporary commentators, in the Anglo-Indian novel, in household-management guides, as well as numerous images of British life in India.[37] At the present time, there has also been wide-ranging discussion in the secondary literature of the significance of servants within the colonial bungalow. This discussion has concentrated on a number of themes, including the reproduction of imperial power relations on a household scale through advice provided in household guides on the management of servants.[38]

Other scholars have discussed the ways in which spatial and social arrangements within the colonial bungalow continually undercut the separation of servant from master; how servants appeared to inhabit the bungalow in a more comfortable manner than their colonial masters; and how this lack of segregation engendered continual anxiety among the colonizers about the presentiment of loss of authority and racial degeneracy.[39] Elizabeth Collingham has highlighted a number of ways in which servants both attended to but at the same time unsettled the occupiers of the colonial bungalow. She notes how servants were permitted to enter the living rooms of the bungalow and how, due to the open plan of that dwelling, they used the same routes to move from room to room as did their colonial masters. The privacy of British residents in the bungalow was also compromised by the quantity of servants usually found there and their easy access to their colonial masters. As Collingham suggests, the presence of Indian servants in the colonial bungalow 'opened up the private sphere of the British in India to the gaze of members of the Indian population' with the result that British domestic practices were 'laid bare to the view of members of a subjugated race'.[40]

The notion of establishing a home in India as far as possible along English lines was fraught with difficulties, and the potential always existed for dissolution or breaching of the hidden but generally understood lines of demarcation and control that were present within middle-class homes in England. As Ann Laura Stoler has argued, in the colonial context 'the self-affirmation of white middle-class colonials ... embodied a set of fundamental tensions between a culture of whiteness that cordoned itself off from the native world and a set of domestic arrangements and class distinctions among Europeans that produced cultural hybridities and sympathies that repeatedly transgressed these distinctions'.[41] Consequently, it has been argued that these factors compromised the establishment of a 'correct' domestic environment necessary for the cultivation of social practices required to maintain British prestige and authority.[42]

Making a home in India: furnishing practices and identity

A tendency is apparent in the secondary literature on the Anglo-Indian domestic interior to conceptualize that space as bare and sparsely furnished.

Anglo-Indian rooms were certainly large, with high and wide expanses of wall space which were often more plainly finished than related rooms in the home country. In addition, contemporary commentators noted the seemingly coarse and unfinished appearance of Indian houses, especially with regard to the ceilings, whose wooden framework of beams was usually left un-plastered and exposed in order that insect infestation could be detected and dealt with immediately. Conventional Victorian middle-class notions of domestic comfort and taste were often affronted by Anglo-Indian interiors.

However, this characterization of sparseness is a partial reflection of the colonial domestic scene which is heavily reliant on textual sources such as the accounts of contemporary commentators, and is a view that has been reinforced by a number of present-day scholars, some of whom have deployed binary oppositions as an analytic category to contrast the English home with the Anglo-Indian bungalow.[43] For example, this analytic category has defined the home in England as a closed and private space, while the Anglo-Indian bungalow was open and fluid in plan. The rooms of English homes have been characterized as domestic in scale, those of Anglo-Indian dwellings as oversized. The English home has been depicted as comfortably furnished, whereas the Anglo-Indian bungalow has been represented as sparsely furnished. Previous writers have deployed these binary oppositions as a device to highlight differences in domestic experience between Britain and India. However, useful as this method may be, it excludes consideration of ambiguities or overlaps between opposed categories of the home within Britain and India. Examination of archival evidence reveals greater complexity in relation to the furnishing of the Anglo-Indian home, including the development of hybrid practices.

Anglo-Indian drawing rooms and hall rooms, however full of furnishings, were often represented as stripped down and bare.[44] This representation of sparseness was in many cases due to the absence of softening features which were usually found in reception rooms of the homeland during the nineteenth century, such as curtains, pelmets, window drapes and wallpapers, all of which were impractical within the Indian context. In addition, representation of the bareness of Anglo-Indian domestic interiors in the literature largely derives from consideration of those interiors of the official British population in India, namely members of the civil administration rather than the non-official population.

In the eighteenth century, the non-official population in India was relatively small and insignificant. However, during the nineteenth century this group expanded in size to include planters, agency house partners, bankers, factors, shipping agents and retailers. Members of these groups often resided for long periods in India, and possessed both the motivation and money to furnish their houses in a manner more akin to that of the homeland.

The domestic interiors of these groups have been largely overlooked in the literature, whereas the bare and sparsely furnished interiors of members of the 'official' population have been subject to repeated scrutiny and comment.

The notion of the bare and sparsely furnished Anglo-Indian domestic interior has held sway by virtue of its repetition without qualification. Such a representation has also been reinforced by a lack of visual images depicting nineteenth-century Anglo-Indian interiors which might have offered a corrective to that perception. For contemporary commentators from the eighteenth century onward, the perceived bareness of Anglo-Indian interiors became an oft-repeated theme.[45] Nineteenth-century writers of household-management advice literature for Anglo-Indians took up this theme and, in fact, promoted an inverted view of the normal associations formed between middle-class Victorians and their furniture. These writers urged that no emotional attachments should be made to Anglo-Indian furnishings, and proselytized the notion of the scantily furnished domestic interior as a means of coping with the colonial condition.[46]

Although not of central concern to their discussions, twentieth-century scholars of Anglo-Indian life such as Percival Spear and Suresh Chandra Ghosh have similarly emphasized the bareness of Indian rooms.[47] Most recent scholars have taken these accounts at face value and have accepted the overarching notion of the Anglo-Indian home as a barn-like and sparsely furnished place. In 2003, for example, Mary Procida argued that 'imperial domesticity was played out on a stage devoid of elaborate sets and props [and] the Anglo-Indian domestic aesthetic was spartan'.[48] Of these scholars, only Amin Jaffer has avoided reiteration of a one-dimensional account of the British interior within India and has hinted at a more nuanced understanding of Anglo-Indian domestic space, which at least acknowledges the non-official, European inhabitants of the Subcontinent, although he does not pursue this line of enquiry beyond a few sentences.[49]

Assertion that the Anglo-Indian interior was sparsely furnished certainly requires qualification, as the term had quite specific connotations for a nineteenth-century audience. A semantic confusion has arisen in the secondary literature around the term 'unfurnished' as to its meaning for contemporary commentators in an Indian context. For example, in 1862 a contemporary commentator such as Colesworthy Grant, writing about Anglo-Indian domestic life, used the term 'unfurnished' specifically to refer to the lack of a fireplace, curtains and wallpaper in a typical middle-class Calcutta interior – not to any lack of moveable furniture or furnishings.[50]

That is not to say, however, that most Britons residing in India during the nineteenth century had an identical relationship to the furnishings in their dwellings as did their compatriots in the homeland. Furnishing practices and modes of socialization underwent a series of modifications within the

Indian context. A number of contemporary commentators recorded the manner in which these Anglo-Indian practices differed from the normative practices of the homeland. Many accounts noted the 'floating stock of household articles', which were distributed within Anglo-Indian society, due to frequent transfers and departures. These accounts also discuss how it was usual practice, when leaving an area, for a price-list of furniture and other household goods to be circulated among the British community.[51] In fact, the process of acquiring furniture for the Anglo-Indian bungalow differed to some extent from practice in the homeland. In 1874, Edmund Hull described the best way for a British resident in India to furnish a dwelling:

> For 1200 to 1500 rupees, ample furniture can be procured for a small bungalow … Of course, one should not go off straight to the best European cabinetmakers and order articles required, out of hand, at shop prices. Here, as throughout, a little management and prudence must be experienced. In every large town auctions are constantly taking place, at which second-hand furniture can be picked up … Bedroom furniture can generally be obtained through the native brokers for about half the price the European shopkeepers demand.[52]

Anglo-Indian women also often narrated the furnishing of the colonial bungalow as an adventurous activity (in contrast to similar negotiations in the homeland). If British women organized the furnishing of the home in India, the trip into the 'native quarter' of the colonial settlement and the furniture bazaar, the protracted negotiations with local 'furniture dealers' and the eventual purchase of appropriate furniture 'obtained … at half or two-thirds of the prices originally demanded', was another imperial challenge confronted and overcome.[53]

One noticeable effect on the Anglo-Indian domestic interior of the absorption of specific pieces from among this large pool of furnishing articles was, as some contemporary commentators noted, that 'every … habitation assume[d] in some degree the character of a second-hand furniture warehouse or curiosity shop'.[54] The emergence of this second-hand culture among the Anglo-Indian community disrupted the usual associations which the British middle class formed with the furnishings of their dwellings in the homeland. Some scholars have noted both the financial and the psychological investment in furniture within the middle- and upper middle-class home in Britain. Recent analysis of evidence (in the form of diaries and inventories) of household possessions owned by the middle and upper middle class in Britain during the late eighteenth century has suggested that acquisition of such items as furniture had ulterior meaning beyond the provision of functional objects. It has been argued, for example, that women within the household inscribed the purchase of newly commissioned furniture, from such manufacturers as Gillows of Lancaster, with specific meanings. Such furniture was often purchased to mark particular family events; it signified the continuation of family life and the acquisition of costly and durable material goods, which could be passed on to the next generation.[55] In addition to its functional role, such furniture served individual and family memory.

New furniture was commissioned by a small percentage of the Anglo-Indian community from both local and European furniture makers in the Presidency towns and cities and at urban settlements on the island of Ceylon.[56] In some cases, the furnishings of the colonial bungalow were entirely commissioned new from local makers. For example, in 1841, a British commentator living in Ceylon described the furniture owned by George Hinde Cripps, the Government Agent and Fiscal for the Southern Province of the island, who lived in the town of Galle. This commentator extolled Mr Cripp's bungalow as being 'filled with the most magnificent furniture I ever saw' and continued:

> Mr C … has had every facility for collecting [furniture made in Galle] and having it carved by the best workmen. It is composed principally of ebony and the rooms are so full of massive chairs, tables, cabinets and caskets of all sizes and shapes that it is difficult to turn around in them, they are all most elaborately carved and the tables beautifully inlaid with the most costly woods.[57]

However, the majority of furnishings acquired for the British domestic interior within the Subcontinent were second-hand. Some observers noted that this factor altered the associative value of furniture for the British within India and caused it to differ from practices of furnishing which were the norm in the homeland. The chairs, tables and other articles within the Anglo-Indian interior possessed a previous history, but that history was unconnected with the present owner. In fact, the new owner consciously had to set aside knowledge of the previous possession and marks of bodily contact to which such second-hand furniture bore witness. Few contemporary commentators alluded in more than a passing reference to the inscription of previous lives on the furniture of the Anglo-Indian room, but in 1872 Edward Braddon drew attention precisely to this factor when he wrote:

> If anyone were interested in the matter, there is a history attached to nearly every piece of [furniture] thus collected. The chair on which we sit was bought from a distinguished civilian … That table was picked when the inspector of railways gave up housekeeping in consequence of his wife's prolonged absence from her Indian home … That davenport was purchased when the late judge left the country on his retiring pension … And so on,

to the end, chairs, tables, whatnots & c. – all souvenirs of people who have come and gone.[58]

Second-hand Anglo-Indian furniture acquired the role simply of domestic apparatus within the colonial bungalow. It rarely served memory or evoked the kind of associations which many furnishings in the homeland did, and was often described in derogatory terms as 'tarnished, cracked, frayed [and] soiled'. For the most part, its non-functional role as signifier of status, taste, family history or class was erased within the Indian context. It was 'a mere convenience … a means of enabling people to give dinner parties' and 'a typical part of the absurd pretence that white people make of being at home in this place [i.e., India]'.[59]

In addition to problematizing the signifying practices of furnishing, the general practice of acquiring and using second-hand furniture also inflected the behaviour of British residents within the Subcontinent. Some commentators noted with dismay how Anglo-Indians accepted 'other people's furniture so pacifically' and how, during the process of acclimatization to India 'a born British gentlewoman' in contrast to her compatriot in the home country 'will live without antimacassars and sleep on a *charpoy* [light Indian bedstead]' – behaviour that would have been considered aberrant within middle-class society in Britain.[60]

Anglo-Indian household-management advice literature

Advice on how to arrange and manage the Anglo-Indian home was forthcoming in the increasingly numerous household-management advice literature published between 1880 and 1920.[61] Many of these publications combined aspects of the eighteenth-century conduct book, medical compendium, cookbook, furnishing manual and, especially, guides on the management of servants. These publications translated the politics of home and domestic discourse to the Subcontinent. This Anglo-Indian literature formed an offshoot of similar texts produced in England by authors such as R.W. Edis, M.E. Haweis and others.[62] However, whereas the latter advised householders on matters of taste within the home, the former offered more pragmatic advice on how to survive in the Indian idiom, and about the best means to organize and control Indian servants and furnish the Anglo-Indian home.

Household-management advice literature, which was largely aimed at the 'official' British population living in India or members of the civil administration, expressed both the physical and metaphorical sparseness of domestic interiors within the Subcontinent, in order to habituate the British resident to unfamiliar furnishing practices. Such advice literature prepared Britons before they arrived in the Subcontinent, or guided them when they were there, to do without many of the things that would normally have been found in middle-class reception rooms of the homeland. This literature also suggested how they might adjust their patterns of consumption and domestic behaviour to accommodate these wants.

The majority of household-management advice manuals emphasized the importance to the imperial enterprise of setting up and maintaining a household in the far-flung outposts of Empire and of creating, in the words of Flora Annie Steel and Grace Gardiner 'a home – that unit of civilization'. Rosemary Marangoly George has suggested that, in both household-management guidebooks and the many Anglo-Indian novels of the time (many of them written by the authors of the household guides),

> it is the daily construction of the home country [in the Anglo-Indian bungalow] as the location of the colonizer's racial and moral identity and as a legitimization of the colonizer's national subjecthood that made possible the carrying out of the work of Empire.[63]

However, 'the daily construction of the home country', at least as far the normal furnishing practices of home were concerned, was disrupted within the Indian context. Due to circumstances within the Subcontinent, fitting out a hall room or drawing room of an Anglo-Indian dwelling with tasteful and substantial (or even matching) furniture in appropriate style was often impossible. Many Anglo-Indian household-management guidebooks acknowledged these difficulties and offered a pragmatic solution to this problem by reinscribing the meanings usually attached to furnishings in the homeland.

They assigned new cultural value to furniture acquired in the Anglo-Indian context, and sought to re-present household furnishings as lightweight, inexpensive and emotionally neutral props within the colonial domestic environment. The guidebooks asserted that Anglo-Indian domestic arrangements functioned best when traditional notions of the value of furniture (both financial and psychological) were discarded and the 'young housekeeper' in India was best advised to 'go out armed with energy, hammers, tacks … and a goodly supply of Bon Accord enamel' and 'buy the old sticks [of furniture] at the bazaar, provided they are strong … Then … she will have the prettiest house in the station [European settlement], with nothing worth a button in it!'[64]

In contrast to the situation in Britain, household-management advice books aimed at members of the 'official' Anglo-Indian population proposed that furnishings for the bungalow should ideally be mobile and disposable, as a cartoon from *The Graphic* of 1875 depicting an Anglo-Indian couple moving house humorously suggests (although an upright piano seems to have been regarded as an indispensable item) (see figure 9). The message in both the advice literature and this cartoon is that the furnishings of the colonial dwelling should be moveable and that little or no sentimental attachments should be made with them. In 1888, Flora Annie Steel and Grace Gardiner advised in the seminal guide of the day *The Complete Indian Housekeeper and Cook*:

> Regarding furniture: it should rarely be imported. Then the instability of the Indian home must be considered. To those who are here today and gone tomorrow, solidities and fragilities are alike a nuisance. Therefore let all big and heavy things be of a kind which can be sold by auction without a pang, and all the delicacies of the sort that will pack.[65]

Steel and Gardiner inverted the usual associations formed by householders in relation to the contents of their homes and promoted in the household-management advice literature of the homeland. Instead, they advised the Anglo-Indian householder that domestic paraphernalia in general should be kept to a minimum. As they noted 'in the multiplication of pots and pans and enlargement of the necessaries of life, lies anxiety and slavery'.[66] Authors of Anglo-Indian household-management advice literature for the next forty years echoed the sentiments of Steel and Gardiner. For instance, writing in 1923, Kate Platt noted of 'Furniture and Furnishings' in India:

> heavy furniture especially is a great encumbrance … fortunately, a Home is something portable and does not depend on location. The English woman in India soon learns this, and is always ready to pack up her belongings at very short notice, not without grumblings it is true[67]

Even members of the 'official' population, of whom it was 'seldom that the whole period of man's service [was] spent even in one province', in many cases chose to ignore published advice to minimize household clutter. As Platt noted, although she realized 'that it [was] wise to limit her possessions, though curiously enough, of all women, the Anglo-Indian cannot resist the temptation of collecting brasses, rugs, embroideries and treasures of all kinds'.[68] However, these portable items, collected in different districts throughout India, marked stages in an Anglo-Indian career, narrated events in a life of service in the tropics and acted as markers of a family's progress through India.[69] These objects were of a different order to that of house furnishings.

Due to the problems of obtaining appropriate furnishings, and the oversized interior spaces within the Anglo-Indian bungalow, recent secondary

9 The impermanence of Anglo-Indian domestic life – packing up the furniture. 'A visit to India – sketches in the Madras Presidency', *The Graphic*, 18 September 1875.

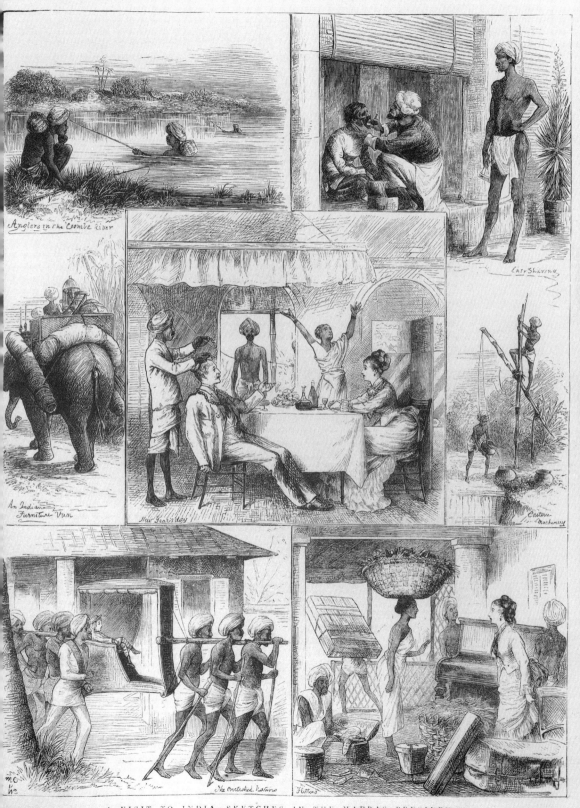

Anglers in the Coombe River

Easy Shaving

An Indian Furniture Van

New Year's day

Eastern Machinery

The Overlooked Natives

Flitting

A VISIT TO INDIA—SKETCHES IN THE MADRAS PRESIDENCY

literature, relying on late nineteenth-century household-management guides, has suggested that the British created a feeling of home in India by including a few English objects in the domestic interior or attempting to place them in the way that they would have been arranged in the homeland.[70] Furthermore, by virtue of the paucity, general lack of quality and indeterminate taste of the contents of many Anglo-Indian domestic interiors, goes the general argument, there took place a renegotiation of the status or worth of the inhabitants of the bungalow as measured through these domestic artefacts.[71] However, this suggestion requires qualification, as there is evidence that many members of the Anglo-Indian community, in ways similar to those of their compatriots in the home country, did use domestic artefacts to negotiate status.[72]

It is certainly the case that the pressures to define oneself through the quality, arrangement, taste and style of one's living room furnishings were mitigated in the Indian context. By 1850, a large proportion of the total British population within the Subcontinent were members of the Civil Administration whose positions within the imperial hierarchy, including their exact status, were published in a book for all to see.[73] Contemporary commentators noted the contrast between the 'necessarily mixed society of England' and acceptance of different social practices relating to matters of precedence and status among the 'official' British community in India. As one Anglo-Indian commentator noted 'our aristocracy is that of age, and [social] precedence is strictly regulated according to the degree of seniority attained in "the service" beginning with civilians [civil servants] as the judges and law administrators of the land'.[74]

Therefore, it has recently been argued, domestic objects played less of a role in status marking than they did in the home country, where issues of respectability, taste and social position were more often negotiated through personal property. Among the British community in India, as 'every creature's position is here at once marked, the characteristic suspicion of our countrymen is never excited by fruitless endeavours to ascertain who such a person is and what he has'.[75] However, it would be misleading to suggest that identity and social status were not negotiated through artefacts within the Anglo-Indian community or that this community did not use objects in a socially competitive manner. During the late eighteenth and early nineteenth centuries, prints and oil paintings were avidly collected and displayed by a small percentage of the British community in India, often with financially ruinous consequences.[76] During the second quarter of the nineteenth century, contemporary commentators also highlighted another more visible consumer item on which expenditure was lavished, namely the carriage. Commentators also noted the slippages that occurred in the process of status marking through the consumption of such a noticeable part of

Anglo-Indian material culture. One publication of 1844 explicitly gendered the consumption habits of the Anglo-Indian community in Calcutta in this case and noted the range of carriages within the city:

> One marvels who all these people are that own these hundreds of carriages ... Some of the most pretending equipages ... are sported by people belonging to the second class of society – uncovenanted government servants, petty East India or European traders – respectable persons in their way ... but the wife and daughters must have their Britzka or Barouche ... and on the course, at least, the wife of the uncovenanted subordinate may jostle the lady of the head of the office.[77]

It has been suggested that much of the Anglo-Indian household-management advice literature urged British women in India to rethink accepted material-culture practices in relation to the home.[78] If the Anglo-Indian household advice literature is taken at face value, then the practical, mediatory role of objects within the social process underwent a change within the Subcontinent. The meanings invested in domestic objects within the Anglo-Indian interior were renegotiated (a process promoted in the household-management guides, such as *The Complete Indian Housekeeper*), and cultural associations assigned to many of the standard furnishings of the drawing room became problematized within the Indian context.[79] However, despite published advice to the contrary, Anglo-Indians, to paraphrase the words of Judy Attfield, still appeared to make sense of the world and their position in it through physical objects.[80]

Using evidence other than that presented in household-management advice manuals, it can be inferred from the domestic objects with which Anglo-Indians surrounded themselves that these items, beyond their functional properties, played a role in self-affirmation and self-fashioning. It is arguable that these objects also expressed and constituted the personhood of the occupant of the Anglo-Indian home and, in related but not identical ways, played a significant role in the daily negotiations of cultural and national identity within the Subcontinent. In fact, as a source of evidence, reliance on household-management advice literature (which specified a model of appropriate furnishing practices and ideal forms of behaviour) does not explain how British residents in India actually furnished or inhabited their dwellings.

The development of colonial domesticity

Anthony King has argued that a limited integration of Indian material culture into the Anglo-Indian bungalow was acceptable.[81] In 1900, for instance, Isabel Savory wrote that India percolated into the bungalow in the form of 'a hundred terrible little Indian, Kashmir and Burmese tables, stools and screens' as well as 'the souvenirs and shikar [hunting] trophies' collected on tours through various districts of India.[82] The interior of the Anglo-Indian home was often a hybrid space that incorporated some Indian things, some English things and things manufactured in India in English form or arranged in a manner that was common practice in England.[83]

Anglo-Indian household-management advice literature published between 1880 and 1920 prescribed, among other issues, how colonial bungalows should ideally be furnished and how to implement appropriate domestic arrangements, with particular emphasis placed on economy, hygiene and practicality. As noted above, the target audience for these publications was the British civil administration in India (the official population). Although this comprised a large number of Britons within the Subcontinent, it excluded much of the total European population within the Subcontinent (such as lawyers, merchants, planters, agency house partners, entrepreneurs and members of the European working class), who resided in India during the nineteenth century in increasing numbers.

The advice literature offered a set of ideals and conventions regarded by their authors as essential to a social group for whom they were intended. However, this advice was contradictory in nature, as Alison Blunt has suggested. As did women's magazines which were produced in the late nineteenth century, these household-management guides not only asserted a colonial domesticity but, at the same time, instructed Anglo-Indian women on its achievement.[84] A potential limitation, however, of this advice literature is that it only represented an *ideal* of colonial domesticity within the public domain.[85] This of itself is not problematic, and analysis of such literature provides evidence of the inscription of the politics of home and the operation of a specific domestic discourse within the Subcontinent.

The focus of recent secondary literature has been concerned with guidance given in these publications on such issues as the management of Indian servants, running the bungalow on a day-to-day basis and housekeeping in an Indian context. Some present-day scholars have read in this Anglo-Indian advice literature a conflation of domestic and imperial values within the bungalow and an overlap of public and private spheres within the colonial home.[86] Late nineteenth-century household-management advice literature set out a programme of ideal behaviour and a series of aspirations for domestic arrangements within the Indian home. But in what ways did Anglo-Indians mediate this advice? How can historians evaluate the lived experience of the British in India through study of domestic space and furnishings? Is it possible to determine whether the main tendencies of the period were followed or modified, and in what ways were distinctions made according to social status, sex, age and occupation?

Case studies of nineteenth-century Anglo-Indian interiors

In addition to household-management advice literature, rich sources of evidence exist for investigation of the Anglo-Indian domestic experience, including probate inventories, auction-sale records, plans of rooms with the placement of furniture depicted, contemporary photographs and written personal accounts of life in India. As with any source of historical evidence, there are limits to the usefulness and reliability of inventories and sale lists. Some historians have suggested that inventories, far from being 'unimpeachably objective', should in fact be regarded as 'fictions'. Lena Orlin has argued that 'these are matters not of deception on the part of the inventories but misconception on the part of their readers, of the distance between what contemporaries required of [them] and what historians have mistakenly asked of them'.[87]

However, lists of the contents of specified rooms within dwellings at identifiable locations owned by individuals whose status can be ascertained and which can be accurately dated offer a special form of corroborative evidence against which other information can be compared. It has been suggested that, instead of assessing inventories in a quantitative manner, qualitative methods of interpretation offer a way of understanding and explaining the organization of the nineteenth-century home as a series of mediations of the prevailing ideals of the period and place.[88] As well, other scholars who have examined colonial domestic interiors have suggested that inventories are useful tools to define and describe the spatial framework within which furniture and fittings are located.[89]

As noted above, a large percentage of British interiors in India lacked much of the usual domestic paraphernalia of the home country. However, this lack did not necessarily affect every Anglo-Indian social habit but the means by which they were facilitated. In fact, if anything, Western social practices were over-emphasized, or doggedly maintained, to compensate. For example, in 1847 the Reverend Charles Acland wrote an account of the recurring problem of staying at one of the circuit houses or temporary forms of accommodation at Balasore, near Midnapore in Orissa District. This house contained no furnishings other than a floor mat, three tables and two armchairs.[90] Having 'called' on a number of British residents as soon as he arrived in Balasore, the Reverend Acland wrote:

> on … the second day one or two people called and when the excise officer and his daughter came in, the deficiency in furniture was manifest. There were Mr and Miss B., Mrs Acland and I and only two chairs amongst us and these, like all chairs in India, were arm chairs, so that we could not even manage by sitting two on one chair; so Miss B and my wife had the two

chairs and Mr B and I sat upon the table – rather a high one it was – so that our feet dangled about half-way between seat and the floor.[91]

The level of domestic furnishing could also depend upon the district or region and the style of life adopted there by the British community. In 1861, John Beames, a civil servant who worked in a number of districts in northern India throughout his career, noted the distinction between the Punjab (N.W. India) and Bengal (N.E. India) in terms of furnishing practices and habits of consumption. He noted that 'the change from the rough, wild Panjab to sleepy, civilized Bengal was very marked', and

> we did not at first slide easily into our new grooves and I fear we were looked upon as rather wild and uncivilized for a time. But the station [settlement] was a nice one, the houses of the Europeans were stately, roomy mansions, standing in large compounds [grounds] and were handsomely furnished. All the Europeans had horses and carriages in plenty; they entertained handsomely and lived, as it seemed to us fresh from the rude fare of the Panjab, luxuriously.[92]

In a short time, Beames and his wife adjusted to their new circumstances and he wrote 'we secured a pretty house and furnished it nicely, and as our horses and buggy arrived before long from the Panjab the New Year found us comfortably settled'.

Furnishing the urban colonial interior

Moving from outlying districts to Calcutta, the centre of British power in India until the early twentieth century, examination of historical evidence suggests that domestic interiors were, in many cases, far from sparsely furnished. In contrast to the image of the scantily furnished bungalow represented in household-management advice literature, contemporary artists and commentators depicted or described the increasing comfort (i.e., Westernization) and opulence of Anglo-Indian houses within the colonial city. In the illustration by James Prinsep of 1830, an elegant Anglo-Indian couple are depicted strolling from the verandah into the large drawing room of a Calcutta house. The room contains an imposing, carved and most probably gilded pier table and glass, a fashionable cut-glass candelabra, an array of classical-style vases, including one raised on an elaborate carved stand, and a pair of armchairs, all of which were most probably supplied by European makers resident in the city (see figure 10). Similarly, in 1844, for example, an anonymous contributor to *the Calcutta Review* wrote:

> We are every year improving … the indoor's comfort and elegance of our domiciles … having attained every possible contrivance for the

10 A fashionably furnished Calcutta interior. James Prinsep, interior of Calcutta drawing room with two figures, *c.* 1830.

mitigation of the severity of the climate, we have betaken ourselves to the work of adorning our dwelling houses, not always, it must be admitted, without some sacrifice of bodily comfort. Year after year has witnessed the introduction of fresh European refinements; our dwellings have grown internally less and less Oriental; and though the change has not been unattended with inconvenience, we are inclined to think we are the gainers by it. Our rooms are no longer bare and unencumbered; they are chock-full of European [style] furniture; the walls are hung with paintings; the floors covered with warm carpets; the doors, perhaps the windows, are curtained. Hence an increase perhaps of warmth, and an unquestionable accession of mosquitoes; but there is a more cheerful look about our rooms; the eye is pleased; the spirit raised; there is a greater feeling of <u>home</u>.[93]

Although perhaps not 'chock-full of … furniture', Colesworthy Grant's illustration depicts the hall of a lower-roomed Calcutta house of

Plate 2.

11 A typical arrangement of furniture within the Anglo-Indian urban home. View of hall of lower-roomed house, Calcutta, *c.* 1860.

1860, furnished in typical style (see figure 11). The room is of imposing dimensions, with bare, beamed ceiling, matted floor and a series of large door openings in each wall, one of which leads directly to the verandah. A large swinging fan or *punkah* occupies part of the centre of the room. The room is furnished with a range and variety of objects, including armchairs, easy chairs, chaise-longues, and occasional tables, all in fashionable, diluted classical style of the period. There is a square piano to one side and the walls are hung with a variety of pictures. The only lighting in the room appears to be a series of glass 'wall-shades'. The disposition of furniture is typically Anglo-Indian, with objects arranged along the walls in rows and a small 'island' of chairs and tables to the centre of the room. This arrangement was most probably dictated by the location of the swinging fan, the furniture being positioned in order that the occupants of the room could take maximum advantage of the cooling draughts of air produced by this device.

Probate inventories and lists of auction sales archived at the British Library, London, also provide a detailed word picture, in some cases, of the luxurious and cluttered material lives of nineteenth-century British residents in metropolitan centres, as well as in outlying regions of India. In some cases, detailed descriptions of house contents are itemized room by room in a particular property. These descriptions provide evidence of the disposition of furnishings at specific locations within the household and also allow for the social practices there enacted to be inferred. In May 1840, the estate of Henry Martindell of Calcutta was offered for sale.[94] He had been Secretary to the Military Fund and had resided in Calcutta for a number of years.[95] In addition to a large quantity of books, crockery, table lights and silver by Hamilton and Co. of Calcutta, 'the furniture and fittings up … in the Centre Room in the second floor' of his upper-roomed house comprised

> A capital square Piano Forte by George Wilkinson, London, cased in fine mahogany and standing on six reeded and turned legs with brass sockets and castors having pedal and covers; a music stool, Morocco seat having elevating screw; a handsome and substantial breakfast table by one of the European cabinet makers meas'g nine by five feet, standing on stout twisted and turned legs with brass sockets; an elegant settee couch, the frame of picked toonwood,[96] caned and varnished, covered with superfine crimson damask having 8 side pillows; a pair ditto differing, covered with chintz; a pair of handsome side tables, made of the finest dark grained mahogany standing on twisted and carved legs with brass lion paw feet, surmounted by beautiful white Parian marble slab, each meas'g 40 × 22 inches; a pair of substantial toon wood square tea poys [occasional tables] on reeded and carved pillars on tripod stand; eight strong and neat varnished toon wood chairs, with railed backs and rattan seats; a pair of beautifully executed coloured engravings, fitted into gold burnished frames, glazed, representing 'the Battle of the Nile at Sunset'; ditto 'at 10 o'clock'; a pair of small ditto, 'the Village School' and 'May Day'; a set of plain ditto, 'Lord St Vincent's Victory', 'Lord Duncan's Victory', 'Battle of Trafalgar', 'Death of Nelson'; a pair ditto, one without glass of sea fight; a pair ditto with glass viz. the Gipsy and rural scene; a single plain ditto 'the Finding of Moses'; a valuable oil painting of landscape and river scenery with a tower in which a dial is fixed, fitted with clock work and music, set to favourite airs in gilt frame and out of order; a pair of handsome double branch wall lights with carved toon wood brackets, plated arms and vase shades; two pair ditto; a pair of neat white washed hanging punkahs with painted borders and ornament and red ropes, each meas'g 16 feet; the mat on the floor.

In addition to 'the Centre Room on the Second Floor', the appraiser who prepared the list for sale also noted the copious contents of other rooms in Mr Martindell's house designated in the following manner: 'in the Bedroom to the West', 'in the Room of the North', 'in the Office to the East', 'in the Front Room to the North', 'in the Staircase', and 'in the Hall on the First Floor'. The contents of the 'Centre Room' are most probably those of a main reception or drawing room, although the room was not described as such by the appraiser.

Although less frequently used than images, three-dimensional objects are a potential resource for visual enquiry. It has been suggested that objects operate as 'unobtrusive measures of social processes and [such objects] can allow inferences to be made' about these processes.[97] A typology developed by Harold Riggins as a general conceptual tool for interpreting contemporary everyday settings offers a series of headings around which to frame questions about the historic interior and the non-functional role of its furnishings.[98] Riggins proposed the classification of everyday objects, in any analysis, into such headings as usage (active/passive, normal/alien), status and esteem, collective objects (that is, making connections to wider social ties) and as social facilitators. He also suggested how the total effect of furnishings in an interior might be assessed in terms of the display syntax of the room (the way objects were organized), highlighting/understating, status consistency/ inconsistency, degree of conformity (to generally accepted norms) and general flavour or atmosphere of the room as a whole.

Mr Martindell's room contained many of the standard items to be found in drawing rooms of middle-class dwellings in the homeland, such as a piano (by an English maker), a breakfast table (of substantial size), settee couches and side or console tables; a set of 'toonwood' chairs was also located in this room.[99] The timbers described were both imported (mahogany) and local (which had the appearance of mahogany). These objects could be classified under the headings of normal usage (in comparison with that of middle-class interiors within the homeland), as social facilitators (allowing for standard patterns of behaviour to take place) and as status objects (an imported English piano and a table made by a European rather than, in contrast, by a local cabinetmaker), as well as collective objects (the allusions and connections to England through manufacture or material linking the owner to others within the Anglo-Indian community).

The few textiles mentioned indicate the adoption of fashionable Western furnishing fabrics, such as 'superfine crimson damask' and 'chintz'. The contents of the room also signify the wholesale adoption of European things or materials within the Anglo-Indian domestic interior during this period, although the Western connection could be tenuous. It could, for example, include objects manufactured by a European firm based in India or the use of the chief cabinetmaking timber of the homeland (mahogany) within the Indian context.[100]

Mr Martindell also owned a number of engravings, including scenes of various naval battles, such as the *Battle of the Nile at Sunset, Lord St Vincent's Victory* and the *Battle of Trafalgar*, which signified a patriotic interest in British military accomplishments. (As noted, he was Secretary to the Military Fund.) In addition, he owned engravings of a more sentimental or religious nature, including *The Gipsy* and *Rural Scene* as well as *The Finding of Moses*.

Both the naval and other engravings indicate connections to wider social ties within the Anglo-Indian community and the homeland. Light sources in the room were limited to the standard fixed forms found in most of the more substantial Anglo-Indian interiors within the Presidency cities, namely six 'double branch wall lights' with vase shades. No other light source is recorded. (There is no mention of an Argand lamp or a chandelier, which would have been the other most likely sources of light at this time.) Finally, in the description of two large, swinging fans – or punkahs – attached to the ceiling, there is a hint that the room was decorated. In grander interiors, these items were normally decorated to match the rest of the room and these punkahs were described as being whitewashed 'with painted borders and ornament'. There was a high degree of status consistency evidenced in the furnishings of this room, and its contents reflected the financial and cultural capital of the owner. Other inventories record similar richness, profusion and variety of furnishings.[101]

In February 1845, a sale list was prepared of the 'handsome furniture and fittings up, hanging and wall lights, carpets, pictures and ornaments etc' formerly belonging to Major Fitzgerald at Calcutta.[102] Major William R. Fitzgerald held a senior position within the Department of Public Works in the city.[103] The catalogue provides an extensive and detailed list of the furniture and furnishings which were located in each room of the house. For example, 'the Drawing Room' contained furniture made by both Shearwood and Currie, two of the most prominent European cabinetmakers working in Calcutta during the nineteenth century, and included:[104]

> A handsome large sized circular drawing roomed [sic] table by Currie, made of dark Spanish mahogany measuring 6 feet diameter supported on a richly carved cross-shaped pedestal, attached is a crimson and yellow damask cover; an elegant, extra sized occasional table of picked mahogany with carved sides by Currie, supported by very handsomely carved scrolls having a platform for a vase; a pair of St Domingo mahogany card tables by Currie, covered with green baize, having recesses and carved corners supported on neat pedestals with platform and feet; a square piano forte by Broadwood & Sons, London, of 6 octaves with metallic plate and bars, a very fine toned instrument cased in French polished mahogany, standing on 4 handsome legs with brass castors having a pedal and quilted cover; a mahogany music stool, with back having elevating cushion covered with red morocco on a curved pedestal and tripod; a mahogany Canterbury, with drawers on castors; a pair of large Ottoman couches by Shearwood, with neat frames and legs of mahogany covered with figured crimson silk damask, having back cushions and outer covers; a handsome Ottoman *morah* [cylindrical cane or reed stool][105] with crimson silk sides and tassel, the top covered with Berlin wool embroidery, having an outer cover; a ditto differing in shape; a ditto with handsomely carved frame and green

silk sides; a comfortable mahogany easy chair standing on castors having
falling back with spring, cushions covered with red Morocco; a toonwood
Spanish easy chair with rattan seat and back; a rosewood gossiping chair
with Berlin wool embroidered seat and back rest, having outer covers; 8
carved mahogany arm chairs with rattan seats; 4 toonwood drawing room
chairs with close rattan seats; an American painted rocking chair; 4 carved
toonwood footstools, with carpet tops; a mahogany sarcophagus shaped tea
cuddy [sic] with ebony beading, lock and key, on pedestal and tripod, with
brass paws and castors; a capital teakwood embroidery frame on stand.

In addition to the large quantity of furniture, the 'Drawing Room' contained
some books, numerous small decorative items and engravings. These
included, for example, *Illustrations of Syria and the Holy Land*, *Illustrations of
the Passes of the Alps*, *Illustrations of London and its Vicinity*, *Souvenirs of the
Highlands* as well as other texts, some of them covered with 'embossed cloth
gilt'. These may be classified as collective objects and indicated connection
to wider social and national ties. Scattered on the furniture were a large
number of intrinsically passive objects, which served as decoration and
reinforced the social status of the occupier. These included 'a plated stand
dish with two diamond cut glasses … a pair of painted and gilt porcelain
flower vases and a pair with match cups; a cut glass Eau de Cologne bottle,
bronzed stand … a table bell on stand; a rosewood stand dish inlaid with
pearl, 2 ink glasses; a pair of cut glass scent bottles and a pair of moulded
glass card trays; 10 large sea shells; 10 small ornaments of sorts; a pair of
frosted glass flower holders on black marble stands; a pair of small prints
framed and glazed'.

The lighting in the room comprised 'a pair of double branch wall
lights with plated arms, carved toon wood brackets, vase shades and oil
burners', and ten more of the same. The floor was covered with 'a handsome
Mirzapore carpet of flower pattern on drab ground, measuring 20 by 16 feet'
as well as the standard 'mat on the floor'. Although the carpet was locally
made and was not recommended by Anglo-Indian household-management
advice literature, its presence made a connection to the furnishing practices
of the home country (and at the same time rejected local practice of covering
the entire floor with matting). Its presence also inferred that this wider
connection outweighed more practical considerations, such as keeping
a large part of the interior as cool as possible. Finally, a 'drab punkah
measuring 19 feet with gilt ornaments, ropes and fringe' cooled the room.
Three pairs of 'swing door screens for 3 doors with mahogany frames and
turkey red twill panels by a European' completed the list of contents.

The selection of furniture and furnishings transcribed in this extract
from Major Fitzgerald's inventory could hardly be described as sparse;
in a number of ways, it also conformed quite closely to the norms of

middle-class interiors in the homeland, albeit a little outdated. A high proportion of the room's contents might be classified as collective objects, objects of status and as social facilitators. The inventory also evidences a high degree of status consistency and conformity. In a similar fashion to those of Mr Martindell's drawing room, the contents of Major Fitzgerald's room reflected the financial and cultural capital of the occupier and, given the location, corresponded to an extent with shared, conventional concepts of British middle-class propriety in terms of object-types, order, colour, form and setting. Many of the items were made of mahogany, the chief cabinet wood used in Britain from the early eighteenth century; the designations of the types of furniture also indicate that the forms followed metropolitan conventions: the mahogany round table or Loo table, the card table, piano, and Ottoman couches were standard items found in mid-Victorian drawing rooms. The adjectives used by the appraiser to describe the furnishings, such as 'neat', 'very handsome', 'richly carved', indicate approval within British elite conventions of taste. The furniture appears to have been on a grander scale than the portable and easily disposable items recommended a few decades later in the household-management advice literature. In addition, a number of items, in a manner similar to that of Mr Martindell's property, had been made by the leading European cabinetmakers in Calcutta.

A selection of easy chairs is recorded, including a 'Spanish easy chair', a 'gossiping chair', and an 'American rocking chair', underlining the necessity of repose in the hot climate of India and the more relaxed and informal body posture adopted by the British within the Subcontinent. Furthermore, a variety of textiles was also included within the interior to mitigate the often-noted sparseness of Anglo-Indian rooms. These included green baize, figured crimson silk damask, Berlin wool work and red twill panels. Inclusion of these textiles indicates their use as collective objects, or connective elements to the wider Anglo-Indian society, as well as to the prevailing taste of the homeland. A number of features were also peculiar to the Indian context, and a small number of Indian or Anglo-Indian objects are also found in this inventory. However, some of these indigenous objects were Europeanized by covering them with textiles (crimson silk, tassels and Berlin wool work) in a manner alien to that of local practice. Such objects included 'two Ottoman *morahs*' or locally manufactured cylindrical reed stools, as well as the Mirzapore carpet and a number of 'door screens', a peculiarity of Anglo-Indian interiors intended to provide some privacy to the occupants of a room, as connecting doors between rooms were invariably left open to allow for circulation of air. The only source of artificial light mentioned in the inventory was a large set of glass wall lights with vase shades.

Inventories of the contents of these two drawing rooms offers evidence of a high level of consistency in terms of object types, materials, quantity and disposition of furnishings. Descriptions of such room contents are also echoed in contemporary commentaries and fictionalized accounts of the period. One example of this similarity between historical source and fictional account is found in an Anglo-Indian novel entitled *Peregrine Pultuney; or Life in India* published in 1844, which, with its closely paralleling the inventories discussed above, merits quoting at length.[106]

In this novel, the description of the invented interior of a well-to-do Calcutta drawing room in a house off 'one of the best Chowringhee Roads' not only corroborates the material in the inventories but also helps to complete the setting of the room in which the furnishings are located (a factor lacking in the inventories) by describing the structure, decorative treatment and arrangement of that interior. In the period before 1850 and the advent of photography, evidence of the appearance of Anglo-Indian interiors is scarce; by combining readings of inventories and fictionalized accounts, together with analysis of the few visual images which survive, a more informed understanding can be reached of the domestic interiors of the British elite in India. In contrast to inventories and other historical records, fictionalized accounts also offer insights into the ways that furnishings functioned within Anglo-Indian interiors, contemporary conventions in terms of placement of objects and the socio-cultural meanings assigned to objects within the home. In the novel, Peregrine Pultuney arrives fresh from England at the house of his aunt, and is shown into her drawing room. He describes it as a 'long and somewhat badly proportioned apartment, very lofty ... and very unfinished in appearance. The walls were white but relieved every here and there by doors, prints and wall-shades'. The doors were covered with 'a kind of half-door made of toon-wood and crimson silk, which neither reached nearly to the top nor the bottom of the aperture'. He then describes the prints and notes that they 'were principally large mezzotinto ones, from the paintings of Cooper, Martin and Danby'.[107] He surveys the light-giving 'wall-shades' and imagines how hot these would make the room when all were lit. The ceiling comprised 'large square bars of wood painted pea green, running across the roof'. Three large chandeliers and two large punkahs hung from these beams, the latter 'most elaborately moulded and gilt, with deep fringes attached to the bottom'. Peregrine Pultuney notes the French windows leading onto a verandah and heavy, green-painted outer 'Venetians', which were intended to exclude the glare of the sun.

He also remarks on the lack of curtains to the windows and carpet on the floor and notes the lack of consistency between 'the unfinished aspect of the apartment and the splendour and number of the articles of furniture, which so ambitiously blocked up the room'. He describes a number of pieces of furniture which closely match the descriptions of furniture within the inventories quoted above; in addition, a sense of the arrangement of these items within the room is also presented. He notes that 'near the bay-window was a large round table, which consisted of a beautiful white marble slab upon a massive mahogany pedestal ... near this table was a mahogany sofa, covered with the finest bright yellow damask silk'. Another marble-topped table of rectangular form 'with a twist-about leg at either end of it' is also described. To the centre of the room was 'an uncommonly large gamboge [coloured] Ottoman, to match the couches'.[108] Other furniture in the room comprises a 'grand mahogany Broadwood ... another round table, but not of marble, two more sofas of ... gamboge damask'.

Having described the furniture to the centre in the room, Peregrine Pultuney proceeds to record the items arranged along the sides of the room. These comprise four 'long marble-slab ornament table[s] on which were placed a variety of china vases, china figures, artificial flowers ... little bronze lamps ... and other specimens of inutility'. Two mahogany bookcases were also placed against the walls of the room, in addition to 'an inlaid ebony and satinwood chess table, a vast number of foot stools of all sorts and sizes' and an armchair.[109]

The objects described in this fictional account can be classified under a number of headings. Several object-types could be classified as collective artefacts – that is, items which proclaimed connection to the wider Anglo-Indian social group. These included items of furniture such as the large round table, the mahogany sofa, the rectangular and the marble-topped table. The collection of prints could be classified as status objects. Items such as the Broadwood piano and the chess set could be categorized as social facilitators which allowed the normative social pastimes of the homeland to be enacted within the Anglo-Indian home. The range of decorative objects which covered the marble-slab tables could be described as intrinsically passive and markers of status. The general flavour of the room's furnishings is described in contrasting terms as both wanting in comfort due to a lack of textiles within the interior, but conversely presenting an abundance of furniture.

Inventories of drawing-room contents recorded during the second half of the nineteenth century depict the increasingly Anglicized nature of this room and the eradication of most Indian features. (The Indian artefacts, which are recorded in this room are small, decorative items, which could be classified as souvenirs or tourist memorabilia.) For example, 'the Inventory and Effects of Capt. John Paterson taken 13th December 1869' presented the main reception room filled with many of the articles found in similar rooms in the homeland.[110] Captain Paterson lived at number 9 Garden Reach, Moocheekhollah, Calcutta and was Agent and Superintendent of the

P & O Steamship Navigation Company. Although prosperous and living in a favoured district of Calcutta, he was not a part of 'official' British India, but one of the many successful British residents in India outside that group. His residence was located close to the P & O Officers' Club and the P & O Yard and Hospital.[111] His 'Household furniture in the Drawing Room' comprised:

> A mahogany marble top centre table; a mahogany marble top centre table differing; a mahogany tortoise shaped marble top table; a mahogany tortoise shaped marble top table to match; a pair of mahogany marble top pie[r] tables; a pair of mahogany marble top console brackets; a pair of corner whatnots; a pair of corner whatnots to match; a pair of corner Italian marble top teapoys; a pair of corner square marble top teapoys; a pair of corner square marble top teapoys; a pair of corner walnut wood marble top small teapoys; a pair of walnut wood jardinières; a Victoria couch; an Albert couch; a Victoria easy chair; an Albert easy chair; a mahogany easy chair; a pair of mahogany fancy chairs; a set of six Genoa chairs; a set of three square footstools covered with fancy carpet; a camp easy chair; a mahogany square piano forte; seven volumes music books and a lot of loose music books; a mahogany music stool covered with carpet; a music whatnot.

In addition to furniture, Captain Paterson's drawing room contained many decorative items such as: 'a set of six fancy cushions; a set of seven fancy antimacassars; a Parian marble group of three; a smaller Parian marble group of two; a pair of flower vases … a plated mounted basket with blue liner; two inlaid marble dishes of Indian workmanship … a papier-mâché ornament; a fancy paperweight; a crimson opal glass … a pair of real China vases … a Bohemian glass flower holder … a Japanese card box … an Italian marble tazza; a set of twelve models of Indian domestics'. Textiles and lighting in the room comprised: 'a pair of door curtains; a set of five door curtains; a six light crystal glass luster; a set of four hanging lamps; an English carpet 18 × 12 ft; [and] a Mirzapore carpet'.

The inventory of the contents of Captain Paterson's Drawing Room gives the impression of a cluttered domestic space. There are listed many pairs of items and many small pieces of furniture. European cabinet woods such as mahogany and walnut are described, indicating a connection to the homeland and rejection of local materials. Several pieces of furniture are described as Italian and the appraiser has designated some of the seating furniture as a 'Victoria easy chair' or 'Albert couch', indicating a relationship to furniture forms of the homeland. The room contained a piano and a number of music books, a significant social facilitator of the homeland as well as the Anglo-Indian community during the nineteenth century. Many textiles are also recorded, including 'fancy cushions', 'fancy antimacassars', 'door curtains', carpet-covered stools, 'an English carpet' as well as a local

(Mirzapore) one. The small decorative objects arranged around the room also reflect the kind of objects that would have been found in many middle-class drawing rooms in Britain, such as Parian marble groups, 'a papier-mâché ornament', 'a fancy paperweight', 'a pair of real China vases' and 'a Bohemian glass flower holder', as well as other items. Locally produced objects are limited to two 'inlaid marble dishes of Indian workmanship' (most probably Agra-work) and models of 'Indian domestics'.[112]

However, these lavishly furnished interiors, located in central Calcutta, were by no means the norm as far as Anglo-Indian furnishing practices were concerned. Other inventories of Britons living in India, whose employment fixed them lower down the social scale, reveal a more basic material existence. For example, in 1846 'the household furniture & C' of William Wise, formerly a pilot employed by the East India Company in Bombay, recorded a relatively meagre set of furnishings.[113] His total household contents included: '1 pair couch; 12 chairs; 1 chest drawers; 1 cupboard; 1 sideboard; 1 round table; 2 teapois [small tables]; 1 liquor case; 1 Argand lamp; 1 set crockery ware; 1 set German silver spoons; 1 set knives and forks; 1 cot with beddings … 1 set copper cooking pots of sizes' and a small quantity of clothes. None of the furniture was described as neat or handsome and the quantities of items listed indicate modest levels of entertainment. Mr Wise possessed the bare minimum levels of comfort and decency, as he owned a pair of couches, a round table and a dozen chairs. He only appears to have possessed one good light source, namely an Argand lamp. No engravings were recorded among his possessions; neither were any furnishing textiles listed nor books. Inventories of the personal property of other low-level employees of the East India Company also present a similar picture of a meagre material existence.[114]

Although many Anglo-Indians rented their accommodation, some owned one or more properties which they rented out. Despite being owners of property, many Anglo-Indians still lived relatively simple existences in terms of the furnishings of their own domestic spaces. Robert Tilbury, a 'Government Pensioner' of Calcutta, whose estate was registered in January 1883, possessed a limited range and variety of furniture which was recorded in the part of number 4 May Road in which he lived.[115] He also owned another property in May Road and one in Leonard's Road.[116] The area in which he lived was close to the municipal warehouses or 'godowns', the arsenal timber yard and Government iron-store, and was some distance from the fashionable houses of Chowringhee and Park Street. His furnishings evidenced basic levels of comfort and modest levels of entertainment. He possessed some pieces of mahogany furniture, but also furniture made of teak wood and camphor-wood. In addition, he owned a piano and Canterbury for music, which indicated connection to a wider Anglo-Indian community, but only 'six dining chairs' and 'four unarmed chairs', indicating limited scope for entertainment and socialization.

Not all Anglo-Indians followed the advice found in household-management guides regarding the arrangement of the bedroom even when they had the means and available interior space so to do. In most of the advice literature it was recommended that only the bed should be located in this room as the inclusion of any other furniture or textiles harboured mosquitoes and other pests. In September 1855, for instance, appraisers listed the furnishings formerly owned by a widow, Mrs Hutteman of Calcutta.[117] In 'Mrs H's Bedroom' the inventory recorded: '1 almirah [wardrobe or cupboard]; 1 cane bed; 2 China trunks;1 plate chest; 1 teakwood chest; 1 small teak box; 1 toon wood dressing table and glass; 1 old couch with mattress and pillows; 1 wash hand stand; 1 small round table; 5 pictures; 1 almirah containing clothes; 1 wooden bench; 3 old tin trunks; 2 chairs; [and] 1 old safe'. Despite her having been comfortably appointed in terms of her material possessions (owning a quantity of jewellery, wearing apparel, and livestock), Mrs Hutteman appears to have inhabited only three rooms including a hall, a sitting room and a bedroom. The latter combined the functions of both bedroom and dressing room.

Furnishing the rural colonial interior

Many Anglo-Indians lived a materially sparse domestic existence that, in some cases, approximated to the guidance offered in Anglo-Indian household-management advice literature. This applied especially to those employed in the civil administration later in the nineteenth century, who, as part of their jobs, were required to move from district to district at regular intervals. For example, in 1863 the estate of C.B. Harris, Assistant Supervisor at the British Government's forestry establishment at Dehra Dun, recorded the basic possessions of a government employee who was frequently required to travel and spend considerable amounts of time under canvas.[118] In addition to a small quantity of furniture including such items as '1 camp table', '2 portmanteaus', and '3 camel trunks', as well as '1 tent with dhurries and one cooking tent', his possessions also included a variety of rifles, swords and hunting trophies ('1 bear's skin, 1 tiger's skin, 2 panther's skins).

The dwellings of non-official members of the Anglo-Indian community, such as planters, which were located in rural localities, present evidence of a more settled and comfortable material existence than those of the imperial administration – an example of this is figure 12, which depicts the drawing room of an indigo planter's bungalow near Patna, northern India. The room is arranged very much in the manner of a comparable room in Britain, the indicators of its Anglo-Indian origin being the bare, beamed

Drawingroom. Turcoulcah House. Chumparum.

12 Many non-official Anglo-Indians enjoyed settled home lives. Henry Manners, Drawing room of an indigo planter's bungalow in Turculea, Champaran District, N. India, *c.* 1880.

ceiling and the matted floor. A range of textiles is apparent (over doorways, draped over tables and arranged around the mantle piece). A collection of small decorative objects is arranged over the surfaces of the tables. In fact, the furniture of the 'Drawing Room' consists of standard items which could found in the Victorian home in Britain, including centre tables, a 'conversation' settee, 'gypsy' or small X-frame table and other occasional tables.

In June 1880, the estate was registered of William Smith, 'indigo planter and manager of the Jogapore Factory in the District of Chuprah [Chapra]' in North East India.[119] He had been married, and his widow became sole possessor of the house contents. The 'Drawing Room' contained comparable types and quantities of furniture to that in equivalent rooms in the homeland, including carved furniture ('a pair of carved chairs, toon, oval backs') and a number of occasional tables or 'teapoys'. In fact, the furniture was mostly made of toon wood rather than mahogany, as it might have been in Calcutta. The room also contained a 'round or breakfast table' – the anchor or pivot of most Victorian drawing rooms in Britain. Perhaps more unusually, the room contained no piano. In addition, the drawing room contained a number of textiles, such as a 'table cloth … maroon colour, silk border', 'chintz rose pattern' upholstery on an easy chair, 'door purdahs' of maroon, '5 pairs of muslin curtains', '6 antimacassars' and a 'maroon coloured fringed mantel piece worked with stripes'. These collective objects indicated connection to the increasingly textile-filled interiors of the homeland, and their usage ran counter to the advice offered in household-management manuals to keep Anglo-Indian interiors clear of such materials.

William Smith's 'Drawing Room' also contained a number of intrinsically passive objects, including pictures and decorations. These comprised 'watercolour landscapes – hill and lake scenery', 'two watercolour drawings – mountain scenery in Switzerland', '2 photographs, Indian hill scenery' and '6 photographs, small, Irish and Scotch lakes'. The sketchy descriptions of the subject matter of these images infer connection to ways of seeing and thinking prevalent among the educated classes of the homeland and, more particularly, manifestation of a picturesque sensibility in relation to the landscapes of 'home' (i.e., within Europe). In addition, the decorations in the Drawing Room comprised, among other things, two 'alabaster female figures, the Seasons', 'five moulded brackets' and a 'pair of vases' on the mantelpiece. These intrinsically passive objects indicated the status and taste of the owner, and could be characterized as collective items which represented aesthetic connections to other Anglo-Indian interiors as well as to those of the homeland.

The range of furniture recorded in the dining room of William Smith's residence closely followed the norms of the homeland and included 'pair of whatnots (toon), dinner table (toon), side board (toon), 6 arm chairs (cushions), ditto, cellaret for 15 bottles … pair of side tables, substantial handsomely carved legs'. In contrast to advice offered in the contemporary household-management advice manuals, the 'SW Bedroom' contained much furniture and combined the functions of sleeping accommodation and dressing room.[120] Although it is problematic to infer ulterior meaning simply from ownership, several publications recorded in the inventory, such as *The English Woman's Domestic Magazine* and *Mrs Beeton's Household Management* offered advice from the homeland on the arrangement of the domestic sphere. To summarize, analysis of the record of William Smith's estate indicates a reasonable degree of conformity in furnishing practices to the norms of the homeland. With the exception of the bedrooms, where the range of object types and their arrangement indicated the influence of local conditions, the contents of each of the other rooms correspond closely to shared, conventional notions of the appropriate items necessary for the performance of the usual social functions within the Victorian middle-class interior.

Inventories of the contents of other planters' dwellings are more difficult to interpret. For example, in 1859, an inventory of the estate of Mary Shillingford, a planter's wife who resided in 'Purneah [Purnia, NE India] District' presents a record of the moveable property contained within 'a bungalow, thatched, with two new *puckah* [brick-built] rooms attached to it'.[121] The contents of the rooms within this bungalow conform, in terms of the range and variety of object types, with those which would have been found in comparable dwellings within the homeland, although the materials from which the furniture was constructed were entirely local (eg 'sissoo', 'camphor', 'mangoe wood', 'teakwood'). However, there was a mixture of status objects ('1 large clock by McCabe') and second-hand objects ('1 old couch', '1 pair of old card tables'). No pictures or textiles were recorded in the inventory, with the exception of '1 large *satringhee*, quite good and new' [a flat-woven cotton carpet, usually of blue and white stripes]. The inventory suggests some sophistication in terms of entertainment, for example in the range and variety of table glassware categorized. Indianized pastimes are also indicated within the household by the recorded presence of '1 large *hookah* bottom' and '1 pewter *hookah* bottom'.

The estate of George Williamson, a tea planter in Assam, registered in June 1867, presents a more basic material existence to that of the previous examples.[122] Williamson was recorded as both a 'tea planter and honorary magistrate' of 'Seebsaugor' [Sibsagar] in Assam District and was, therefore, of some status within the British community in that region.[123] However, there was an inconsistency between this status and the material possessions of his home. The inventory records the relatively simple furnishings he possessed (e.g. '2 camp bedsteads', '2 camp tables'). He also owned a conventional range of object types ('9 armchairs', '2 sideboards', '5 teapoys') but the quantity of furnishings was modest, and no pictures, books or textiles other than a carpet are noted in the inventory. Although it is problematic to draw firm conclusions from the contents delineated in the inventory, it would appear that, in view of his status as magistrate, Williamson's interior space did not conform to the norms of the homeland.

Anglo-Indians often had to customize or personalize an unwieldy interior space and furnish such a space as best they could with limited material possessions. In a small number of cases, because Anglo-Indian furnishing practices adopted were idiosyncratic or thought to be noteworthy, the British inhabitants of Indian domestic space occasionally depicted, in a sketched drawing, the arrangement of furniture in their reception rooms and bedrooms, either for themselves or for their relatives in the home country. For example, in the Younghusband album at the British Library, of around 1880, plans of the 'Dining Room' and 'Bedroom' were sketched out, each room presenting the disposition of a limited range of furniture, including, in the former, depictions and descriptors of 'large round table' (located in the centre of the room), 'sideboard with lamps' and 'square table'.[124] Often one or two of the multiple doorways in Anglo-Indian dwellings were blocked by a piece of furniture and, in the case of the Younghusband album, with the words 'door to drawing room kept always shut' and with a washing stand positioned in front of it.

Other private papers, in a similar vein, depict the manner in which the furnishings of a room or building were disposed. For example, in the Thatcher Papers at the Centre of South Asia Studies at Cambridge, there is a hand-drawn plan of a bungalow in Agra executed in 1900 which depicts the arrangement of the limited quantity of furniture in the bedroom and office/drawing room.[125] The very centre of the latter is marked by a cross and designated by the name 'Bill', emphasizing the significance, at least on paper, of the room's occupant. As is the case with other sources of evidence, the bedroom is represented as being filled with a variety of furniture, in contrast to the prevailing advice.

The Anglo-Indian dwelling could also become a site of memory. Memories evoked by the material culture of that dwelling included both those of the domestic sphere within the homeland and, as the socio-political position of the British in India became more unstable in the early years of the twentieth century, memories of an imagined golden era in India prior to the present. In 1928, Mrs Ironside-Smith, wife of the British judge at Vizagapatam on the Eastern coast of India, wrote a nostalgic account of 'a big rambling white-washed bungalow' dating from the nineteenth century, which she and her husband rented in a settlement called Waltair.[126] In contrast to the '[e]fficient ordinariness' of the modern flat which she had previously occupied in Calcutta, she described the bungalow at Waltair as 'the house of my dreams' and that 'going to live there was like stepping back three-quarters of a century, back to the days of John Company [the English East India Company]'. She countered the usual complaint among Anglo-Indians regarding the scale and bareness of the Indian rooms by asserting that 'the big bare rooms [of the bungalow] never seemed empty to me'. In contrast to many Anglo-Indian accounts, Mrs Ironside-Smith's bungalow was imbued with homely attributes and was characterized by the use of such adjectives as 'mellow', 'kindly', and 'gracious dignity', descriptors which were not usually associated with the British home in India. Cultural memories of the homeland were also evoked in this bungalow.

The bungalow at Waltair contained, among other spaces, 'an English-looking room, with its wicker furniture and unobtrusive Wilton carpet'. A sense of connection to the homeland was also evoked in this room through the 'white paint which made the room seem so English', the view of the sea and the inclusion of images of home, such as 'two watercolours of Devon … a Calindarium Londinense and two views of London … and an etching of Aberdeen'. As in many Anglo-Indian rooms, the inhabitants were confronted with the problem of breaking up expanses of bare walls and personalizing such a space. The 'Middle Room' at Waltair, in the same way as all the others in the bungalow, had been built to include 'ten doors or arches … all absolutely symmetrically placed and so huge' that they presented 'a problem in decoration'.[127] The chief obstacle was to break up 'the hard lines' and avoid the creation of a room which looked 'like a figure in Euclid'.

Many Anglo-Indians invested much time and effort in the creation of comfortable living spaces within their bungalows and houses. As Mrs Ironside-Smith noted,

> How we moved and removed that furniture about, decided a sofa would be better over there and found it wasn't and moved it back again and so on – months of work, but it was worth while, for the old house, once a dreary desert of mid-Victorian furniture in all stages of decay, began to blossom … and the furniture, washed and polished and dressed in nice new covers, regained its self-respect.

Much of the furniture at Waltair was second-hand and belonged to the Indian owner of the house and was described as very 'unattractive'. The dining room furniture was 'mostly in the Empire style, probably Indian-made copies of furniture brought out in the East India Company's days'. The large expanse of wall-space in the dining room was also broken up and personalized by hanging 'some Underground Railway posters from home' in place of full-length portraits. The unwieldy and stark Indian domestic space of the Waltair bungalow was, by such vestigial measures, rendered into a series of spaces which could be more comfortably inhabited. Many Anglo-Indians actively engaged in re-creating their own spaces and some went to great lengths, investing much time, personal creativity and expense in modifying their domestic sphere (see figure 13).[128] In this illustration, Mrs Hyde has recorded herself with a carefully positioned Box-Brownie camera, seated in fashionable, Westernized domestic surroundings entirely designed by her (and most probably executed by local craftsmen). If the context of this photograph was unknown, the furniture could perhaps have been interpreted as the product of Heals of Tottenham Court Road or Bowmans of Camden Town.

13 Fashionable drawing room interior and furnishings designed by the resident, Mrs Hyde, Diwan bungalow, Jagdalpur, Bastar, India, *c.* 1930.

In such interiors, British residents in India made statements, through their possessions, about the 'hierarchy of values' to which the middle-class consumer in Britain, with access to a vast range of products, could more easily subscribe (see figures 14 and 15).[129] In these two illustrations, from India and Ceylon, light textile drapes are used to soften and mark off part of the domestic environment. There is also extensive use of other textiles in the form of knotted pile carpets, cushions and 'throws'. The Indian interior depicts three men seated on a chaise-longue and easy chair before a mirrored display cabinet in Aesthetic-style, which displays various artistic products, including a small statue. The Ceylonese interior depicts a range of furniture types, including armchairs, side tables, caned sofas, occasional tables, all of distinctively local production, especially the seating furniture, but evoking the fashionable middle-class furniture of the homeland.

Some members of the British community in India, as exemplified in the inventories and sales lists discussed above, were able to make connections through their choice of furnishings within the domestic interior to a 'larger sphere of cultural meaning' than many of their compatriots living in more distant and remote provinces of India.[130] However, even the lavish furnishings of British reception rooms in Calcutta differed from those of comparable rooms in Britain; both the furnishings and the social behaviour engendered

14 Textiles, decorative items and European-style furniture within an Anglo-Indian interior. Drawing room in bungalow with three men at Kaladgi, Bijapur, Bombay, c. 1875.

15 The furnishings of the Rev. and Mrs James Nicholson in Ceylon. Drawing room, Wesleyan Mission house, Colombo, Ceylon, c. 1880.

in the former were modified by conditions within the Subcontinent. While the appearance of Indian rooms was in some cases superficially similar to that of domestic interiors in the home country, the British in India, to use a term coined by Katherine Grier, 'paraphrased' essential elements of metropolitan reception rooms, or expressed the meanings attached to assembled artefacts in those interiors in non-standard ways.[131]

This process may have included the arrangement of furniture in ways which were not the norm in the home country, and may have included local forms of furniture within the interior and other furnishings such as door screens or *purdahs*, matting, *morahs* or reed stools and *sattringhees* or flat-woven carpets. It may also have included the adoption of locally manufactured furniture of assorted Indian woods but in European style. The peripatetic existence of late nineteenth-century British bureaucrats in India necessitated the planning and furnishing of the domestic interior in the style of a route march or camp. In fact, it appears that the British were often most happy when living in tents, whether it was the semi-permanent versions on the Esplanade in Bombay or those used on a tour through a rural district.[132] Perhaps the sense of impermanence felt by many Anglo-Indians within their bungalows in the Subcontinent was more comfortably aligned to actuality in their tented structures.

In addition, there was greater fluidity in terms of room function within the Anglo-Indian interior than of that in the homeland, and Anglo-Indians used furniture in different ways to those of their compatriots in the metropolitan country. This fluidity in the use of domestic space and alteration to their body postures, due to the climate, inflected patterns of behaviour and comportment – in England, set social practices or conventions were generally understood to operate within the parlour, the drawing room, the dining room (see figure 16). Within India no such guidelines existed for interior spaces designated as the 'North East Room', 'the Lower Hall', or 'the South East Room Below'. The climate also affected the way in which all Anglo-Indians used their furnishings. In the illustration of the drawing room in Pen Rhiw bungalow, Bangalore, one of the women is depicted in a typical Anglo-Indian pose, reclining with feet up – a pose, for a woman, which would have been regarded as indecorous within a British drawing room. As a result of the Indianized nature of the British domestic sphere within the Subcontinent, the lack of function-specific space and the mixed or second-hand nature of the furnishings in Anglo-Indian rooms, the normative associations of the homeland with regard to the British and their domestic spaces were disrupted within the Indian context.

The creation of a colonial domesticity in India rarely depended upon the wholesale adoption of a prescribed set of ideals which were endlessly promoted through the household-management advice literature of the time.

16 Drawing room with two women at leisure. Pen Rhiw bungalow, Bangalore, S. India, *c*. 1880.

As discussed in this chapter, despite localized deficiencies, domestic artefacts were actively used in self-fashioning within the Anglo-Indian home. In fact, the notion of home was reconfigured by Anglo-Indians to fit the varying circumstances of the Subcontinent. In their drawing rooms, halls and verandahs, Anglo-Indian homemakers had to negotiate, as William Glover has suggested, alien 'sensory qualities and meanings which were tied to local histories of production and use'.[133] Furthermore, inhabiting the colonial bungalow involved mediation of the cultural norms of the homeland as well as the notion of an imperial mission centred on the domestic sphere, which was increasingly advanced in the published household-advice literature of the late nineteenth and early twentieth centuries.

For the British in India, the development of a colonial domesticity, social self-creation through domestic material culture and the production of British culture and identity within the inherent 'instability of the Indian home' took place in a number of real and fictive spaces. These included the disquieting spaces between the contemporary discourse of Anglo-Indian household-management advice literature, the Anglo-Indian domestic sphere itself and the lived experiences of British residents in India, through their everyday negotiations of that world. Moving on from discussion of the Anglo-Indian domestic sphere, the following chapter assesses how colonial contact led to changes in the physical appearance of local middle-class domestic interiors, the gradual absorption of Western material culture and inflection of the social practices which took place in that space.

Notes

1 Hari Kunzru, *The Impressionist* (London, 2002), p. 299.

2 Many of these outputs were produced during the 'Raj revival' of the 1970s and 1980s. For example, Michael Edwardes, *Glorious Sahibs: the romantic as empire-builder, 1799–1838* (London, 1968); Mark Bence-Jones, *Palaces of the Raj: magnificence and misery of the lord sahibs* (London, 1973); Charles Allen (ed.), *Plain Tales from the Raj: images of British India in the twentieth century* (London, 1975), the same author's *Raj: a scrapbook of British India, 1877–1947* (Oxford, 1977); a number of films and television programmes also mined the rich vein of nostalgia for the Raj including James Ivory and Ismail Merchant's film, *Heat and Dust* (1982) based on a screenplay by Ruth Prawer Jhabvala; Granada Television's adaptation of Paul Scott's four-part novel, *The Jewel in the Crown* (Granada Television Ltd., 1984); other books include Margaret MacMillan's *Women of the Raj* (New York, 1988) and Pat Barr's *The Dust in the Balance: British women in India, 1905–1945* (London, 1989).

3 *Mofussil* – rural localities situated away from the main urban settlements of British India.

4 Alison Blunt, 'Imperial geographies of home: British domesticity in India, 1886– 1925', *Transactions of the Institute of British Geographers*, vol. 24, no. 4 (1999), pp. 421–40; Swati Chattopadhyay, 'Goods, chattels and sundry items: constructing 19th century Anglo-Indian domestic life', *Journal of Material Culture*, vol. 7, no. 3 (November 2002), pp. 243–71; Mary Procida, *Married to the Empire: gender, politics and imperialism in India, 1883–1947* (Manchester and New York, 2002), pp. 56–77; William Glover, '"A feeling of absence from Old England": the colonial bungalow', *Home Cultures*, vol. 1, no. 1 (2004), pp. 61–82. Swati Chattopadhyay, an architectural historian, has discussed how Anglo-Indian 'material-culture practices' were modified within the Indian context, although her account largely relies on published household-management advice literature.

5 R.W. Emerson, 'English Traits', *Manchester Guardian*, 9 February 1857.

6 Ian Baucom, *Out of Place: Englishness, empire and the locations of identity* (Princeton, 1999), p. 77.

7 Katherine Grier, *Culture and Comfort: parlour making and middle class identity, 1850– 1930* (Washington, D.C. and London, 1997), p. 7.

8 Grier, *Culture and Comfort*, p. 8.

9 Emerson, 'English Traits', 9 February 1857.

10 Baucom, *Out of Place*, p. 79.

11 Baucom, *Out of Place*, p. 79.

12 Baucom, *Out of Place*, p. 80.

13 This tendency for Anglo-Indian men to adopt the black broadcloth of the homeland was noted by other commentators. 'We are not aware that the temperature of Calcutta has been reduced … To see a man sit down to dinner in the month of May, dressed

from head to toe in black broad-cloth, is a spectacle calculated to teach a lesson in martyrology not easily forgotten', *Calcutta Review*, vol. 1, no. 1 (May 1844), p. 32.

14 Daniel Miller, *Material Culture and Mass Consumption* (London, 1987), p. 215.

15 Grier, *Culture and Comfort*, p. 5.

16 Flora Annie Steel and Grace Gardiner, *The Complete Indian Housekeeper and Cook* (London, 1888, reprinted 1921), p. 21.

17 William Hart, *Everyday Life in Bengal and other Indian Sketches* (London, 1906), p. 66.

18 Evidence which supports this assertion is discussed later in this chapter, and includes a range of sources including drawings, watercolours and photographs of domestic interiors, inventories, sale lists and wills in L/AG/34/27 series at the British Library.

19 Charles T. Buckland, *Sketches of Social Life in India* (London, 1884), p. 2.

20 Ann Laura Stoler, 'Cultivating bourgeois bodies and racial selves', in Catherine Hall (ed.), *Cultures of Empire: colonizers in Britain and the empire in the nineteenth and twentieth centuries* (Manchester, 2000), p. 92.

21 Thomas R. Metcalf, *Ideologies of the Raj* (Cambridge, 1995), p. 177.

22 Elizabeth M. Collingham, *Imperial Bodies: the physical experience of the Raj, c. 1800–1947* (Cambridge, 2001), *passim*.

23 Metcalf, *Ideologies of the Raj*, p. 178.

24 Stoler, 'Cultivating bourgeois bodies', p. 88.

25 Ann Laura Stoler, *Race and the Education of Desire: Foucault's 'History of Sexuality' and the colonial order of things* (Durham, NC, 1995), p. 108, cited in Glover, '"A feeling of absence from old England"', p. 78.

26 Maud Diver, *The Englishwoman in India* (Edinburgh and London, 1909), pp. 87–8.

27 Stoler, *Race and the Education of Desire*, p. 10 cited in Glover, '"A feeling of absence from old England"', p. 78.

28 Anthony King, *Colonial Urban Development: culture, social power and environment* (London and Boston, 1976), p. 90, cited in Collingham, *Imperial Bodies*, p. 168.

29 Procida, *Married to the Empire*, pp. 57–8.

30 London, British Library: Mss.Eur. B 369/5 (53), Journals of Thomas Machell.

31 London, British Library: Mss.Eur. B 369/5 (53), Journals of Thomas Machell.

32 Colesworthy Grant, *Anglo-Indian Domestic Life; a letter from an artist in India to his mother in England* (Calcutta, 1862), p. 8.

33 Grant, *Anglo-Indian Domestic Life*, p. 11.

34 Hart, *Everyday Life in Bengal*, p. 69.

35 Kate Platt, *The Home and Health in India and the Tropical Colonies* (London, 1923), p. 18.

36 Giles Tillotson, *The Tradition of Indian Architecture: continuity, controversy and change since 1850* (London and New Haven, 1989), pp. 71–2.

37 Most household management advice books for Anglo-Indians addressed the issue of local servants. Edward H. Aitken's, *Behind the Bungalow* (Calcutta and Bombay, 1895) was entirely devoted to discussion of Indian servants.

38 Blunt, 'Imperial Geographies of Home', p. 421.

39 Swati Chattopadhyay, 'Blurring Boundaries: the limits of "white town" in colonial Calcutta', *Journal of the Society of Architectural Historians*, vol. 59, no. 2 (June 2000), p. 175; Glover, '"A feeling of absence from old England"', pp. 75 and 78.

40 Collingham, *Imperial Bodies*, pp. 104–5

41 Stoler, 'Cultivating Bourgeois Bodies', p. 97 cited in Glover, '"A feeling of absence from old England"', p. 75.

42 Glover, '"A feeling of absence from old England"', p. 79. 'The material qualities of the bungalow's construction and the social arrangements they were meant to help constitute problematized the everyday expectations and sensory perceptions … in the colonial setting'.

43 Collingham, *Imperial Bodies*, p. 99.

44 Grant, *Anglo-Indian Domestic Life*, p. 9.

45 Amin Jaffer, *Furniture from British India and Ceylon: a catalogue of the collections in the Victoria and Albert Museum and the Peabody Essex Museum* (London, 2001), p. 62.

46 Steel and Gardiner, *The Complete Indian Housekeeper and Cook*, p. 28.

47 Percival Spear, *The Nabobs: a study of the social life of the English in 18th Century India* (London, 1932, revised 1963), p. 46; Suresh Chandra Ghosh, *The Social Condition of the British Community in Bengal, 1757–1800* (Leiden, 1970), p. 104, cited Jaffer, *Furniture*, p. 23.

48 Procida, *Married to the Empire*, p. 67.

49 Jaffer, *Furniture*, p. 64.

50 Grant, *Anglo-Indian Domestic Life*, p. 9. In fact, Grant includes an illustration of the hall-room of a typical upper-roomed house in Calcutta, which, although lacking fireplace, curtains and wall-paper is filled with furniture.

51 [J.A.D.] *Notes on an Outfit for India and Hints for the New Arrival* (London, 1903), pp. 24–5.

52 Edmund Hull, *The European in India; or Anglo-Indian's Vade-Mecum*, (London, 1874), p. 76.

53 Mrs H. Reynolds, *At Home in India; or Taza-be-Taza* (London, 1903), p. 84.

54 E. Braddon, *Life in India; a series of sketches showing something of the Anglo-Indian* (London, 1872), p. 109.

55 A. Vickery, *The Gentleman's Daughter: women's lives in Georgian England* (New Haven and London, 1998), pp. 161, 189, 192.

56 This is evidenced by the existence of a number of European cabinetmakers in Calcutta, Bombay and Madras during the nineteenth and early twentieth centuries (recorded in trade directories and other sources). See *The New Calcutta Directory for 1856*, vol. 2, parts 6–11 (Calcutta, 1856), p. 176: Cabinet Makers & Upholsterers' & c.: Dunn & Taylor, 64 Cossitollah Street; Edmond, J.M., 21 & 22 Cossitollah Street & 10 Waterloo Street; Lazarus & Co., 49, 54 & 55 Cossitollah Street; Paxton & Co., 30 & 48 Cossitollah Street & 10 Waterloo Street; Shearwood & Co., 39 & 40 Cossitollah Street.

57 University of Peradeniya, Kandy, Sri Lanka: Journal of Major and Mrs G. Darby Griffiths, 'Ceylon during a Residence in the Years 1841–2', 4 vols, vol. 3, p. 130.

58 Braddon, *Life in India*, pp. 109–10.

59 S.J. Duncan, *The Simple Adventures of a Memsahib* (London, 1893), p. 250.

60 Duncan, *The Simple Adventures of a Memsahib*, p. 249.

61 These included among others: E. Garrett, *Morning Hours in India; practical hints on household management* (London, 1887); Chota Mem, *The English Bride in India; hints on Indian housekeeping* (Madras, 1909); C. Deighton, *Domestic Economy* (Madras, 1909); Diver, *The Englishwoman in India*; Steel and Gardiner, *The Complete Indian Housekeeper and Cook*.

62 R.W. Edis, *Decoration and Furniture of the Town House* (London, 1881); M.E. Haweis, *Beautiful Houses* (London, 1882). Other similar texts included H.J. Jennings, *Our Houses and How to Beautify Them* (London, 1902) as well periodicals such as *The Magazine of Domestic Economy* (1836–1844); *Home Circle* (1849–53); *The Englishwoman's Domestic Magazine* (1852–77); *Sylvia's Home Journal* (1878–91); *Home Chat* (1895–1958). See H. Fraser, S. Green and J. Johnston (eds), *Gender and the Victorian Periodical* (Cambridge, 2003), pp. 100–20.

63 Rosemary Marangoly George, 'Homes in the empire, empires in the home', *Cultural Critique* (Winter 1993–94), p. 107.

64 Steel and Gardiner, *The Complete Indian Housekeeper and Cook*, p. 28.

65 Steel and Gardiner, *The Complete Indian Housekeeper and Cook*, p. 28.

66 Steel and Gardiner, *The Complete Indian Housekeeper and Cook*, p. 22.

67 Platt, *The Home and Health in India*, p. 64.

68 Platt, *The Home and Health in India*, p. 64.

69 Other commentators noted these souvenirs collected by the British as they progressed through India. 'You will probably, on your travels, pick up many curious and pretty articles of Eastern manufacture, such as bronzes, china & c. and such things will go far to supplement the few drawing-room ornaments you may take out with you'. Major S. Leigh Hunt and Alexander S. Kenny, *Tropical Trials; a handbook for women in the tropics* (London, 1883), p. 151.

70 Chattopadhyay, 'Goods, chattels and sundry items', p. 252.

71 Chattopadhyay, 'Goods, chattels and sundry items', p. 267.

72 *The Calcutta Review*, vol. 1, no. 1 (May, 1844), p. 16.

73 *The Bombay Calendar and General Directory Containing Civil, Army and Navy Lists for 1850* (Bombay, 1850), pp. 529–32. See also *The Warrant of Precedence* (Calcutta, 1921) cited in Allen (ed.), *Plain Tales from the Raj*, p. 95.

74 *Life in Bombay and the Neighbouring Out-Stations* (London, 1852), p. 32.

75 *Life in Bombay*, p. 35.

76 Jaffer, *Furniture*, pp. 58–9; Natasha Eaton, 'Excess in the city: the consumption of imported prints in colonial Calcutta, 1780–1795', *Journal of Material Culture*, vol. 8, no. 1 (2003), pp. 45–74.

77 *The Calcutta Review*, vol. 1, no. 1 (May 1844), p. 29.

78 Chattopadhyay, 'Goods, chattels and sundry items', p. 251.

79 Alfred Gell, *Art and Agency* (Oxford, 1998), p. 6.

80 Judy Attfield, *Wild Things: the material culture of everday life* (Oxford and New York, 2000), p. 1.

81 King, *Colonial Urban Development*, cited in Collingham, *Imperial Bodies*, p. 169.

82 Collingham, *Imperial Bodies*, p. 169.

83 Procida, *Married to the Empire*, p. 61.

84 Blunt, 'Imperial geographies of home', p. 426.

85 Blunt, 'Imperial geographies of home', p. 438.

86 Blunt, 'Imperial geographies of home', p. 438; Chattopadhyay, 'Goods, chattels and sundry items', p. 243.

87 Lena Orlin, 'Fictions of the early modern English probate inventory', in Henry S. Turner (ed.), *The Culture of Capital: property, cities and knowledge in early modern England* (New York and London, 2002), p. 53.

88 Margaret Ponsonby, 'Ideals, reality and meaning: homemaking in England in the first half of the nineteenth century', *Journal of Design History*, vol. 16, no. 3 (2003), p. 204.

89 Antonia Malan, 'Furniture at the Cape in the eighteenth century: an archaeological approach', in Titus Eliens (ed.), *Domestic Interiors at the Cape and in Batavia, 1602–1795* (The Hague, 2002), pp. 139–59.

90 Sparsely-furnished Government rest houses were established on major routes throughout India and Ceylon. Sir Edward Creasy, Chief Justice in Ceylon during the early 1860s, noted that 'about four beds or couches are all that are generally found in a Rest-House'. University of Oxford, Rhodes House Library: Mss.Ind.Ocn.t.5, Sir Edward Creasy Papers, letter to his sister, Emma Cottam 1861, p. 19.

91 The Reverend Charles Acland, *A Popular Account of the Manners and Customs of India* (London, 1847), p. 40.

92 John Beames, *Memoirs of a Bengal Civilian* (London, 1896 reprinted 2003) p. 128.

93 *The Calcutta Review*, vol. 1, no. 1 (May 1844), pp. 15–16.

94 London, British Library: Bengal Wills, 1840, L/AG/34/27/120, estate of Henry Martindell.

95 *The Bengal Directory and Annual Register for 1839* (Calcutta, 1839), p. 433.

96 Toonwood – Indian cedar; this timber was used in the manufacture of furniture most probably because of its availability in northern India and relatively low cost, and also because of its similarity in appearance to that of mahogany.

97 M. Emmison and P. Smith (eds), *Researching the Visual: images, objects, contexts and interactions in social and cultural enquiry* (London, Thousand Oaks and New Delhi, 2000), p. 107.

98 S.H. Riggins, 'Fieldwork in the living room', in S.H. Riggins (ed.), *The Socialness of Things* (New York, 1994), pp. 101–48, cited in Emmison and Smith, *Researching the Visual*, pp. 112–13. There are limitations in applying to historic interiors a method deployed in the analysis of present day room settings, and Riggins' typology has been used as a point of entry into an analysis of such interiors.

99 A study of the piano as an integral part of British colonial culture would be a worthwhile activity. A large number of Anglo-Indian inventories record the existence of a 'Broadwood' or a 'Wilkinson' within the colonial domestic interior.

100 Jaffer, *Furniture*, pp. 43–6.

101 London, British Library: Bengal Wills, 1840, L/AG/34/27/120, estate of Thomas Clarke, who owned houses in Calcutta at 'Dhurrumtollah', 'Jaun Bazaar', and 'Intallah'. This inventory presents evidence of rooms furnished in a similar fashion and with similar materials to those of Mr Martindell (see note 94 above).

102 London, British Library: Bengal Wills, 1845, L/AG/34/27/133, estate of Maj.

Fitzgerald.

103 *The Bengal and Agra Directory and Annual Register for the Year 1844* (Calcutta, 1844), p. 177.

104 *The Bengal and Agra Directory*, records Currie and Co. as Cabinet Makers in Cossitollah Street (no number) in that year, p. 339. *Thacker's Directory for Bengal, the North Western Provinces and the Punjab … for 1865* (London, Allahabad and Bombay, 1865), records Shearwood & Co. as 'billiard table manufacturers' and 'cabinet makers' at 39 and 40 Cossitollah Street, Calcutta, pp. 341–2.

105 *Morah* or *morha* – cylindrical stool of waisted form made of cane or reeds.

106 John Kaye, *Peregrine Pultuney; or life in India* (London, 1844) 3 vols, pp. 62–6.

107 These artists are most probably: Thomas Sidney Cooper (1803–1902); John Martin (1789–1854) and Francis Danby (1793–1861). John Martin was a noted printmaker, especially of mezzotints. Martin Postle, 'Cooper, Thomas Sidney', Robyn Hamlyn, 'Martin, John', Hilary Morgan, 'Danby, Francis' all from *The Grove Dictionary of Art Online* (Oxford University Press) www.groveart.com (accessed 18 April 2006).

108 Kaye, *Peregrine Pultuney*, p. 65.

109 Kaye, *Peregrine Pultuney*, p. 66.

110 London, British Library: Bengal Wills, 1869, L/AG/34/27/177, estate of Capt. J. Paterson.

111 *Thacker's Directory for Bengal and the North West Provinces & c. for 1868* (Calcutta, 1868), part 2, pp. 141 and 152.

112 For examples of related miniature Indian figures see fig. 365, 'Figures of caste 'types', including a *sadhu*, musician, government employee [etc.]' made of clay and painted wood in C.A. Bayly (ed.), *The Raj: India and the British, 1600–1947* (exhib. cat., London, 1990), p. 288; a group of similar clay and painted wood miniature figures representing various Indian trades forms part of the collection of the National Museum, Copenhagen, together with a model of an ox-cart and drivers purchased at the Paris International Exhibition of 1867.

113 London, British Library: Bombay Wills, 1846–1850, L/AG/34/27/397, estate of William Wise.

114 London, British Library: Bombay Wills, 1846–1850, L/AG/34/27/397, estate of John Dwyer; for example, the 'Inventory of Household Property belonging to the late Sub-Conductor John Dwyer of the Hon. East India Company's service' was recorded at Palghatcherry on 21 October 1850 and included: '1 lot books … 1 half table; 1 dressing table; 1 trunk; 1 jackwood chest of drawers; 1 pair teapoys; 1 dressing table; 6 pictures; 1 Argand lamp; 1 looking glass; 1 couch; 1 teapoy; 1 cot, bedding and steps; 1 cot and mattress; 1 wardrobe; … 1 bookcase; 1 pair shades; 2 candle sticks; [assorted glassware]; 1 screen … 1 cradle and bed; 1 despense cupboard; 6 jackwood chairs … 1 lot carpets; 1 table [and assorted objects]'. The small amounts of money achieved at the sale for each item indicated that John Dwyer's furnishings were unimpressive.

115 *The Bengal Directory, 1881* (Calcutta, 1881), p. 1145.

116 London, British Library: Bengal Wills, 1883, L/AG/34/27/190, estate of Robert Tilbury.

117 London, British Library: Bengal Wills, 1855, L/AG/34/27/156, estate of Mrs Hutteman.

118 London, British Library: Bengal Wills, 1863, L/AG/34/27/170, estate of C.B. Harris.

David Gilmour notes that British Civilians or civil servants in many parts of India spent up to seven months of each year 'on tour' in camp, administering justice and conducting reassessments of revenue. D. Gilmour, *The Ruling Caste: imperial lives in the Victorian Raj* (London, 2005), pp. 104–5.

119 London, British Library: Bengal Wills, 1880, L/AG/34/27/187, estate of William Smith; *The Bengal Directory, 1880* (Calcutta, 1880), pp. 836 and 1158.

120 The 'SW Bedroom' contained: 'pr toon beds, mosquito curtains, mattresses, pillows complete; dressing table, mahogany, substantial looking glass, brass moveable candle brackets ... ; china dish for dressing table; ladies dress horse, toon; large towel horse, toon; marble wash hand stand ... ; commode; bidet; small toon wood table w. cloth; 2 bamboo and cane chairs covered with chintz; large sissoo bed w. mattress'.

121 London, British Library: Bengal Wills, 1859, L/AG/34/27/163, estate of Mary Shillingford. *The New Calcutta Directory for the Town of Calcutta, Bengal and the North-West ... for 1858* (Calcutta, 1858). Charles A. Shillingford is recorded as indigo planter of the Munshye concern, Purneah and Joseph A. Shillingford is recorded as indigo planter of the Kolassy concern, Purneah.

122 London, British Library: Bengal Wills, 1867, L/AG/34/27/174, estate of George Williamson.

123 *Thacker's Directory for Bengal, North West Provinces ... for 1867* (Calcutta, 1867), p. 188.

124 London, British Library: Mss.Eur. F197/37, Younghusband album.

125 University of Cambridge, Centre of South Asian Studies: Thatcher papers.

126 London, British Library: Mss.Eur. D 898, Ironside-Smith papers.

127 London, British Library: Mss.Eur. D 898, Ironside-Smith papers, p. 5.

128 University of Cambridge, Centre of South Asian Studies, E.S. Hyde papers. The photograph of Mrs Hyde seated in her drawing room is inscribed 'round coffee table, desk, desk stool, bookcases and small 'peg' table my designs'. These were most probably executed by a local craftsman. Another photograph of the same room by Mrs Hyde is inscribed 'sand-coloured carpet, hand-made in the jail; toning sand-coloured tapestry cloth brought from London for sofa and chairs, soft pink curtains matching lotus in vase'.

129 M. Douglas and B. Isherwood, *The World of Goods: towards an anthropology of consumption* (London and New York, 1996), p. ix.

130 Grier, *Culture and Comfort*, p. 9.

131 Grier, *Culture and Comfort*, p. 17.

132 In November 1854, Frances Wells recorded the process of packing up an Anglo-Indian house and setting off on a route march. 'Our house is quite dismantled and we are living almost in campaign fashion ... Our camp furniture will consist of our bed ... three chairs, 2 camp tables made to fold up ... 1 footstool, 2 cane stools ... a commode, my bath and baby's ditto. I believe we shall have nothing more than this; but I expect to be very happy and comfortable with it.' University of Cambridge, Centre of South Asian Studies: Berners papers.

133 Glover, '"A feeling of absence from old England"', p. 73.

3 ✦ 'Furnished in English style': globalization of local elite domestic interiors

T HE PRESENT CHAPTER shifts attention away from the construction of British colonial domesticity within the Subcontinent, to discuss the home culture of the Indian and Ceylonese middle class. It assesses the extent to which, during the nineteenth and early twentieth centuries, members of the local middle class appropriated Western goods and consumption habits and modified their domestic spaces as a result of European contact. This chapter also gauges the effect of these changes on local social practices and the role of colonial material culture within the formation of individual and group identity. It is suggested that marked differences were apparent in the absorption of Western ways and the non-functional uses of objects between these regions. Anglicization of the Indian middle-class domestic interior and adoption of Western social practices did not take place, in any meaningful sense, until the early years of the twentieth century, whereas that process, due to different histories and longer exposure to Western life-styles, had already begun in Ceylon by the second half of the nineteenth century. Because of these differences in the adoption of Western life-styles, discussion of the interiors of the Indian and Ceylonese middle class will be treated separately.

Indian home culture

Local consumption of Western-style furniture in India has been discussed recently and it has been suggested that, before the arrival and increased presence of Europeans within the Subcontinent, furniture in the Western sense was largely unknown in this region.[1] Amin Jaffer has argued that, prior to and during the early part of the colonial era, people in India 'sat cross-legged on textiles placed on the floor, and this posture, in which they socialized and ate, determined the design of the objects that surrounded them'.[2] However, previous research in this area requires some qualification.

Recent scholarship mostly addresses courtly consumption of Western-style furniture rather than its adoption by the Indian urban- and rural-dwelling middle classes, and discussion concentrates on the late eighteenth and early nineteenth centuries, neglecting significant cultural changes within these groups after this period.[3] In addition, published, and therefore less specific, accounts of Western contemporary commentators are relied upon, rather than other more 'close-grained' sources, such as inventories. The accounts of contemporary commentators are deployed to substantiate the assertion that there took place, during the eighteenth and nineteenth centuries, a 'superficial Westernization' of the material culture of the Indian elite and a partial appropriation of Western furniture and other furnishings by this group.

A number of studies have examined the active appropriation of non-local material culture by communities beyond the metropole during the nineteenth century. As Jane Webster has suggested with regard to another context, in contesting externally imposed social changes and in renegotiating local identities in response to such changes, peoples in inferior positions of power have made active use of the material culture of those who hold power over them.[4] In these contexts, non-local artefacts may be said to operate in an ambiguous fashion; they are simultaneously desirable and troubling. Such objects also play a crucial role in what has been termed 'resistant adaptation', or behaviour that has been characterized as 'the everyday processes of pragmatic accommodation by which wider structures of dominance are countenanced'.[5] Within the Indian context, both imported Western artefacts and locally-manufactured artefacts in a Western style were increasingly appropriated by some of those within the middling and higher echelons of local society and used in their domestic interiors.

However, these non-local artefacts were, until the early years of the twentieth century, restricted to certain groups within that society, and within these groups were only used in limited areas within the home such as specially furnished rooms set aside from the family's main living accommodation. It is argued that the Indian social elite, in renegotiating their identity when confronted by a number of externally generated economic and social changes, appropriated some aspects of Western material culture (in the form of furnishings for their domestic interiors) to their own ends and, at least until the early years of the twentieth century, regulated the use of non-local things within their domestic environment. In a broader context, it is arguable that the altered consumption habits of the local elite within the Subcontinent in relation to the domestic interior can be interpreted as part of that group's negotiation of the increasing Anglicization, Westernization, or even globalization of their material world during the late eighteenth and nineteenth centuries.

Globalization, generally regarded as a recent phenomenon, has its roots in the expansion of European empires into other geographical regions such as South Asia. This expansion played a significant part in promoting increasingly complex relationships, exchanges and interconnections between different territories, peoples and regions of the world.[6] As one of the most far-reaching of these European power blocs, the English East India Company, and subsequently the British empire in India, played a vital role in this process. Globalization is understood here to mean the acceleration, often in an arbitrary or unplanned fashion, of economic and cultural networks that operate across national boundaries, in fact, transcending these boundaries. This phenomenon resulted from European interventions in the intra-Asian trading networks of the early modern period, increased Western settlement and trade within South Asia in piecemeal fashion and the resulting shifts in communication and world systems of production and consumption. Early manifestations of globalization were complex and unpredictable in their outcomes and can be distinguished from the analytic category termed by Edward Said as cultural imperialism.

Cultural imperialism has been conceptualized as a part or product of imperialism and, within Said's definition, operates in such a way that economically dominant nations systematically develop and extend their political as well as cultural control over other countries.[7] Said and others have argued that this process is effected through the transmission of Western products and consumption habits from the dominant to the dependent region. As a result of this process, it has been suggested, particular patterns of demand are created, which both underpin and promote the cultural values and practices of the dominant region. Said argues for a hegemonic and deterministic view of the modification of local patterns of behaviour and habits of consumption. This view assumes within the imperial project an organizing principle, systems of product distribution at a localized level and a straightforward and uncomplicated absorption of alien objects and patterns of behaviour, all of which are difficult to reconcile with evidence of the possessions and everyday practices of the local elite within the Subcontinent.

The structure, functioning and value systems of the Indian domestic sphere

Local and traditional patterns of behaviour within the home in India were dictated by the requirements to maintain security and privacy for the family unit, as well as to control social contact between the sexes. Houses of the local well-to-do within the Subcontinent, in both rural and urban areas, conformed (with regional variations) to a standard layout in terms of their configuration. In more prosperous districts within urban centres, the local built environment was made up of houses (*haveli*) constructed around courtyards which were arranged, close together, along narrow lanes (*galis*) which in turn led to wider bazaar streets. Unlike dwellings inhabited by the British in India, a significant category of houses owned by the local elite, in terms of their number, were situated in close-knit urban settings and were, therefore, not surrounded by a distancing and protective compound or grounds. In addition, and in a similar fashion, unlike domestic dwellings built for or inhabited by the British in India, houses of the local elite did not present an open or public front to the street. The frontage of the Hindu urban dwelling presented features which both helped to articulate the local architectural space and acted as an interface with the lane or street.[8] These features included the raised platform along the whole of the facade (*chabootara*), entrance arch, overhanging canopies (*chajjas*) and balconies (*jharhokas*).

Despite these features, which offered connection with life beyond the home, the internal arrangement of the local dwelling was intended to exclude the outside world and create an open space (*chowk*) or courtyard with verandah within the centre of the plan, where daily rituals of domestic life could be carried out.[9] In order to preserve privacy and block views of the interior from the lane or street, a baffle wall was often placed directly behind the entrance, forcing anyone entering the house to turn left or right in order to access the interior.[10] As V.S. Pramar has suggested, the local urban house, at least in Northern India, repeated the basic plan of the local rural dwelling.[11] In general, the main elements comprised, to the rear of the dwelling, two or more adjoining rooms (*ordos*), a central interior space that contained a main room or space (*dalaan*) situated on the axis with the entrance and the area around the courtyard (*parsal*), in which the daily activities of the home could take place. In addition, an internal verandah (*otlo*) was usually located around the courtyard; the local elite dwelling also contained a large room, situated adjacent to the street and running the whole width of the plot (*khadki*). Apart from the kitchen, stores and bathroom, the rooms in an Indian *haveli* rarely had fixed functions but were adapted to the daily requirements of the inhabitants. Over time, there also developed the usage of an upper chamber or *divankhanu*, which was located on the first floor of the front room or *khadki*. This was a space situated above and away from the street where visitors could be received. As a consequence of this function, it began to be decorated in an appropriate fashion.

The accounts of contemporary commentators provide a high degree of consistency in relation to descriptions of the structure of the Indian house. In 1865, James Kerr described the brick-built houses 'inhabited by the wealthier classes' of the local population in Bengal as presenting 'a square area in the centre [of the building] – the apartments being ranged on each side, with an inner verandah in front of them all round'.[12] In the following year, and in a virtually identical fashion, the Reverend Ishuree Dass characterized the standard form of dwelling owned by the wealthier classes within the local population of Northern India as being 'built in a square form, with an open quadrangle in the centre; this square or yard has rooms all around'.[13] In 1887, Devendra N. Das described the standard house form of the *zamindar* or land-owning class. He noted the severe and secure exterior of the building, which presented 'a somewhat heavy appearance on the outside … the outer gate is built of solid masonry with a colossal door of sal wood studded with huge nails'.[14] In a similar manner to that of other commentators, Das described the inner courtyard, verandah and arrangement of rooms leading off from that space.

There were also marked differences between local houses in India and houses inhabited by the British in the ways they were used and the value systems attached to the material culture of home. During the nineteenth century, the majority of Indian houses, both Hindu and Muslim, were inhabited by a joint family system. This arrangement has been described by Irawati Karve as 'a group of people who generally live under one roof, who eat cooked food in one kitchen, who hold property in common, participate in common family worship and are related to one another as some particular type of kindred'.[15] In the Northern Indian Hindu joint family, women exercised an amount of freedom within the interior but a system of seclusion operated. This has been described by V.S. Pramar as 'seclusion by avoidance' or 'seclusion by distance'. In other words, men and women of the household lived in close proximity but avoided directly facing each other through the enactment of various forms of behaviour and subtle domestic manoeuvres by the women of the house. As such, there were, strictly speaking, no dedicated male or female zones within the home. In the Northern Indian Muslim household, women were physically segregated from male kin and visitors. The Muslim town house usually possessed at least two interior courtyards. One of these spaces operated as a semi-public area and the other, known as the *zenana*, was allocated for the use of the women of the household. Pramar suggests that this arose from the Muslim practice of ensuring that sexually mature female members of the family lived a secluded existence, away from the rest of the household and any visitors to the house.

It has been argued that the joint family system had a profound effect on that family's life-style.[16] The chief effect was that privacy and possessiveness were, for the most part, absent from the local home. The large number of family members living together under one roof effectively prevented any one individual from enjoying much personal privacy. The requirement

to maintain internal harmony among family members also made possessiveness and ownership undesirable qualities. As Pramar has argued, within
the Indian home

> all things were shared in common: internal spaces, furniture, goods and
> property ... this lack of possessiveness further enhanced the attitude towards
> the house and its spaces: since no part belonged to anyone, it never had
> a personal quality, it contained no pictures or décor selected and put in
> place according to any one person's taste, in short, the household and all
> it contained was relatively 'impersonal', including its architecture.[17]

In relation to the physical appearance of high-status Indian dwellings,
commentators also noted of Muslim urban houses the lack or sparseness of
windows in exterior walls and the consequent darkness (and also coolness)
of many interiors. Doorways were often low, in a similar manner to restrict
the amount of light and heat entering the room. In comparison to British
domestic material-culture practices within the Subcontinent, middling and
high-ranking members of traditional local society attached value to different
things within the domestic environment. In addition to the scale of the
house he inhabited and ownership of land, the status of a member of the
indigenous middle class within local society was judged by the quality of the
clothes he and his family wore, the jewels he and the women of the family
possessed and the number of brass cooking vessels and plates he owned,
rather than the quantity and quality of the furniture he owned.[18]

An inventory of the estate of Muddenmohun Ruckhut, a member of the
local elite in Calcutta who died in 1855, provides a sense of the material
world and value systems of such a figure.[19] In addition to the ownership
of two indigo factories in the district of Hoogly, he owned a number of
houses in Calcutta, including 'an upper-roomed family dwelling house' in
Mugudbaree Street, 'lower-roomed godowns [warehouses]' and an upper-
roomed house at Bytukhanah Street, as well as an upper-roomed house in
Cornwallis Street. He also owned several parcels of land, including a number
of 'gardens' (i.e. land containing fruit and other trees) around Hoogly as
well as a number of 'tanks' or reservoirs (probably land containing a temple)
in addition to ancestral rent-free land. His personal property comprised a
quantity of diamond, gold and silver ornaments, such as 'one large white
diamond ring; two stringed pearl chain; one pair *jorawa taubiz* or bracelets;
one gold watch; one gold mounted hookah'. He owned a range of objects
made of precious metals, including 'one silver *rakaub* or plate ... one silver
dupia or bottle box ... one silver *jauntee* or nutcracker ... one silver *bamtee* or
cup'. He also owned a quantity of fine textiles including 'one black *roomaul*
... one white *chaudur*; one embroidered *roomaul* ... one velvet embroidered
kaubba'. He owned large quantities of brass-ware including 'six brass *culsees*

... thirteen brass *rakaubs* ... thirteen brass tumblers ... one brass *bamtee* ... twenty three brass glass covers' as well as other copper and iron cooking implements. In addition, he is recorded as owning a small quantity of furniture, although some of the items were clearly of local origin and had local uses, such as 'two pieces of wood for tying shawl ... one *chauppur khaut* with bedstead & c ... one *chowkee* ... one *tucktapore* or platform ... one *pitturah* ... [and] ten wooden *puralis* or seats'. Muddenmohun Ruckhut's personal property strongly evidenced connection to local value systems and local customary practices, which were far removed from British material-culture practices. This is indicated both by the language used by the appraiser to describe the moveable property and by the groupings of objects. Some small part of his domestic environment (in the form of a few items of European-style furniture) evidenced a limited appropriation of Western things but, in general, the contents of his home indicated a traditional and locally rooted material culture.

Inventories of the personal possessions of other members of the local middle class within India also suggest the maintenance of local material-culture practices, at least until the 1860s.[20] For example, an inventory taken in 1861 of the property of Shaik Ellahy Bux, recorded the essentially Indianized material culture within his 'upper-roomed house at Cossitollah' and a 'lower-roomed house at Durjeepurrah Lane' in Calcutta. Shaik Ellahy Bux owned jewellery, brass products and other metal utensils. Few items of furniture were described and, of those, the majority were designated by Indian terms ('2 *tucktapores*', '1 *almirah*', '1 *khot*') suggesting a localized usage. Similarly, in 1867, an inventory of the estate of Puddolochan Singhee, who lived in a brick-built lower-roomed house at number 13 Puttoonbollah Lane, Calcutta, recorded the moveable objects of note in this dwelling. The inventory was arranged in the conventional manner for members of the local population and reflected the priority given to personal adornment in the form of jewellery and useful objects of brass. At the head of the list were placed 'gold ornaments', 'silver ornaments', 'brass articles', 'bell metal utensils' and lastly 'wooden things'. This latter category only contained a few objects, such as '2 *tucktapores* or bedsteads', '1 chair', '1 chest', '1 small bench' and '2 small boxes'.

Partial Westernization of the local interior

Beyond the small number of previously described individual contacts between the Indians and the British within the indigenous courtly milieu of the Subcontinent, from the second half of the eighteenth century, it was trade that brought increasing numbers of these two groups into closer and closer contact. By the early nineteenth century, increasingly Westernized trading groups emerged from among those elements within local society that had greatest contact with Europeans. These initially included agents or factotums and merchant groups within the main urban centres of British India such as the *dubashes* of Madras and the Parsis of Bombay or, later in the nineteenth century, Indian English-writing government employees of the *baboo* class in Calcutta. By the early twentieth century, a new stratum of highly Anglicized Indians had come into existence following the opening up of the imperial civil service to qualified members of the local population.

By the late eighteenth century, a large proportion of the local merchant class in parts of the Subcontinent had developed two parallel modes of socialization (one local, one Westernized). The root cause of this shift in behaviour was the increased trading contacts between Indians and the British during this period. For example, as Susan Neild-Basu has noted, many of the *dubashes*[21] of Madras in the 1770s and 1780s built houses in imitation of their British patrons in suburban areas of the city, the same areas favoured by the British. As she suggests, in these houses 'often partly furnished according to Western tastes … they could lavishly entertain both Europeans and Indians'.[22] Many of these dwellings were filled with collections of European furnishings such as those possessed by a Komati merchant, Sunku Chinna Krishna Chetti, and described in *the Madras Courier* of November 1815. However, this class of merchant also maintained a town residence in the local enclave or 'Black Town', which served as the centre of their business activities and where local, traditional forms of behaviour could take place away from the British presence.[23] The *dubash* class in Madras, as did all local groups who subsequently came into regular contact with the British, used part of their built environment (suburban houses) and the contents of these dwellings as mediating material to enable and enhance social contact with Europeans. This allowed for the creation of a middle ground, a space where both parties could come together, transact business and cement personal relationships, while still, at the same time, maintaining local life ways.

Increasing contact between the British and some sections of the local population resulted in the emergence of new ways of interacting and changes to local patterns of behaviour. By the middle of the nineteenth century, commentators noted the development of modified forms of behaviour among those Indians, who had most contact with Europeans. This change was apparent in a number of social arenas, including matters of etiquette. Writing in 1865, English commentator James Kerr noted how he had

> known instances in which a native, when calling upon a European, has entered the room with his turban in his hand, and when he sat down he would place it on his knee … In fact, the transition state, which a portion of native society is passing through, gives rise to a sort of compromise between European and native manners, and to a style which is neither wholly the

one nor the other ... The blending of the two seems strange and rather shocks our sense of propriety.[24]

Western education was a significant factor in the gradual alteration of the consumption habits and increasing Anglicization of the local middle class. In 1813, Parliament had allocated a sum of money to the East India Company for the promotion of local education, both 'Oriental' and 'Western'. Ten years later, a Committee of Public Instruction had been established in Bengal and, in 1834, Thomas Babington Macaulay became its president. In 1835, Macaulay wrote his 'Minute on Education' which recommended that an educational system based entirely on the English model was to be introduced into India, which, he wrote, would eventually create 'a class of persons, Indian in blood and colour, but English in taste, in opinion, in morals and in intellect'.[25] As Benedict Anderson has suggested, Macaulay's policy was formulated to turn 'the respectable classes in Bengal' into 'people culturally English, despite their irremediable colour and blood'.[26]

During the nineteenth century those Indians who had most contact with the British (such as the Parsi community in Bombay and the local middle class in Calcutta), did, to an extent, adopt the trappings of a Westernized life-style, particularly in the furnishing of their main reception rooms.[27] But many commentators noted the persistence of local social practices and consumption habits among the greater part of the local elite. For example, writing in 1866 about conditions in northern India, Ishuree Dass, of the American Presbyterian Mission of North India, noted:

> As for furniture, the [majority of] Hindoos may be said to have none. They have no chairs and tables and wardrobes nor any of those other things that are seen in the houses of Europeans. The only things that they have in their houses are boxes or round baskets with covers and locks to keep their clothes and jewels in, cooking utensils ... and bedsteads ... on which they sleep. Even wealthy Hindoos, who are possessed of hundreds of thousands of rupees, have no more than this.[28]

Other commentators concurred with this characterization of the consumption habits of the locale elite. In 1865, it was noted that

> even the wealthier classes [of the local population] indulge but sparingly their taste for furniture. On entering the house of a wealthy *baboo* of Calcutta, you find apartments bare and almost empty. There may be a chair or two for European visitors and one or two cushions to recline upon, and a white cloth spread over the floor; but there is little more, such is the primitive native style as exhibited in the houses of the wealthy Calcutta *baboos*.[29]

Anthony King quotes extensively from the Reverend J.E. Padfield, who wrote in 1896 of the absence of Western furnishings in the houses of the local Hindu elite:

if we look at the furniture of a house we are struck by its extreme simplicity. Taste and wealth are not manifested in grand furniture and costly hangings or any of the other things that go to make up a luxurious home in Europe … The furniture … is very little … In the houses of the more modern or advanced, there are occasionally a few chairs, and a table or two; and a chair is usually produced for a European visitor; but as a rule, even amongst the better classes, there is a complete absence of most of the domestic conveniences, which even the poorest Europeans consider indispensable.[30]

The chief criticism levelled by the Reverend Padfield and others at the domestic arrangements in 'an ordinary house of the fairly well-to-do Hindu in the town' was a lack of comfort in the Western sense. As he noted,

It is … the absence of comfort which (to the European) seems most conspicuous in a Hindu home. Of this the idea, or sense, or whatever it may be called, does not seem to exist in the Aryan inner consciousness, and hence there can be no manifest development of it.[31]

This representation of sparseness or lack of comfort within the local domestic interior, while actual in comparison with Western interiors in many cases, in fact expressed the different ways in which objects and space were perceived within the Indian and the British home. As suggested above, the traditional Indian house comprised a series of relatively undifferentiated spaces which could be used for multiple purposes. Space within the local home was largely polyvalent. There was, in the Indian house, no area designated specifically as the 'bedroom' or the 'dining room', for example, and the usage of interior space depended upon circumstances. The joint family system which inhabited the Indian house also ensured that privacy and possessiveness were mostly absent. The majority of things within the local house were shared. As no part of the house or objects within the house belonged to anyone, they lacked any personalized quality. The architectural space of the house (and most of what it contained) was, in fact, relatively impersonal and an individual's sense of identity, within the traditional Indian home, was expressed and constituted through the relationship of one family member to another and that individual's connection to the chain of kinship relationships both within and beyond the home.

This mode of perception, in relation to identity, things and interior space, contrasted with the prevailing domestic discourse within nineteenth-century Britain. The British middle-class persona was represented as being constituted and expressed through the ownership of things and through individuated domestic space. By 1800, division of domestic space within the British home had become function-specific. This fixing of function was effected and communicated by the placement of certain object types within designated interior spaces – i.e., a dining table and a set of chairs signified the particular function of the room. In addition, by the mid-nineteenth century, individual members of the family were usually assigned their own space within the British home, which could be personalized through décor and arrangement of furnishings. Contemporary discourse in Britain articulated the connection between household possessions and the persona of the householder, as well as the role that domestic furnishings played in self-fashioning and social self-creation.

The mediatory role of Western furnishings: Bombay and Calcutta

Only in the Presidency cities, and after the middle decades of the nineteenth century, was there limited adoption by the local elite of Western furnishing practices, but purely as a means to allow for restricted intercourse with the British.[32] The Parsis[33] of Bombay, for example, used Western furnishings in part of their homes as mediating material in their dealings with the British, in order to create a Westernized ambience, where both groups, local and British, could meet and socialize. However, Western commentators, even those sympathetic to Indian society, were quick to point out the deficiencies in the furnishing schemes of this local group, ensuring that these facsimiles of European interiors could never be mistaken for the 'real' thing. In renegotiating their identity in the face of the externally generated social and economic changes of colonialism, the Parsi community in Bombay appropriated Western and Western-style things to their own ends within their own houses.

However, nineteenth-century British commentators were alert to the potentially troubling amalgamation of Western and Asian material culture within the home at this time, and were quick to distance the Westernized Parsi interior from the British domicile. The concerns of Western commentators, in relation to these local interiors, rested upon a perceived misunderstanding by the local elite of the value systems attached to furnishings within a Western setting; often criticisms were levelled at the overcrowding of a room with furniture or the lack of taste in the choice of décor or the incongruous aspect of an over-feminized reception room, from which, due to the restrictions of *purdah*, all the women of rank in the household were excluded. In 1852, for example, it was noted by a British commentator that in Bombay

> It is a great point among the wealthy Parsee gentlemen that the furniture and fittings-up of their abodes should vie with ours [i.e. the British], in costliness and elegance of arrangement; and this is carried to an absurd height, considering the total dissimilarity of our habits and domestic relations. For instance, amongst them, the ladies of the family live completely secluded in distant apartments … [never visiting] the magnificent reception rooms … lavishly decorated with chandeliers, mirrors, Persian carpets, couches,

cabinets, ottomans and even ornamental tables, covered with annuals, and every description of rare and tasteful 'bijouterie'.[34]

Even when some of the domestic interiors of the local elite presented the appearance of Anglicization, as British commentator Lady Nora Scott, wife of the Chief Justice of Bombay, noted in 1885, despite 'the furniture of the room [being] mostly European and the carpets gaudy' there was 'always something about [the] rooms in Indian houses, that tell you, you are not in Europe'.[35] Due to her status, gender and generally open-minded curiosity, Lady Scott gained entry to and described in her journal many local interiors from all sections of the local community in Bombay during the 1880s, including those in the *zanana* of local houses. For example, in May 1885, she paid a visit to the wife of a wealthy Parsi, Mrs Pherozehai, who lived in a house in Hornby Row. Having been led up a 'wide handsome staircase onto a landing' she and her party were led into 'an immense drawing room … The room was decorated in the heavy style of 60 years ago and the furniture, heavy, and covered with satin damask, was of the same period. The sofas and chairs were arranged in two lines facing each other'.[36] In this excerpt, both the age of the furnishings and their arrangement, were found wanting.[37]

In addition to assessing the furniture arranged in local interiors, Lady Scott also noted that the social practices enacted in these rooms diverged considerably from practice in Britain. For instance, in March 1884, she and her husband paid a visit to a wealthy Hindu, Sir Mungaldas Natabhoy, who lived 'in a very grand, large house … enclosed in a high walled garden. The house is furnished in a half English style and portraits of the Queen and the Royal family hang on the walls'.[38] However, despite the exchanges of social niceties and although he was 'head of the reforming Hindoos' in Bombay, Sir Mungaldas was reluctant to allow his daughter to pay a return visit to the Scotts, as he explained 'it would be very difficult' and 'his [deceased] wife used to have friends among the English and when they were away in the country … had pleasant intercourse with them, but … in Bombay he said it could hardly be'.[39] In many cases members of the local elite adapted local customary habits in their use of Western furniture. One of a group of 'Mahommadan ladies' who visited Lady Scott 'would evidently have been more comfortable on the floor than on her big chair. She sat with one foot on the floor and the other on the chair with the knee up to her chin; then she crossed one leg and nursed her foot and then, finally, tucked both legs under her and looked more comfortable'.[40]

In addition to the mixing of English and Indian furnishings within parts of the local domestic interior and the periodic, Indianized usage of furniture, contemporary commentators also drew attention, despite the appearance of Westernization, to the continuance of traditional joint family kinship arrangements within the Indian home into the late nineteenth century. For instance, in December 1885, Lady Scott described a visit to 'Westfield', the house of Mr Hurkissondas, a Hindu merchant. On being shown around the house,

> Mr H. explained that his uncle was the owner but there were several of his sons and nephews living there also with their families – 55 persons altogether. Bertha [Lady Scott's sister-in-law] was rather amused at the idea of paying a morning call on 55 people at once. The ground floor belonged to the old gentleman [Mr Narrotundas] and his family, the floor above to his son and fifty yards away from the house but connected by a corridor was a little bungalow, where Mr H. and his family lived. All the rooms, in both houses, were large and airy and beautifully clean. They were carpeted with handsome Brussels carpets and nicely furnished – half English, half Indian, in appearance.[41]

In 1880, Sir George Birdwood summarized the situation with regard to the use of furniture among the local population in India, using his experience of local elite interiors in Bombay as exemplars:

> If we may judge from the example of India, the great art in furniture is to do without it. Except where the social life of the people has been influenced by European ideas, furniture in India is conspicuous chiefly by its absence. In Bombay the wealthy native gentlemen have their houses furnished in the European style, but only their reception rooms, from which they themselves live quite apart, often in a distinct house connected with the larger mansion … Europeans, as a rule, and all strangers are seen in the public rooms; and only intimate friends in the private apartments.[42]

Adoption of a middle course within the Indian domestic sphere, part local, part Western, is also evidenced in local inventories in a manner similar to that outlined by Birdwood. A number of aspects of an Anglicized material culture were often combined with the maintenance of local practices and things. In 1859, for example, an inventory was made of the contents of a three-storeyed house at 135 Chitpore Road, Calcutta, which had been owned by Amun Ali Khan.[43] He had also owned a lower-roomed house in Chitpore Road as well as a garden house to the north of Calcutta in the town of 'Moorshedabad' [Murshidabad]. This inventory suggests the co-existence in the Chitpore Road property of both Indianized and Western cultural practices, which were located and enacted in separate parts of the house. The inventory commences, in the conventional local manner, with a long list of metal cooking utensils. However, the longest section of the inventory describes the 'Extensive Library of Rare and Valuable Persian Works'. These comprised, for example, '22 shuts of *Moracka* [*muraqqa*]', '*The Golestan*', '*Rasalai Fardoon*', 'valuable copies of the *moracka* etc all gilt',

'*Shah Nahmah* by Fardosee', '*Tarik Jahan Kasub Nadurhee*' and '*Kolamwallah or Koransarif* purchased at great cost and very richly gilt'. Such works signified an appreciation of, as well as an intellectual and spiritual engagement with, a courtly, Indo-Islamic culture which was already in decline by 1857 with the extinction of the Mughal dynasty.

Other aspects of Amun Ali Khan's domestic sphere indicated connection to local social practices and material culture. An extensive list of clothes and textiles was recorded, including: 'very fine flowered Dacca pattern cloth', 'striped Dacca muslin', 'valuable cashmere shawls, comprising *chudders*, *romauls*, long shawls', '*kincobs*' and 'printed calico'. Eleven 'Mirzapore *suttrenjees*' were listed, the largest of which measured twenty-four by seventeen feet. In addition, on the second floor of the house, a quantity of engravings and watercolour drawings was noted, which suggest a visual discourse part Western, part local. The items were described in Western terms and in the conventional manner of recording visual images (by type of engraving, how framed). However, the subject matter was mostly local and signified a specifically Indianized or Muslim visual culture. For example, titles included: 'the Triumphant Reception of the Sikh Guns', 'the Durbar at Moorshedabad', 'watercolour drawings showing Nudur and another prince', 'the King of Turkey', 'pictures of Mogul kings'.

If the lower floors of the house at 135 Chitpore Road indicated maintenance of local material-culture practices, the third floor appears to have functioned as a completely Anglicized space, judging by the room contents. This floor contained a large quantity of European-style furniture and furnishings, which most probably supported the enactment of Westernized social practices and included

> a substantial circular drawing room table … a pair of handsome mahogany teapoys … a pair of mahogany Grecian couches … [covered with] red and white silk taboret … a double back Albert couch … covered with flowered taboret … a mahogany conversation couch … an invalid's spring couch … a handsome mahogany duet seat … a mahogany chiffonier … a lady's handsome mahogany davenport … a pair of handsome mahogany glass door bookcases … a very handsome velvet punkah with rich gold lace work and fringe.[44]

Other inventories, of the 1870s and 1880s, indicate the continuance of local material-culture practices in relation to clothing and personal adornment, but also the absorption of Westernized furnishings into the local domestic sphere, especially glass-ware. An inventory filed in June 1883 of the estate of Gooroo Churn Singh, a Calcutta merchant, suggests these patterns of consumption.[45] Gooroo Churn Singh owned a large number of properties in Calcutta, including 'a two storied brick built house and premises at no. 57 Bentinck Street', a similar house at 12 Jackson Ghat Street, 'a tower roomed brick built house at no. 85 Cotton Street' and twelve other houses in Cotton Street, Bentinck Street, Chitpore Road, and Chunam Gully, as well as a number of shop premises in Barabazar. The inventory suggests, through the use of Indian descriptions, the localized usage of ornaments ('1 pearl string containing 133 pearls and 4 emeralds,' '1 *champa kully* studded with diamonds and pearls,' '1 pair gold enameled *jasseem* studded with diamonds') and clothing ('six silk *pyjamahs*', 'a Benares *rumal*', 'a cashmere *roomal*', 'a red cashmere coat with worked border', 'a Benaressee *pyjamah*').

However, large quantities of European-style furniture and furnishings of particular types were also recorded. These items included such objects as: 'a gilt pier table surmounted by a blue veined white marble slab', 'a very elegant pier glass in richly carved gilt frame, the plate of unusual thickness' [and six others similar], 'a pair of medallion backed fancy chairs covered with red silk taboret', 'a three seated centre couch', 'an Albert couch', 'a handsome self performing organ playing 4 airs', 'a Brassels [Brussels] carpet 44 × 12 feet', 'a cheval glass in a dark mahogany frame', 'a handsome mahogany book almirah'. Another distinctive feature of these interiors, as indicated by the inventory, was the quantity of glassware described, including glass lighting devices. For example, these comprised: 'a very handsome cut glass 12 light chandelier fitted with frosted and engraved shades, ornamented with prismatic [sic] drops', 'a four light chandelier with frosted and engraved domes', 'a pair of figure shaped four light candelabras each fitted with four engraved shades', '5 pairs of cut glass wall shades', 'a handsome ruby and gilt glass 3 light gas chandelier with frosted and cut domes with ornamental drops'. The use of Western furnishing fabrics was also pronounced, including for example, 'chintz covers for chandeliers' and 'pair of red damask door *purdahs*'.

In Calcutta during the late nineteenth century, another group within local society – namely Indian, English-writing government employees – was drawn closer to the British due to the increasing demands of the imperial bureaucracy. Individual members of this group came to be known by the Hindu polite form of address for a man, *babu*.[46] Initially this descriptive term was applied to respectable Indians within Bengal, but soon became a disparaging descriptor applied by the British to local writers, clerks and others who, so their critics maintained, produced an over elaborate or pretentious version of the English language in their daily work.[47]

Writing in 1865, James Kerr noted how, even in the apartments of a 'wealthy baboo of Calcutta', the material culture of home in general followed traditional local forms, and how there was, consequently, little furniture, the rooms being 'bare and almost empty'. By the 1870s, however, greater numbers of the *babu* class in Calcutta had begun to adopt Westernized consumption habits with regard to the furnishing of their domestic space, although when Kerr was writing these were unusual and, therefore, worthy of comment, as he noted 'a striking exception to this rule may occasionally be met with, particularly among the more Anglicized baboos; some of whom have their houses gorgeously furnished in the European style'.[48] In a similar manner to that of other British commentators, Kerr goes on to criticize the taste of those 'more Anglicized baboos' in their furnishing schemes, as well as their notion of comfort, distancing these simulacra of the drawing rooms of the homeland from the 'real' thing. He continued 'they do not know where to stop, and imagine they cannot have too much furniture. The apartments are literally crammed full of chairs, tables and sofas; while the walls are covered with wall-shades and mirrors; and magnificent chandeliers hang from the ceiling'.[49]

Writing in 1881, Shib Chunder Bose, who was described as one having 'received the stirring impulse of Western culture and thought', outlined the chief characteristics of the Bengali *babu* and the penetration of Western habits of consumption into most aspects of the life-style of this group.[50] He noted that in general 'the establishment of British rule in India [had] introduced a very great change in the national costume and taste', and more particularly that since the arrival of the British 'a Bengalee Baboo is an eager hunter after academic honours … [and] English is [his] adopted language'. He continued:

> even the amusements of the Bengalee Baboo are more or less Anglicized. Instead of the traditional *jattras* (representations) and *cobees* (popular ballads), he has gradually imbibed a taste for theatrical performances and native musical instruments are superseded by European flute concertinas … and piano fortes. Thus we see in almost every phase of life at home or outside, the Bengalee Baboo is Europeanized. In his style of living, in his mode of dress, in his writings, in his public and private utterances, in his household arrangements and furniture, in his bearing and department [sic], in his social intercourse, in his mental accomplishments and in fact in his passionate particularity for Western aesthetics, he is a modified Anglo-Indian [i.e., British person in India].[51]

Evidence of the Westernized intellectual interests of this group is found in an inventory of the estate of Abinash Chunder Dutt 'late lecturer at the Hooghly College, Chinsurah', recorded in May 1883.[52] Dutt's property comprised a few simple pieces of European-style furniture ('2 bookcases', '1 medicine shelf', '4 tables', '12 stools', '1 looking glass', '2 bedsteads with bedding', '6 lamps'). However, the inventory provides a detailed, four-page list of the books which he owned and most probably used in the course of his working life. All the books are of Western origin and are located within Western systems of knowledge. The appraiser categorized them under a large number of headings ('Light and Optics', 'Chemistry', 'Electricity and Magnetism', 'Physical Geography', 'Education' and 'Natural History', 'Astronomy', 'Mental Philosophy and Logic' [etc.]) and each text was itemized under the appropriate heading (for example, 'Botany – Hooker's Botanical Science Primer, Roxburgh's Flora Indica' [etc.], 'Arts and Manufactures – Collier's Primer of Arts, Hughes' Photography, Gilk's Art of Wood Engraving' [etc.]. Although the quantity of Western texts owned by Abinash Chunder Dutt is perhaps unusual due to the nature of his employment, nonetheless it is indicative of the penetration of Western intellectual pursuits within part of the population of Bengal.[53]

Western education, government service and creation of an Anglicized local elite

Anthony King has suggested that the emergence of an Indian middle class resulted principally more from 'changes in public administration and law than [from changes] in economic development and belonged to the learned professions'.[54] As he has noted, the growth of government services in India between 1857 and 1901 attracted more Indians (increasing from 3,000 to 25,000 between those dates). The acceptance of Indians into the higher reaches of the imperial administration, he also suggests, became conditional on the extent of their Westernization – 'not merely the acquisition of language, dress, behaviour and life-style, but also a willingness to adapt to Westernized environments and equipment'. The consequences of imposing an English education system on the population of the Subcontinent (the first universities were founded in India in 1857) and the increased numbers of Indians joining government service led, by the first decades of the twentieth century, to the creation of an Anglicized local minority, who had gradually become segregated from the rest of their people, through their linguistic, cultural, political and economic ties to the metropolitan country.

Writing in 1932, one member of this local minority, Bipin Chandra Pal, ruefully reflected on the effect of British education policy in India, the absorption of Indians into the British administrative system and the effect of these cultural shifts on one section of this group. He wrote that Indian magistrates

> had not only passed a very rigid test on the same terms as British members of the service, but had spent the very best years of the formative period of their youth in England. Upon return to their homeland, they practically lived in the same style as their brother Civilians, and almost religiously followed the social conventions and the ethical standards of the latter. In those days the India-born Civilian practically cut himself off from his parent society, and lived and moved and had his being in the atmosphere so

beloved of his British colleagues. In mind and manners he was as much an Englishman as any Englishman. It was no small sacrifice for him, because … he completely estranged himself from the society of his own people … He was as much a stranger in his own native land as the European residents in the country.[55]

Another local commentator noted the more direct effect of these externally imposed changes on the material culture of the indigenous middle class. In 1919, Begum Shaista Ikramullah described the Westernizing process in Lilloah, Calcutta and her family's move from a traditional Muslim town house to a government bungalow in the 'civil lines'. Her father, a London-qualified doctor, had recently been appointed District Medical Officer with the East India Railway, and she noted that:

> we had a very nice house and a really lovely garden … This was the stage when Indians went in for extreme Westernization in every way, particularly those who joined the service, which so far had been reserved for the English. They felt it was their incumbent duty to prove to Englishmen that they could emulate him to perfection … Our house, therefore, was furnished to look exactly like an English house. In the drawing room there were heavy sofas … lace curtains, gleaming brass and silver … and knick-knacks displayed in cabinets. The dining room had a fairly massive sideboard … displaying a love of heavy silver. The hall and study were furnished in the typical English style of the times[56]

The colonial city, modernity and the local domestic sphere

In addition to the effects of Western education on the life-style of the local elite and expansion of opportunities offered by government employment, in cities such as Bombay in the first decades of the twentieth century, new types of urban dwelling were developed, which affected the way in which the Indian family had traditionally functioned as a social unit. Furthermore, the period after 1920 was one of economic growth and expansion of business opportunities for local capitalists and entrepreneurs, especially in Bombay. Indian manufacturers in the city, particularly textile mill owners, had increased their productivity and profits due to the reduction in foreign imports caused by the First World War.[57] The middle class in Bombay, at this time, enjoyed a period of great prosperity and this drove expansion of the property market and the demand for Western or Western-style consumer goods.

The 1920s and 1930s in Bombay witnessed an economic boom, increasing pressure on prime building land for the erection of new dwellings close to the centre of the city. These social and economic pressures resulted in the development of a scheme to reclaim land in the Back Bay area of the metropolitan zone. This reclaimed land, later named Marine Drive, became a prime residential site for the erection of a new form of residential development within the Subcontinent, the apartment. The apartments on Marine Drive, arranged in blocks, were characterized by a new style of building (as well as the incorporation of new materials such as aluminium and pre-caste concrete), metal window and door-frames, flat roofs, linked verandahs, new configurations of internal space and, for the exterior elevations, sleak, rounded corners to the buildings familiar from contemporary American and British *moderne* or Art Deco dwellings.[58] Even the traditional bungalow form of the Subcontinent underwent modification during this period, at least in relation to its external appearance, and incorporated overhanging, stepped rectangular and cantilevered entrance porches, rounded corners to the building articulated by sets of parallel mouldings and the placement of horizontal windows at the building's corners.[59]

     As a relatively new form of residential building within the Subcontinent, the apartment both expressed and constituted a cultural shift away from the traditional extended family unit living under one roof in a spacious bungalow or house and compound to one where families lived as single, nuclear units on the Western model, comprising only parents and their children. An editorial in the *Journal of the Indian Institute of Architects* of January 1938 noted this social and cultural shift:

> young people, fed on the international outlook day by day, by the newspaper, the cinemas and the radio, with the speed of lines of the motor car and the aeroplane as familiar as were once the family bullock cart ... are not satisfied with the old traditional family home that took generations to come to its fruition. They require a little home of their own and one that does not require a great deal of time and an army of servants to keep tidy.[60]

     The apartments on Back Bay also highlighted a change in the way that interior space was decorated. Prior to the 1920s, the Indian middle class (and also the British elite in India), if they adopted fashionable European styles of interior decoration at all, tended to adopt them in a piecemeal fashion; previous styles such as the 'Old French' or rococo revival of the middle decades of the nineteenth century or the Aesthetic style of the 1870s and 1880s, were often indicated within an indigenous domestic interior by allocating one room in the dwelling or a portion of the room to that style; adoption of the latter style, for example, was usually manifested by the creation of an Aesthetic corner, complete with drapes (often Far Eastern), fans, and Oriental vases or plates mounted on the walls.

     The *moderne* or Art Deco style was the first style originating in the West to be fully realized throughout the Indian middle-class domestic interior. It was manifested in the refurbishment of existing dwellings, such as that of Sir Mangaldas Mehta in his 'bungalow' (described as such although on a palatial scale) at Ridge Road, Bombay. The whole of the residence underwent a remodelling in the mid-1930s and all rooms were decorated in the *moderne* style, with great attention paid to the coordinating colour scheme; these included a mix of European and Indian materials, but executed by Indian workmen.[61] The drawing room included a freestanding bookcase of fashionably stepped outline, a streamlined and tiered occasional table and a suite of seating furniture with prominent, rounded arm-rests. The interior decoration of the room was described as follows:

> [the] walls are of honey colour. Teakwood dado lined with black strips in between to go with upholstery. Cornice and ceiling are plaster of Paris coloured light cream. The floor is set in Italian coloured marble and is carried out by Rawal and Co. Upholstery in a heavy textured fabric completes the furnishing scheme.[62]

During the 1920s and 1930s, the local middle class in Bombay and elsewhere within the Subcontinent were also acclimatized to the new style through the material culture of everyday life in metropolitan India, in the form of advertisements, magazines and graphic design in general, European department stores, the motor car and the cinema (discussed in Chapter 4). For example, the Army and Navy Stores, Bombay, created an ambience where consumers could imagine *moderne* furnishings in their own homes. In their advertisements, this firm offered their customers fashionable new 'Designs for Living' and 'stocks of materials and imported manufactures [which] are up to date and have unique distinction' (see figure 17).[63] This advertisement for the Army and Navy Stores in Bombay of October 1936 illustrates part of an imaginary drawing room, which includes a sofa with rounded ends decorated with a quadrant sun-burst veneered in contrasting tones of 'Burma teak and Malabar Rosewood', linen curtains with repeating abstract pattern and a 'chromium and plate-glass table by PEL [Practical Equipment Limited of Oldbury, Birmingham, England]'.[64] The whole ensemble recalls the fashionably smart interiors promoted by house furnishers in London, such as Heals of Tottenham Court Road, at the same period.

In 1937, Indian consumers witnessed the first 'Ideal Home' exhibition within the Subcontinent, held at the Town Hall, Bombay. Clearly modelled on the *Daily Mail* 'Ideal Home' exhibition held in London, this colonial event attracted around 100,000 visitors in twelve days. The aim of the exhibition was to lay before the public 'in a pleasant and easily accessible form, the latest devices to make this vital environment of our lives more comfortable, more modern, more congenial and perhaps more artistic'.[65] The exhibition revealed tensions between the local professional classes

U·C·A· 130

"AERO"

7448

HT· 22

DESIGNS
FOR *Living*

Facades were not enough. The Architect's plan now embraces the Copenhagen China figure on the bookcase and the colour of the electric lamp flex—which is as it should be.

To professional men baffled by the glut of cheap, commonplace furnishings and fittings in Indian markets, we offer sympathetic help. Our stocks of material and imported manufactures are up to date and have unique distinction. The design and craftsmanship of our locally made articles have nearly 70 years of experience behind them.

Our clientele has always been exacting ; and we can execute architects' ideas, while our advice on complete schemes or odd requirements to fit an existing scheme is always worth having. As an example of harmonious combination and prices :

UCA 130—Heavy linen curtains, which fall in sculptural folds.

AERO—Sofa in Burma Teak and Malabar Rosewood, upholstered in Cotton Tweed, with two easy-chairs.

7448—Symbolist " Horse " lamp in chromium.

HT 22—Chromium and plate-glass table by PEL, in detachable sections.

ARMY & NAVY STORES, LTD.
BOMBAY

Printed by H. W. Smith at the Times of India Press, Hornby Road, Fort, Bombay, and Published by F. J. Collins at 143, Esplanade Road, Bombay, Hony. Editor—D. W. Ditchburn, F.R.I.B.A., F.I.I.A., J.P.

17 Fashionable furnishings for the modern interior. Advertisement for Army and Navy Stores, Bombay, *c.* 1936.

and the local government elite, as the organizers were (somewhat unfairly) upbraided by the First Minister of Bombay for holding such an event and failing to address the issue of housing for the working class in the city.

The contents of the exhibition, as revealed by the various themed stands, were squarely aimed at the middle class of Bombay and addressed modern life in relation to the furnishings which were presented. For example, stand 15, 'The Drawing Room', included in the display a range of chromium plated, bent tubular steel and upholstered easy chairs and a sofa (see figure 18). An occasional table to the centre of the stand was constructed of plate glass and metal, and the 'room' also contained a *moderne* mural of a stylized athletic figure and a clock of angular profile. Stand 17, 'The Library', was similarly furnished with tubular-steel furniture in the *moderne* style. Additional representations of modernity were also found in stands 18 and 19, which were described respectively as 'Film Studio', which presented a range of studio equipment and 'Studio Scenes', which displayed a film set.

The suppliers of modern furnishings to the exhibition included the Army and Navy Stores Ltd, and interior decoration was provided by H.T. Flanagan & Co. of Bombay. Other local firms supplying tubular-steel furniture

18 Chromed tubular-steel furniture within the colonial home. 'Drawing Room', Indian Ideal Home Exhibition, Bombay, 1938.

included Moderna, Allwyn & Co., and Godrej Boyce & Co. Mitha & Co. supplied the wooden furniture in *moderne* style for some of the stands.[66]

The room settings on show at the Bombay 'Ideal Home' exhibition presented the visitor with a tableau of imaginary interiors, the majority of which included modern household artefacts arranged in a domestic setting, in ways similar to those of the *Daily Mail* 'Ideal Home' Exhibition held at Olympia, London since 1908.[67] The displays presented at the Indian 'Ideal Home' exhibition were part of a number of visual representations of modern life to which the Indian urban-dwelling middle class was exposed. This exhibition was also one in a long line of such events which allowed members of the local population to engage with modernity in the form of the furnishings on display and, more significantly, envisage such objects within their own homes.

One contrast between nineteenth-century representations of the local within India and Ceylon is the relative lack of visualizations of the Indian middle-class domestic interior between 1800 and 1890. Textual representations exist, written by both European and local commentators. Portraits of the Indian middle class also exist, but these likenesses were usually captured away from their domestic setting, within a photographic studio.[68] Until the early years of the twentieth century, the rare visual images of the Indian domestic sphere which do survive usually comprise standard views of the 'puja' or prayer room, such as that depicted by James Prinsep in a Benares house around 1830 (see figure 19).[69] It may be overstating the significance of this lack, but photography constituted a new mode of representation within late nineteenth-century visual culture, and this technology was deployed to record multiple facets of local life within the colonies. A noticeable lack of representation of the local interior serves to underline the resistance of the local domestic sphere within India both to the colonial gaze and to the penetration of alien material culture practices.[70] This resistance began to dissolve in the early decades of the twentieth century, when fundamental shifts occurred in both the configuration of the local domestic sphere and the political and social economy of India more generally. Although far from numerous, visual images of the Ceylonese middle-class domestic interior (including prints and photographs) exist in sufficient numbers to indicate that the domestic sphere on the island was more open to the Western gaze and to Western influence after 1850.[71]

Anglicization of the local elite interior in Ceylon

Evidence presented and discussed above suggests that there was an incremental, selective and resistant appropriation of Western things and a belated adoption of European material-culture practices within the Indian

On Stone by J. Haghe   Drawn by H^y Prinsep Esqr

A THAKOOR DWAREE.

Interior of Lala Kishmooree Mul's House, Benares.

Un Penates and Sacra in the Sanctum

Day & Haghe Lith^{rs} to the King, 17 Gate St.

19 A rare representation of a room within a local elite house in India. 'A Thakoor Dwaree' [prayer room in local elite house, Benares (Varanasi)], *c.* 1830.

domestic environment, at least until the first decades of the twentieth century. By contrast, present-day historians of Sri Lanka have noted a growing Anglicization in the life-styles and consumption habits of the indigenous social elite on the island, which commenced during the nineteenth century.[72] The causes of such a change in local society and the extent of factors such as access to Western education in this process have also been debated, particularly in relation to the formation of this local elite. There is, however, general agreement that the development of Anglicized tastes and habits of consumption among this group were new factors particular to the colonial era that set members of the group apart from the majority of the population.

Assimilation of the cultural attributes of the West both aided the social (as well as political) advancement of the local elite within colonial society and smoothed the processes of government on the island. Yet the development of taste for Western goods among high-placed members of the local population in Ceylon has not been given the attention it deserves. Lord Macaulay's memorandum of 1835, cited above (see p. 131 and note 25), although intended to outline British education policy in India, at the same time advanced taste as an agent for the development of a new class of Asian colonial subjects who were to be the interface between the British and the great mass of the local population to be governed.[73] It will be argued in this chapter that, if anything, adoption of British taste in their choice of consumer goods by the social elite of Ceylon was more pronounced than that of their peers in India.[74]

Since the 1980s, the secondary literature has addressed a number of factors relating to the increasingly Westernized life-styles of this group in Ceylon. For instance, English education has been discussed as a process which aided 'the adoption of English ways and luxuries and refinement of living'.[75] Self-representation of the local middle class and display of their material possessions has also been discussed.[76] In fact, the outward trappings of Western cultural assimilation have been briefly described in a number of present-day sources. These sources have discussed such cultural manifestations as the adoption of Western clothes as well as the latest architectural fashions in the grand residences built by the local elite after 1860 in Colombo, the capital of the crown colony.[77] However, non-documentary or material evidence for the cultural transformation of this group – in the form of their houses, clothes and furnishings – has received only passing mention in the literature, and such evidence has been used in a passive sense, to illustrate a point, rather than as the subject of analysis. Discussion of their place in the social production of British life on the island during the nineteenth century has not been central to the arguments of previous writers, nor has their significance been explained in relation to this cultural shift. As yet, no detailed study has been made of an important site for this transformation, namely the Ceylonese domestic interior and the furnishing of that space as a location that engendered and supported the production of Western life-styles on the island. The latter part of this chapter will address this neglect through an analysis of three case studies, using in particular the record of furniture in inventories, in addition to descriptions of contemporary commentators and photographic images of interiors.

As discussed above, before the period of European colonial contact with South Asia, local socialization in both India and Ceylon took place at floor level on woven mats or textiles and, except for a very limited range of indigenous object-types, mostly without the use of moveable furniture in the Western sense. In 1803, Robert Percival noted of the local population on the island that 'they use neither tables, chairs, nor spoons; but like other Indians [the inhabitants of Ceylon] place themselves on the ground and eat their food with their hands'.[78] Built-in features of indigenous houses on the island, such as the *pila* or platform which extended beyond the walls of vernacular homes 'to form a narrow bench right around the [dwelling]' functioned in a similar manner to that of European-style furniture.[79] The Ceylonese social elite of the early colonial period also used a range of stools, *banku* or *bankuva*, most probably under the influence of the Portuguese *banco* (bench).[80] Only the highest ranks of local society possessed rudimentary beds or seating furniture and, in 1821, John Davy noted the very limited quantities of furniture found in the dwellings of the 'middling classes' in the centre of the island (the Kandyan Provinces) when he wrote 'the furniture of their houses, which is … plain and economical … consists chiefly of a couch or two for lying on [and] of two or three stools'.[81] In the second quarter of the nineteenth century, even a local notable as socially prominent as Ehelepola Maha Nilame possessed but few pieces of furniture.[82] In 1859, Sir James Emerson Tennent, Colonial Secretary of the island, summarized the domestic arrangements of the majority of the population in the South-Western coastal regions of Ceylon:

> the domestic economy of the great body of the Sinhalese, who inhabit Colombo and other towns of the island, is of the simplest and most inexpensive character. In a climate, whose chief requirement is protection from heat, their dwellings are as little encumbered with furniture as their persons with dress.[83]

By the mid-nineteenth century, however, other British commentators on the island began to note that the local middle class in general was beginning to seek out Western consumer goods. In 1843, John Whitechurch Bennett noted the consumption habits of this group:

> The Singhalese [middle class] are partial to Manchester, Leeds, Sheffield and Birmingham manufactures … The higher ranks indulge in the best wines, particularly Madeira and Champagne, which is liberally dispensed at their parties to European guests; and no people in the world set a higher value upon British medicines, stationery and perfumery; or relish with keener zest English hams, cheeses, butter, porter, pale ale cider [etc.].[84]

Adoption of new habits of consumption and gradual Westernization of the life-styles of the local elite, particularly in relation to domestic arrangements, was also noted by commentators such as Charles Pridham, who wrote in 1849 that 'several articles of European furniture have found their way into their permanent residencies; and under the next generation we may reasonably expect a wholesale conformity to European habits of life'.[85] During the middle decades of the nineteenth century, a blend of local and Western consumption habits and patterns of behaviour developed in the dwellings of high-status members of the local population. Local practice continued but was enhanced through the acquisition of European-style goods. Local traditions of hospitality were maintained but the apparatus of hospitality – the interior decoration of rooms, the form and style of tables, chairs, crockery and cutlery – demonstrated a knowledge and understanding of Western taste.

In 1859, Sir James Emerson Tennent witnessed a specific example of this phenomenon when he dined at the house of a high-ranking local official:

> the residences of the headmen are of a very different class and exhibit European taste engrafted on Singhalese customs. A dinner at which my

20 A member of the Ceylonese elite posing with a British-style armchair. 'Don Solomon Dias Bandarnayeke', *c.* 1860.

DON SOLOMON DIAS BANDARNAYEKE.

family were received by the Maha Moodliar de Sarem, the chief of highest rank in the Maritime Provinces, was one of the most refined entertainments at which it was our good fortune to be present; the furniture of his reception rooms was of ebony, richly carved and his plate … was a model of superior chasing on silver.[86]

Tennent commended the taste of the Mudaliyar (or headman) as manifested in his 'richly carved' furniture (as well as his skillfully worked silver). We know that at least some furniture owned by the most prominent members of the Mudaliyar class, such as de Sarem, was of Western form and style. Tennent included an illustration in his two-volume work on Ceylon of Don Solomon Dias Bandaranayake, one of the Mudaliyars of the Governor's Gate, standing in full English-devised regalia beside an easy chair in the style of an English library chair of the second quarter of the nineteenth century (this chair, however, being most probably made of ebony and originating from one of the furniture-making workshops in Galle, to the South West of the island) (see figure 20).[87] Of local middle-class consumption habits, contemporary commentators on the island generally acknowledged that, after 1850 'the houses and tables of the higher classes [of the population in Ceylon] are furnished in English style'.[88] Examination of other evidence for individual members of this social elite provides greater detail as to how this section of the local population furnished their houses and the extent to which Western consumption habits and life-styles were adopted.

The furnishings of Charles Ambrose Lorenz

As the historian Kumari Jayawardena has noted, 'Sri Lanka, as an island strategically situated on the important sea routes between Asia, Africa and Europe, had been exposed to foreign influences and the mingling of races and culture throughout its history'.[89] One component of this multi-ethnic mix, which included Sinhalese, Tamil and Malay populations (among others), was the so-called Burgher community, whose members were descendants of Dutch and other Europeans who had settled on the island. By the nineteenth century this group formed a culturally distinct and relatively prosperous section of the urban populations in Colombo, Galle, Matara and elsewhere.[90]

Charles Ambrose Lorenz, in common with a number of Burghers in Ceylon, made his money in the legal profession (as barrister-at-law and advocate of the Supreme Court of the island); he also founded a literary magazine entitled *Young Ceylon* and edited a local newspaper, *The Examiner*. An inventory of his property carried out after his death in 1871 records the material goods of one of the most prosperous members of this community on the island during the third quarter of the nineteenth century.[91] The document provides a different type of evidence to that in the accounts of contemporary commentators, and a case-study analysis of this inventory makes it possible to set these furnishings within the colonial society that imported, commissioned, manufactured and used it. Furthermore, the inventory reflects the extent to which Western consumption habits, as manifested in the contents and arrangement of the domestic interior, had penetrated the life-styles of the local middle class.

Lorenz owned a number of properties on the island, including a house in Keyser Street, located in the Pettah, Colombo which was valued at £1,205. In the nineteenth century the Old Town (*Oude Stad*) or Pettah had become the centre of the Burgher community in Colombo and comprised 'many fine houses with luxuriant gardens and rows of compact one-storeyed villas with their roofs slung from a common ridge and pitched over broad verandahs or *stoepes* which lent the [district] respectability'.[92] In 1850, a contemporary commentator noted the furnishings of the Burgher community within this part of Colombo:

> In the Pettah is situated the chief bazaar for edibles of every description; here also reside the greater number of the burghers … ; in the streets that break off from the main street and in the abodes of these people is frequently to be seen some of the most exquisitely carved ebony furniture conceivable, the designs, usually of fruit and flowers, being chiselled out with the utmost accuracy, depth and sharpness.[93]

Lorenz also owned other properties in Colombo, including Elie House at Mutwal (during the mid-nineteenth century, a fashionable residential area north of the Fort), together with 14 acres of land which was valued at £5,000. In addition, he owned land and property at Kalutara on the west coast of the island. He also owned a range of furnishings that reflected the shifting consumption habits of the local elite (and the British who were resident on the island). Since the 1840s, despite the local production of high-quality ebony furniture in European-style, Bombay-manufactured rosewood furniture had been imported into the island in larger and larger quantities.[94] In addition to locally-produced, carved ebony furniture, Lorenz also possessed examples of this imported furniture from India. It is most probable that the Indian furniture was used in the main reception rooms and the ebony furniture reserved for such rooms as the library.[95]

Lorenz's moveable property comprised a large group of furniture, which was divided between his houses at Colombo and Kalutara. The first group to be itemized consisted of 'Bombay wood' items, including: 'A Pair of Bombay Wood Sofas £10', 'Eight Bombay Wood Ladies Chairs £8', 'One Bombay Wood Carved Cheffonier £7.10s', 'A Pair of Bombay Wood Tea Poys £2', 'One Bombay Wood Dining Table in Seven Pieces £10', 'Eight Bombay

Wood Arm Chairs £1.10s', 'One Bombay Wood Reading Chair £1.10s', 'A Bombay Wood Cellaret £1', 'Two Bombay Wood Folding Screens £2' and other pieces of furniture made of the same wood. These items were the most expensive pieces of furniture owned by Lorenz. As their designation implies, they were imported from India and this most probably accounts for their high valuation.[96] Furniture made of local cabinet-woods and most probably by local makers comprised such items as: 'A Calamander Settee £3', 'Two Tamarind Wood Ladies Chairs 15s', 'One Ebony Cheffonier £8', 'Six Ebony Ladies Chairs £6', 'Two Ebony Easy Chairs (Carved) £6', 'Four Ebony High Backed Chairs (Carved) £8', and 'A Pair of Ebony Footstools 10s'. The appraiser's descriptions of the furniture indicate that they were mostly of fashionable Western form. A range of other furniture locally made of Ceylon woods is also recorded.[97] Although no books are itemized in the inventory, Lorenz possessed a number of bookcases which housed the collection he most probably owned.[98] A number of items also signify an interest in his Dutch ancestry, including a 'Large Eight Day Dutch Clock 37.10s', and 'Two Dutch Long Glasses 2s'.

Lorenz's other possessions also acted as signifiers of his wealth and refinement. The 1871 inventory itemized large quantities of silver and glass-ware as well as porcelain. His houses were lit by 'A Three Branched Chandelier (glass)', 'A Two Branched French Hanging Lamp', 'Six Pairs of French Hanging Lamps', 'Three Globe Lamps' in addition to other devices. His table at Colombo was lit by 'A Large Table Centre with Six Branches and Shades'. Various decorative objects are also described, such as 'A Pair of Marble Statuettes £5', 'A Pair Large Marble Flower Vases £3', and 'A Marble Card Stand'. Lorenz owned portraits of various British governors of the island, including Sir Henry Ward and Sir Charles Macarthy, in addition to three 'Scotch Ladies' and a painting of his house in Mutwal. Freemasons' paraphernalia is recorded and was valued at the highest single amount of his moveable property (£40). Finally, the inventory recorded his ownership of two sets of elephant tusks – the *sine qua non* at this time for the reception rooms of the local middle class of the island.

The furnishings of Charles Lorenz manifested assimilation of many of the cultural attributes of the West. The interiors of his houses were filled with a heterogeneous mixture of English, Dutch, French, Indian and local artefacts. Although the descriptions of some objects appear to suggest an entirely indigenous origin ('Four Kandyan Table Ornaments', 'A Lance on Kandyan Sticks'), for the most part, the furnishings indicated the accumu-lation of things which indicate his adoption of Western middle- and upper middle-class consumption habits and modes of socialization. To paraphrase Anthony King, such objects, seen from the viewpoint of traditional and un-Westernized indigenous society, had no function outside the confines of the colonial culture.[99] They include culture-specific objects such as large sets of chairs and dining tables to allow for large-scale entertainments, such as dinner parties; easy chairs to facilitate conversation or reading; depictions of senior members of the British colonial elite, used as symbols of status and connection; fine glass and table-ware, as well as vases for the display of flowers, indicating acquired levels of taste acknowledged in the colonial and metropolitan country.[100]

These artefacts formed an appropriate backdrop to lively entertainments, such as musical evenings. The 1871 inventory lists a 'A Piano and Stool', and a watercolour in the collection of the Royal Asiatic Society, Colombo depicts members of the Lorenz family engaged in such a musical event at 'Lodge Harmony' at Matara, in the far south of the island.[101] The furnishings of Charles Ambrose Lorenz represented the Anglicized, bourgeois life-styles available to some of the indigenous middle and upper middle class in Ceylon. Such objects communicated shared values with senior members of the colonial power, indicated his standing in the local and metropolitan society and established points of reference for the deepening of social relationships, not only with the British, but with other members of the Westernized indigenous middle class of the island. It was in the interiors of Elie House and Lodge Harmony that the range of European-style – or in some cases simply European – goods engendered the reproduction of Western cultural practices.

The Furnishings of Charles de Soysa

By far the best-known collection of furnishings formed by a member of the indigenous elite was that of Charles H. de Soysa at Alfred House, Kollupitiya, Colombo. In 1892, Constance Gordon Cumming wrote of this collection that 'specially interesting to the newcomer in the isle were the beautiful specimens of furniture at Alfred House, much of it richly carved, made from all the choicest woods of the Ceylonese forests'.[102] Even by the standards of the time, Charles de Soysa, a Christian Sinhalese, was immensely rich.[103] Moreover, in 1863 he had married Catherine de Silva, a local heiress. In 1871, he entertained Alfred, the Duke of Edinburgh, on the occasion of the latter's visit to the island – a rare opportunity for a member of the indigenous elite and one that marked him out from his peers. This occasion is recorded in a number of sources, including an account written by John Capper. The latter described 'an evening at Alfred House' as follows:

> the mansion of the de Soysas is situated in the midst of extensive grounds, on the high road from Colombo to Galle … The building is composed of two floors; … the reception and retiring rooms, with a suite of elegantly-furnished apartments, being on the first floor, reached by an ample flight of

21 A fashionably furnished drawing room within a local elite house. 'The Reception Room, Alfred House' [Colombo, *c.* 1870].

stairs. The furniture is of ebony, satin and calamander and when the whole building is lighted up, as was the case on the occasion of the Duke's visit, it presents a very brilliant appearance.[104]

In addition to the written description, an engraving in Capper's book depicts 'the Reception Room, Alfred House' with the figures of Susew de Soysa and his nephew, Charles H. de Soysa (see figure 21). The room depicted was most probably located on the first floor of the house, and the dimensions appear imposing. The room was hung with two cut-glass chandeliers lit by candles; six oil lamps with opaque white shades, cut-glass pendants and metal chains also provided light for the room. A number of double glass 'wall-shades' provided additional illumination. The walls were panelled and painted in tones of green and white. In contrast to those of the British governors' residence in Colombo, the windows were curtained and shuttered with 'Venetians'. It is possible that the panels above the windows and doors were fitted with pierced and carved *mal lalla* [floral fretwork panel]; if this was the case, such a feature would have improved ventilation in the room. The floor covering was most probably joined sections of tufted carpet decorated with a diaper pattern.

The furniture in the room was entirely European in form and style, although perhaps slightly old-fashioned when compared to the contents of contemporary interiors of a similar status in Britain. Two 'Loo' tables are depicted in the centre of the room, each with bulbous supports and tri-form bases. An elaborate table centre-piece of glass, silver or porcelain was placed on one of these tables, in the mid-Victorian manner. At least four side or drawing room chairs in the 'Grecian', 'modern' or classical revival style were positioned around the Loo tables, in a way to facilitate conversation or for other activities such as card playing. Two sofas with over-scrolled arms similarly in the fashionable 'Grecian' or classical revival style were placed in proximity to one of the Loo tables. The upholstery of the sofas matched the décor of the room. A deeply upholstered 'easy' chair in the Louis XV or rococo revival style was situated between the sofas. Other furniture comprised a davenport and occasional tables.

Through the familial connections of de Soysa with Moratuwa – in the nineteenth century, a village a few miles south of Colombo – it is most probable that at least some of the furniture would have been manufactured in this important centre of cabinetmaking. Two mounted elephant tusks completed the interior decoration of the room. In fact, there is little in this room to suggest a tropical setting, except for the dress of one of the occupants (and perhaps the elephant tusks so prominently displayed). The contrasting styles of dress of the two men also encapsulate the generational difference in the absorption of Western culture among the local elite. Charles de Soysa's cultural assimilation into the colonial culture is seemingly complete, whereas his uncle continued to maintain traditional ways. Susew de Soysa, the older man, is depicted in the traditional dress of the Low Country or coastal region of Ceylon (modified through contact with previous Western colonizers of the island), with a white cotton *comboy* [printed cotton wrap] and short jacket. His hair may be held by a tortoiseshell comb and he wears his facial hair in a traditional style. On the other hand, Charles de Soysa, Susew's nephew, is dressed entirely in Western style with a dark morning coat, trousers and leather shoes; his hair is also dressed in Western manner.

The furnishings of Charles de Soysa's house reproduced the ambience of upper middle-class or even aristocratic houses in Britain and provided an appropriate venue in which to entertain the son of the British monarch.

This occasion – especially the presence of many socially prominent guests – marked him as a figure of the highest social standing on the island. By permitting him to offer hospitality to such an important visitor, Sir Hercules Robinson, the British Governor of the island, conferred on him a singular status (the de Soysa entertainment was the only 'native' reception or *tamasha* given to the Duke of Edinburgh on his visit to Ceylon). The occasion also aided de Soysa's own social ambitions. His family fortune (recently acquired) was based on the profits from liquor-renting. As the beneficiary of this fortune which derived from a less than savoury commercial activity, Charles de Soysa wished to convert his monetary capital into more elevated and socially acceptable things and activities. To this end, he engaged in lavish

22 A range of furniture, lighting devices and textiles in a local elite house. 'Guest Room, home of Lady de Soysa, a titled Sinhalese lady, Bambalapitiya, Colombo, Ceylon' [*c.* 1903].

philanthropic acts, endowed a number of educational and medical institutes and built and furnished Alfred House in Western style in a fashionable part of Colombo.

For this 'new man', so to speak, and member of the *karava* caste, the reception at Alfred House also aided his ambitions in relation to status competition with members of the traditional, hereditary elite, or 'old money', on the island – those members of the *goyigama* caste, such as the Diases and Dias-Bandaranayakes.[105] De Soysa was viewed as someone who was granted special privilege by the colonial power. In the words of Kumari Jayawardena, he was a 'somebody' (as opposed to a 'nobody') – a person to be reckoned with.[106] This dazzling entertainment, among the Anglicized furnishings of Alfred House, indicated in a graphic manner de Soysa's monetary as well as recently acquired cultural capital.[107] Although not all of de Soysa's residences in Colombo were furnished in the style of (and on the scale of) Alfred House, the contents of this house were also perhaps the closest of the period to resemble some of the more modest princely interiors of India (see figure 22). This evocative illustration depicts a small room in another de Soysa property in Colombo, furnished with a range of Dutch- and British-style furniture (including revivals of the Dutch burgomaster or round chair), as well as some examples of imported 'Bombay blackwood' items. The floor is neatly matted, and embroidered drapes hang from the window openings. Numerous cut- and frosted-glass lights hang from the ceiling and two huge elephant tusks, together with a model of a sambhur or Ceylonese deer head, placed in a slightly surreal manner in the foreground, complete the interior decoration. This illustration gives an impression of a more intimate space, but the sumptuousness, glamour and implied expense of the de Soysa reception rooms at Alfred House conveyed an altogether different ambience to the mostly *bourgeois* interiors of even the very wealthiest members of the local elite on the island.[108]

Twentieth Century Impressions of Ceylon

One venue where members of the local population in Ceylon became accustomed to Western-style furniture and furnishings was the photographic studio, a number of which had opened on the island from the 1860s.[109] Chairs, tables, davenports, low settees and other items of furniture that were familiar props in the photographic studios of Europe were transposed (by both European and local photographers) to the more exotic location of the island. The paraphernalia of the photographer's studio, including a few items of furniture against which the subjects posed, transformed that space into a location where Christopher Pinney has suggested 'an elevated and intensified identity could be acquired'.[110] The place of the photographic

23 Posing with a European-style chair. Studio portrait of 'Singalese Headman' [Colombo, *c.* 1865].

studio in the spread of modernity and the practice of polite behaviour during the nineteenth century has been discussed elsewhere.[111] Therefore, it is perhaps unsurprising that, after 1850, members of the local middle class were increasingly represented, or rather represented themselves, standing by or sitting on chairs of Western form and profile (see figure 23). In fact, Anne Maxwell has suggested that the photographic studio in the colonies was a space where the indigenous population could emphasize 'their ability to master the codes of social dress and behaviour that characterized civility'.[112] Among the earliest photographic portraits of local people, taken on the island around 1852 by European photographer Frederick Fiebig, are images of members of the local elite posed by or seated on Western-style furniture, with such titles as 'Cinghalese gentleman in office', and 'Cinghalese lady, Kandy'.[113] Other photographic portraits of the local elite in Ceylon in the second half of the nineteenth century reveal an enduring convention of posing with Western-style furniture.

The practice had its fullest expression in a book entitled *Twentieth Century Impressions of Ceylon*, first published in 1907.[114] This publication is replete with photographs of local notables, depicted in studio settings and in or outside their comfortably appointed residences, surrounded by the physical evidence of their wealth and taste. In this book, the local social elite, who had been acclimatized to Western cultural norms for over two hundred years, as well as the more recently introduced conventions of Western photographic practices, represented themselves with furnishings whose style and form (if not their manufacture) had their origins in Britain. The adoption and use of Western-style furnishings by the local middle class was a central aspect of what may be termed an unspoken cultural dialogue between the colonial power and the indigenous population.

Much attention has been paid in histories of the island written since Independence in 1948 to the decrees of the colonial government, its laws, censuses and other aspects of bureaucratic control.[115] However, in parallel with these legislative acts which framed and ordered colonial society, it is suggested that less coercive but nonetheless influential aspects of Western (material) culture permeated the homes of the local population. Western or Western-style things – textiles, furniture, pieces of porcelain and silver – were gradually absorbed into the Ceylonese domestic interior during the nineteenth century. These things, although assimilated by the local population as part of the everyday fabric of life and therefore almost disregarded or overlooked, nonetheless inflected the social rituals of the Ceylonese middle class because they were willingly acquired, formed an intimate part of daily experience and engendered the production of Westernized social practices.

Mary Louise Pratt has argued that through the acquisition of Western cultural forms, local peoples undertook 'to represent themselves in ways which engage[d] with the [European's] own terms' and which willingly involved them in 'collaboration with and appropriation of the idioms' of the West.[116] She suggests that this form of behaviour can be viewed in a positive light, as a means by which the local population actively engaged in a cultural dialogue with the West. However, this engagement was also of benefit to the British. During the nineteenth century, the acquisition of or representation with Western-style furnishings by the local social elite in Ceylon, in addition to the adoption of other Western consumption habits – the wearing of Western-style apparel, for example – had a number of effects: they helped forge an Anglicized, assimilated and, as a consequence, also quiescent local middle class by creating and maintaining common cultural bonds between them and the British on the island. Many of the local elite of the late nineteenth century 'bought into' the British colonial life-style and, at least publicly, chose not to be represented with local material culture.

Twentieth Century Impressions of Ceylon is an impressive record of the social, cultural, economic and political condition of Ceylon around 1900. This generously illustrated publication was produced by the British to describe and promote, to interested parties, the diversity and natural wealth of the island (the book being one of series that promoted other British colonies at the time, such as *Twentieth Century Impressions of Malaysia*).[117] Members of the local middle class were able to purchase space in the book to describe their pedigrees, their education, the accomplishments of their offspring, their business and cultural interests, and to represent their material success through depiction of their often lavish, Anglicized life-styles. The images in the publication acted as a measure of the material progress of Ceylon while under British control – which was, in fact, the central rationale for the book. Much of the content of *Twentieth Century Impressions* took the form of an extended series of (self-)advertisements for the wealth and status of the local social elite. As Malathi de Alwis has noted 'each family that was invited to represent themselves in this volume not only provided their photographs and accompanying texts, but paid the British government according to the inclusions and quantity of photographs'.[118]

Although many illustrations in the publication originated as studio portraits, a large number of local reception rooms were also photographed, and these represent the range of furnishing schemes (at least for their public rooms) that the local middle class had chosen for their homes. One such interior, for example, is that of Mr and Mrs Peiris, 'Rippleworth' Turret Road, Cinnamon Gardens, Colombo (see figure 24). James Peiris was a prominent member of the island's elite. He had 'gained high scholastic honours in England' (as had the majority of his peers): he had won an English University Scholarship in 1878, graduated with First Class Honours from St John's College, Cambridge, had been elected President of the Cambridge Union Society and was called to the Bar in 1881. He was Justice of the Peace for the entire island and owned large tracts of plantation land there. His mother was a de Soysa and he had married a member of the prominent de Mel family. 'Rippleworth' was a large, two-storey house in the most fashionable district of Colombo. The drawing room is furnished in a manner very similar to that of comparable middle-class homes in England of the same period, the only difference being the inclusion of distinctively Anglo-Ceylonese chairs. If it was not entirely clear from the accompanying text, then the illustration of the Peiris's drawing room confirmed the assets and cultural capital, as well as the affinities of this scion of one of the elite families on the island.[119]

In *Twentieth Century Impressions*, as well as other contemporary sources, most of the illustrations of local middle-class domestic interiors comprise drawing rooms that were used for formal occasions and entertainments and which presented a public front to the world.[120] It is in these rooms that the influence of Western and particularly British cultural forms are most apparent. However, it is also most probable that in more private rooms,

MR. AND MRS. JAMES PEIRIS, AND VIEWS OF THEIR RESIDENCE, "RIPPLEWORTH."

24 The Anglicized contents and arrangement in the drawing room of a local elite home. 'Mr and Mrs James Peiris and views of their residence, "Rippleworth"' [Colombo], c. 1907.

not selected for illustration, some members of the local elite engaged in different local and customary practices. In fact a number of those elite most probably followed a 'middle course' between wholesale adoption of a European life-style and the maintenance of indigenous, hereditary cultural practices. Michael Roberts discusses this middle course and cites the diaries of Edmund Rowland Gooneratne (b. 1845), a 'Low Country Sinhalese notable of Goyigama stock', which suggest that 'it was possible for [Gooneratne's] family to indulge in Westernized lifeways and Christian rituals, at the same time that they organized *pirit* ceremonies, exorcisms and *dane*, patronized *rukada* puppet shows and had their "pedigree sung by Kottassa"'.[121] How many of the local elite actually followed this course is, however, difficult to determine.

Adoption of Western life-styles and material-culture practices by the Ceylonese middle class appears to have begun at an earlier date – and therefore seems to have been more pronounced – than related behaviour by their peers within the Indian Presidencies. This was most probably due to longer exposure to Western influence on the island. Contact with the Portuguese, the first European colonizers of the island in the sixteenth century, had begun to alter the local material culture of the Ceylonese elite.[122] In addition, many members of that elite had converted to Christianity during the Portuguese period, and adopted Westernized names. As a result of these processes, there existed, by the seventeenth century, a disjuncture in the cultural life of the local elite. Local Buddhist practices had, in many cases, been forgone in favour of Christian ones. Subsequent contact with the Dutch, who colonized the island during the seventeenth and eighteenth centuries, especially along its western seaboard, had also familiarized the local middle class with a model of Westernized domesticity (albeit adapted to a tropical climate).

During the eighteenth century, the Dutch constructed domestic dwellings in towns such as Galle and Colombo, which supported a modified European way of life, and commissioned Western-style furniture from local craftsmen to fill those interiors. The Dutch had also intermarried with the local population, thereby embedding Western habits of consumption and aspects of a Western life-style within sections of the local population, and engendering modified material-culture practices which blended local and Western forms. At the same time, Dutch material-culture practices and behaviour had also been inflected through contact with the local population.

When the British expelled the Dutch from Ceylon in 1796, there already existed a Europeanized material culture on the western seaboard of the island. The British presence in Ceylon during the nineteenth century consolidated and extended a process which had begun 150 years earlier. Whereas in India the creation of a highly Anglicized section of the local population had occurred because of the opening up of government service to Indians in the late nineteenth century, in Ceylon extensive Westernization of the local middle class resulted from globalization of the island's economy, service within the colonial administration (as translators, for example) and the new economic opportunities presented to the local population as a result of this process. As a result, during the nineteenth century in Ceylon, Western furnishings and European social practices appear to have penetrated more deeply and been more readily assimilated into the life-styles of the local social elite, to a greater extent than in India.

Anglicization of local middle-class domestic interiors in Ceylon after 1850 was a visible but as yet little discussed effect of the impact of British culture on the island. Furnishing schemes of the majority of this group after this date encoded an alien value system and engendered modes of social behaviour particular to Europe. It is a given that the domestic spaces of this group and the objects which filled those spaces created conditions for acceptable forms of social interaction within the household, which conformed to the societal norms of colonial culture and excluded undesirable possibilities.[123] It is suggested here that, in fact, these spaces and their furnishings objectified colonial social relations. The local middle class engaged in new forms of behaviour engendered in these spaces (with, in fact, a 'drawing-room culture' developing among this group), and other Western social rituals and habits of consumption were also eagerly adopted.

It is arguable that these practices had a corrosive effect on indigenous culture at the highest levels of society. Although in private some members of the local middle class continued to follow traditional life-styles and cultural practices, using Westernized furnishings on a daily basis in their front rooms and the adoption of associated Westernized forms of behaviour relegated their own local cultural forms to a marginal position. Through their consumption of Western-style furnishings and their adoption of other non-local forms of material culture, the indigenous social elite allowed their cultural identity to be validated against British standards. These domestic interiors were not, as such, singled out for opprobrium by Buddhist nationalists in their attacks on the Westernization of everyday things on the island during the last decades of the nineteenth century. However, together with the adoption of Western apparel, manners and other habits of consumption, the acquisition and use of Anglicized furnishings in the local domestic interior may be regarded as informal but significant aspects of the cultural apparatus of the West. Furnishing in 'English style' allowed the local middle class in Ceylon to demonstrate their civility and taste (judged by British standards) as well as their modernity. In addition, it established common ground or mediating material between them and the colonial power; but, it is suggested that this process – whereby the core of the domestic interior was fitted out in a non-local manner – also created non-traditional and hybrid environments on the island where alien cultural forms were socially produced.

Both the Anglo-Indian and local domestic sphere have so far been examined as spaces where issues of identity were negotiated through domestic material culture. But the domestic sphere within the Subcontinent formed part of a larger space – colonial public space – which formed a significant extension of the home environment during the nineteenth and early twentieth centuries. The following chapter examines translation of some of the forms of public space located in the homeland (such as clubs, hotels, shops and cinemas) to the colonies. These spaces created public but domesticated locales where Anglo-Indians sought refuge and reassurance among familiar surroundings, and the local elite assimilated new Westernized practices in spaces recently created in the colony.

Notes

1 Amin Jaffer, *Furniture from British India and Ceylon: a catalogue of the collections in the Victoria and Albert Museum and the Peabody Essex Museum* (London, 2001), pp. 106–25.

2 Jaffer, *Furniture*, p. 106.

3 Even when discussing Indian material culture of the twentieth century in the exhibition catalogue C. Benton et al., *Art Deco 1910–1939* (London, 2003), pp. 382–95, the greater part of Amin Jaffer's account addresses princely consumption of the Art Deco style, rather than its absorption by the indigenous middling sort. The definition of the Indian middle class within this chapter encompasses local civil servants, doctors, writers, publishers, teachers, and those Indians engaged in banking, insurance, mining, planting and trading. See B.B. Misra, *The Indian Middle Class: their growth in modern times* (London, New York and Bombay, 1961), pp. 178, 181, 185.

4 Jane Webster, 'Resisting traditions: ceramics, identity and consumer choice in the Outer Hebrides from 1800 to the present', *International Journal of Historical Archaeology*, vol. 3, no. 1 (1999), pp. 53–73.

5 Webster, 'Resisting traditions', p. 54.

6 T. O'Sullivan, J. Hartley, D. Saunders et al., *Key Concepts in Communication and Cultural Studies* (London and New York, 1994), pp. 130–1.

7 Edward Said, *Culture and Imperialism* (London, 1993), *passim*.

8 Henry Moses, *Sketches of India; with notes on the seasons, scenery and society of Bombay, Elephanta and Salsette* (London, 1850), p. 54.

9 Sunand Prasad, 'A tale of two cities: house and town in India today', in G.H.R. Tillotson (ed.), *Paradigms of Indian Architecture: space and time in representation and design* (Richmond, 1998), pp. 176–98.

10 This directional device is known as a *modh*.

11 V.S. Pramar, *A Social History of Indian Architecture* (New Delhi, 2005), p. 51.

12 James Kerr, *The Domestic Life, Character and Customs of the Natives of India* (London, 1865), p. 165.

13 Rev. Ishuree Dass, *Domestic Manners and Customs of the Hindoos of Northern India or … North West Provinces of India* (Benares [Varanasi], 1866), p. 118.

14 Devendra N. Das, *Sketches of Hindoo Life* (London, 1887), p. 34.

15 I. Karve, *Kinship Organisation in India* (New Delhi, 1968), p. 8, cited in Pramar, *A Social History of Indian Architecture*, p. 47. A different view of the joint family system to Karve's is offered in A.M. Shah, *The Household Dimension of the Family in India* (London, 1974).

16 Pramar, *A Social History of Indian Architecture*, p. 48.

17 Pramar, *A Social History of Indian Architecture*, p. 48.

18 Dass, *Domestic Manners and Customs*, p. 121.

19 London, British Library: Bengal Wills, 1855, L/AG/34/27/156, estate of Muddenmohun Ruckhut.

20 London, British Library: Bengal Wills, 1861, L/AG/34/27/167, estate of Shaik Ellahy Bux; Bengal Wills, 1863, L/AG/43/27/170, estate of Sree Mutty Joypeary Dossee; Bengal Wills, 1867, L/AG/34/27/174, estate of Puddolochan Singhee; Bengal Wills,

1880, L/AG/34/27/187, estate of Sreemutty Roymoney.

21 *Dubash* – an Indian manager or factotum for a European merchant. From *do bhasha*, a person who speaks two languages. C.A. Bayly, *Indian Society and the Making of the British Empire* (Cambridge, 1988), p. 208.

22 Susan Neild-Basu, 'The Dubashes of Madras', *Modern Asian Studies*, vol. 18, no. 1 (1984), p. 25.

23 Neild-Basu, 'The Dubashes of Madras', p. 25.

24 Kerr, *The Domestic Life*, p. 225.

25 Benedict Anderson, *Imagined Communities: reflections on the origin and spread of nationalism* (London and New York, 1994), pp. 90–1.

26 Anderson, *Imagined Communities*, p. 91.

27 Holt Mackenzie, giving evidence to a Parliamentary Committee, noted in 1831 'judging from Calcutta, there has been, I think, a very marked tendency among the natives to indulge in English luxuries; they have well furnished houses, many wear watches, they are fond of carriages and are understood to drink wines'. *Select Committee of the House of Commons, 1831–2 Minutes of Evidence, II (735 II)*, p. 11 cited in Misra, *The Indian Middle Class*, pp. 153–4.

28 Dass, *Domestic Manners and Customs*, p. 121. Also quoted in W. Chichele Plowden, *Report on the Census of British India taken on the 17 February 1881* (London, 1883), p. 12.

29 Kerr, *The Domestic Life*, p. 166.

30 Rev. J.E. Padfield, *The Hindu at Home* (London, 1896), p. 16 cited in A.D. King, *The Bungalow: the production of a global culture* (London, 1984), pp. 54–5.

31 Padfield, *The Hindu at Home* cited in King, *The Bungalow*, pp. 54–5.

32 Mrs Postans, *Western India in 1838* (London, 1839), p. 104. In 1850 Henry Moses described the interior of the house owned by Sir Jamsetjee Jeejeebhoy in Rampart Row, Fort St George, Bombay. The entrance hall contained paintings of Chinese mandarins; the first floor was 'fitted up in English style', all the furniture having been 'manufactured in London'. The room also contained family portraits. Moses, *Sketches of India*, pp. 256–8.

33 Parsis – descendants of Persians who fled to India from Muslim persecution in the seventh and eighth centuries and were adherents of Zoroastrianism. They had become, by the nineteenth century, the main local commercial and entrepreneurial class in Bombay.

34 *Life in Bombay and the Neighbouring Out-stations* (London, 1852), p. 262.

35 University of Cambridge, Centre of South Asian Studies: Scott Papers, 18 April, 1885.

36 University of Cambridge, Centre of South Asian Studies: Scott Papers, 10 May 1885.

37 A reasonable resemblance of 'home' was re-created within some elite Indian interiors, but these were always 'betrayed' by a feature or arrangement which indicated an incomplete understanding or acceptance of British material-culture practices. In 1889, Lady Wilson described the 'English bungalow' of a Muslim notable in Shahpur and how he had built this 'bungalow English-fashion' next to his house 'on the floors of the drawing-room and dining-room cotton floor-cloths were laid, with a dark-red ground … There was an ottoman in the middle of the room, an English fireplace and mantelpiece, chairs with net- and silk-embroidered antimacassars and a table

on which were placed a looking-glass, glass butter-dishes and salt-cellars, by way of ornament'. Lady Wilson, *Letters from India [1889–1909]* (London, 1984), pp. 32–3.

38 University of Cambridge, Centre of South Asian Studies: Scott Papers, 7 March 1884.

39 University of Cambridge, Centre of South Asian Studies: Scott Papers, 7 March 1884.

40 University of Cambridge, Centre of South Asian Studies: Scott Papers, 22 June 1884.

41 University of Cambridge, Centre of South Asian Studies: Scott Papers, 6 December 1885.

42 George C.M. Birdwood, *The Arts of India* (London, 1880), p. 199.

43 London, British Library: Bengal Wills, 1859, L/AG/34/27/163, estate of Amun Ali Khan.

44 London, British Library: Bengal Wills, 1859, L/AG/34/27/163, estate of Amun Ali Khan, pp. 171–2.

45 London, British Library: Bengal Wills, 1883, L/AG/34/27/190, estate of Gooroo Churn Singh.

46 'baboo', 'babu' – 'properly a term of respect attached to a name, like Master or Mr., and in some parts of Hindustan'. Col. H. Yule and A.C. Burnell (eds), *Hobson-Jobson; a glossary of colloquial Anglo-Indian words and phrases, and of kindred terms, etymological, historical, geographical and discursive* (London, 1886, reprinted 1994), p. 44. See also Mrinalani Sinha, *Colonial Masculinity: the 'manly Englishman' and the 'effeminate Bengali' in the late nineteenth century* (Manchester, 1995).

47 'In Bengal … it is often used with a slight savour of disparagement, as characterizing a superficially cultivated, but too often effeminate, Bengali' and due to their employment by the British administration 'the word has come often to signify "a native clerk who writes English"'. Yule and Burnell (eds), *Hobson-Jobson*, p. 44.

48 Kerr, *The Domestic Life*, p. 167.

49 Kerr, *The Domestic Life*, p. 167.

50 Shib Chunder Bose, *The Hindoos as They Are; a description of the manners, customs and inner life of Hindoo society in Bengal* (London and Calcutta, 1881).

51 Bose, *The Hindoos as They Are*, pp. 197, 204, 207–8.

52 London, British Library: Bengal Wills, 1883, L/AG/34/27/190, estate of Abinash Chunder Dutt.

53 English commentators also noted the quantity of books owned by the Bengali middle class. In 1904 Lady Wilson described the private rooms of 'the best-known writer of plays in Bengal', which were 'almost furnished with books. They lay on the table, sat on the chairs and crowded the bookcases, which lined the walls'. Wilson, *Letters from India*, p. 316.

54 King, *The Bungalow*, p. 56.

55 Bipin Chandra Pal, *Memories of My Life and Times* (Calcutta, 1973), pp. 331–2 cited in Anderson, *Imagined Communities*, p. 92.

56 Begum Shaista Ikramullah cited in King, *The Bungalow*, p. 58.

57 B. Stein, *A History of India* (Oxford, 1998), pp. 303–4.

58 Flats, such as Sorab Mansions and Russi Court, both built along Queen's Road, Back Bay, exemplified the new apartment-block look. *Journal of the Indian Institute of*

Architects, vol. 4, no. 1 (July 1937), p. 270.

59 This adoption of the *moderne* or Art Deco style in bungalow construction can be seen in images of three residences built at Warden Road, Bombay, which were designed to 'conform to modern ideas of simplicity and comfort'. *Journal of the Indian Institute of Architects*, vol. 4, no. 2 (October 1937), pp. 286–7.

60 *Journal of the Indian Institute of Architects*, vol. 4, no. 3 (January 1938), p. 115, cited in Benton et al., *Art Deco*, p. 384.

61 Although Sir Mangaldas Mehta's bungalow was remodelled in the latest style, vestiges of local traditional usage survived in the room devoted to a large image of 'the Lord Buddha'.

62 *Journal of the Indian Institute of Architects*, vol. 3, no. 1 (July 1936), pp. 158–9.

63 *Journal of the Indian Institute of Architects*, vol. 3, no. 2 (October 1936), back cover.

64 *Journal of the Indian Institute of Architects*, vol. 3, no. 2 (October 1936), back cover.

65 *Journal of the Indian Institute of Architects*, vol. 4, no. 3 (January 1938), p. 319.

66 *Journal of the Indian Institute of Architects*, vol. 4, no. 3 (January 1938), p. 326.

67 Deborah Ryan, *The Ideal Home through the Twentieth Century* (1997), *passim*.

68 See Judith Mara Gutman, *Through Indian Eyes: 19th and early 20th century photography from India* (New York, 1982). In this work Gutman illustrates a number of portraits of local people, produced by local photographic companies but working within a Western visual discourse. See also M. Karlekar, *Re-visioning the Past: early photography in Bengal, 1875–1915* (New Delhi, 2005).

69 Mildred Archer includes a depiction of the *puja* room in a local middle class home in *Patna Painting* (London, 1947), opp. p. 17. *Hatri Puja* painted by Gopal Lal *c.* 1870 depicts two worshippers within a local domestic interior, the room with shrine, as well as European glass 'wall-shades' and pictures on the wall. No furniture other than a low table is depicted in the painting. See also James Prinsep, *Benares Illustrated in a Series of Drawings* (Calcutta, 1830) for an engraving of 'A Thakoor-Dwaree' which depicts another local *puja* room.

70 Lack of visual representations of the local middle-class domestic sphere within India contrasts with the situation in Algeria during French colonization. Zeynep Celik has argued that the new photographic technology of the nineteenth century was used to make the colony visible in the metropole by giving it an easily recognizable image to disseminate. As she suggests, the Algerian house, especially the inner courtyard, occupied a key place in the repertory of French photographers. Zeynep Celik, 'Framing the colony: houses of Algeria photographed', *Art History*, vol. 27, no. 4 (September 2004), pp. 616–26.

71 R.K. de Silva illustrates a number of views of the local interior in Ceylon during the second half of the nineteenth century. R.K. de Silva, *19th century Newspaper Engravings of Ceylon – Sri Lanka* (London, 1998).

72 M. Roberts, *Caste Conflict and Elite Formation: the rise of the Karava elite in Sri Lanka, 1500–1951* (Cambridge,1982 reprinted New Delhi, 1995); K.M. de Silva, *A History of Sri Lanka* (Chennai, 1997); P. Peebles, *Social Change in Nineteenth Century Ceylon* (Colombo,1995); K. Jayawardena, *Nobodies to Somebodies: the rise of the colonial bourgeoisie in Sri Lanka* (Colombo, 2000). The term middle class in the context of this chapter is used to encompass a broad section of the local social elite in Ceylon during the second half of the nineteenth century. This includes lawyers, plantation owners, *rentiers* and entrepreneurs. It also encompasses different ethnic groups

such as the Burgher community, Christian Sinhalese, members of the Karava and Goyigama castes and wealthy Tamils.

73 Cited in C. Breckenridge, 'The aesthetics and politics of colonial collecting: India at World's Fairs', *Journal of Comparative Studies in History and Society*, vol. 31 (1989), p. 213.

74 Roberts, *Caste Conflict and Elite Formation*, p. 221 notes 'in Sri Lanka, the lengthy period of Western rule in the Low-Country [south-western coastal region] resulted in a much more pronounced penetration of Western consumption patterns than within most parts of British India'.

75 De Silva, *A History of Sri Lanka*, p. 333.

76 Malathi de Alwis in, 'Notes towards a discussion of female portraits as texts', *Pravada*, vol. 4, nos 5/6 (1996), p. 16, suggests that photographic portraits of the local social elite in Ceylon did not involve them passively in another form of Western knowledge-making. She suggests that they 'were actively involved and implicated in their self-representation'.

77 Jayawardena, *Nobodies to Somebodies*, pp. 256–60.

78 R. Percival, *An Account of the Island of Ceylon* (London, 1803), pp. 173–4. J. Guy and D. Swallow, *Arts of India, 1550–1900* (London, 1990), p. 201 note 'with British expansion [in India] … there was a need to provide for furnishing residences in European style, since chairs, tables, desks and most of the other impedimenta seen as essential by Europeans had no part in the traditional life of India at any level of society'.

79 R. Lewcock, B. Sansoni and L. Senanayake (eds), *The Architecture of an Island: the living legacy of Sri Lanka* (Colombo, 1998), p. 23. Percival, *An Account of the Island*, p. 173, noted of Ceylonese dwellings 'round the walls of their houses are small banks or benches of clay, designed to sit or sleep on'.

80 A.K. Coomaraswamy, *Medieval Sinhalese Art* (Broad Campden, 1908), p. 138, plate XI.

81 J. Davy, *An Account of the Interior of Ceylon* (London, 1821), p. 279.

82 London, National Archives: CO 54/104: 'List of Property Belonging to Eheylepola Maha Nillame sold by Public Auction … January 1825'. The sale comprised 498 lots of which four items were described as 'chests' and one as the 'glazed frame of [an] almyrah [cupboard]'. The majority of items in the sale comprised cloth, jewellery and ivory combs.

83 Sir J.E. Tennent, Ceylon: an account of the island, physical, historical and topographical (London, 1859), vol. 2, p. 675.

84 J.W. Bennett, *Ceylon and its Capabilities* (London, 1843), p. 48.

85 C. Pridham, *An Historical, Political and Statistical Account of Ceylon* (London, 1849), pp. 262–3.

86 Tennent, *Ceylon*, vol. 2, p. 675.

87 Tennent, *Ceylon*, vol. 2, p. 692. The Mudlaliyar's costume indicates the mixing of components from Europe and Asia and was composed of Dutch eighteenth-century frogged coat, English medal, local wrapped cloth and European shoes.

88 L. Liesching, *A Brief Account of Ceylon* (Jaffna, 1861), p. 18.

89 Jayawardena, *Nobodies to Somebodies*, p. 247.

90 D. Brohier, 'Who were the Burghers?', *Journal of the Royal Asiatic Society (Sri Lanka Branch)*, vol. 30 (1985/86), pp. 101–19.

91 B.R. Blazé, *The Life of Lorenz* (Colombo, 1948), n.p. I am grateful to Ismeth Raheem for drawing my attention to this source.

92 R.L. Brohier, *Changing Face of Colombo* (Colombo, 1984), cited in D. Brohier, *Dr Alice de Boer and Some Pioneering Burgher Women Doctors* (Colombo, 1995), p. 22.

93 H.C. Sirr, *Ceylon and the Cingalese* (London, 1850), vol. 1, p. 44.

94 Data held at the National Archives, London in the form of customs returns of goods shipped into Ceylon during the nineteenth century bears witness to the growth of Indian furniture imports. During the years 1845, 1846 and 1847, £1,897, £2,274 and £1,169 respectively of Indian 'cabinet ware' was imported into the island. See London, National Archives, Cust 13 series.

95 An example of the usage of Bombay wood and local furniture within different rooms of the local domestic interior is found in photographs of Calverly House, Turret Road, Colombo, c. 1910 in I. Raheem and P. Colin Thomé, *Images of British Ceylon: nineteenth century photography of Sri Lanka* (Singapore, 2000), pp. 74–5.

96 After 1840, large quantities of 'Bombay Blackwood' furniture were manufactured and distributed to all parts of India, Ceylon, Burma and Africa. 'It is always the same furniture which is to be seen everywhere in these Bombay houses, made of *shisham* or blackwood trees (Dalbergia sp.) and elaborately carved ... the carving is very skilful, but in a style of decoration utterly inapplicable to chairs and couches and tables'. Birdwood, *The Arts of India*, p. 201. Newspaper advertisements record the presence of Bombay Blackwood furniture on the island from the 1840s. London, National Archives: CO 59/3: *The Ceylon Times*, 29 December 1846, 'Sale of Household Furniture ... at the Residence of Captain Holsworthy, Slave Island [Colombo] ... the whole of the household furniture consisting of handsomely carved Bombay wood sofas, Easy chairs, Dining Room and Drawing Room Ditto'.

97 Other furniture comprised: 'One Nandoonwood High Backed Chair 5s', 'One Jackwood Sofa 6s', 'Two Square Satinwood Settees 10s', 'Two Dozen Satinwood Ladies Chairs £10'.

98 'Four Satinwood Bookcases £8', 'One Jackwood Bookcase £1'. The books were listed in a separate catalogue.

99 A.D. King, *Colonial Urban Development: culture, social power and environment* (London and Boston, 1976), p. 147.

100 King, *Colonial Urban Development*, p. 147.

101 M. Roberts, I. Raheem and P. Colin Thomé, *People Inbetween: the Burghers and the middle class in the transformations within Sri Lanka, 1790s–1960s* (Ratmalana, 1989), p. 109, pl. 17. The Lorenz household participated in 'a musical meeting at Mr de Livera's every Saturday evening at seven'.

102 C.F. Gordon Cumming, *Two Happy Years in Ceylon* (Edinburgh and London, 1892), vol. 1, p. 78.

103 Roberts, *Caste Conflict and Elite Formation*, pp. 104–5.

104 J. Capper, *The Duke of Edinburgh in Ceylon* (London, 1871), p. 101.

105 goyigama – traditional hereditary landowning elite.

106 Jayawardena, *Nobodies to Somebodies*, p. 177.

107 P. Bourdieu, *Distinction: a social critique of the judgement of taste* (London, 1994), p. 12 and pp. 53–4.

108 I am grateful to Professor Kingsley de Silva for this suggestion.

109 Raheem and Colin Thomé, *Images of British Ceylon*, pp. 22–30.

110 C. Pinney, *Camera Indica: the social life of Indian photographs* (London, 1997), p. 74.

111 K.C. Grier, 'Imagining the parlor, 1830–80', in G.W.R. Ward (ed.), *Perspectives on American Furniture* (New York, 1988), pp. 230–3.

112 A. Maxwell, *Colonial Photography and Exhibitions: representations of the 'native' and the making of European identities* (London and New York, 1999), p. 13. Maxwell also proposes that 'because these portraits were taken at the customers' bidding … they were probably the first images over which … indigenous peoples exercised any semblance of control'.

113 For example, London, British Library: PDP Photo 1000/(4986), 1000/(5006), 1000/(4983).

114 A. Wright (ed.), *Twentieth Century Impressions of Ceylon* (London, 1907), *passim*.

115 de Silva, *A History of Sri Lanka*, pp. 254–64.

116 M.L. Pratt, *Imperial Eyes: studies in travel writing and imperialism* (London, 1992), p. 7.

117 Other writers also proselytized the commercial possibilities of Ceylon, see J. Ferguson, *Ceylon in 1883* (Colombo, 1883). John Ferguson was an active promoter of the island's plantation sector.

118 de Alwis, 'Notes towards the Discussion', p. 16.

119 The large room is lit by a glass chandelier and the lavish, Westernized furnishings comprised low button-upholstered armchairs of fashionable *fin-de-siècle* English form and a carved ebony and upholstered armchair with scrolling arms. The windows are fitted with light-diffusing drapes, and tables as well as other items of furniture are covered with textiles, adding to the opulence of the room. The photograph is reminiscent of related contemporary British domestic interiors recorded by H. Bedford Lemere (1864–1944).

120 See Erving Goffman, *The Presentation of Self in Everyday Life* (Harmondsworth, 1959), pp. 32–40.

121 Roberts, Raheem, Colin Thomé, *People Inbetween*, p. 70. On this issue Roberts also quotes Jon Prins, who wrote in 1850 that some Low Country Sinhalese were 'uncomfortable with the Portuguese and Dutch habits and manners they [had] adopted and the British ones they [were] acquiring'. *Pirit* – the chanting of a Buddhist sacred text/texts, with the intention of warding off evil spirits; *dane* – almsgiving; *rukada* – traditional puppet show.

122 A. Jaffer and M. Schwabe, 'A group of sixteenth-century ivory caskets from Ceylon', *Apollo*, vol. 49, no. 445 (March 1999), pp. 3–14.

123 R. Evans, 'Figures, doors, passages', *Architectural Design*, vol. 48, no. 4 (1978), pp. 267–78.

4 ✧ Domesticating authority in the public spaces of empire

T HIS CHAPTER examines the role played by a range of Anglo-Indian public spaces (and the objects they contained) – the club, the hotel, the photographic studio, the cinema and the department store – in the affirmation of white, middle-class British national and cultural identity. These venues are also discussed as spaces where the local elite could learn to 'inhabit' Westernized environments newly introduced into the Subcontinent – although, on occasion, in a manner not imagined by their colonial masters. The public spaces listed above have been selected because they were recent introductions to India and Ceylon from the second quarter of the nineteenth century. In addition, their spatial configuration, fittings and furnishings, as well as the social practices which were constituted and expressed in these venues, came to form significant aspects of colonial material culture. The colonial club and hotel, for example, were envisaged as supportive environments which formed extensions to Anglo-Indian domestic space. Furthermore, other public spaces such as the cinema and the department store, which existed in most urban centres of the Subcontinent, provided Westernized 'routes' through the colonial city. These spaces collectively constituted part of what has been termed in another context an 'exhibitionary complex' within the colony.[1] However, there was by no means complete correspondence between these new public spaces which had recently been developed in the West and their transplanted forms within the Subcontinent. Within India and Ceylon, in a similar fashion to that of the colonial domestic sphere, such spaces, their material culture and social practices were adapted to local conditions. They were also intersected by local histories of use and, because of their socio-historical context, engendered increasingly rigid and anachronistic forms of behaviour intended to reinforce the Anglo-Indian persona.

The power of colonial public space as a location intended to fix certain forms of behaviour and reinforce a rigid communal solidarity is expressed in the following quotation. This extract conveys the dawning awareness of a new arrival within the Anglo-Indian community with regard to the seemingly intractable nature of the social practices produced within a particular colonial institute:

> In front, like a shutter, fell a vision of her married life. She and Ronny would look into the Club like this every evening, then drive home to dress; [at the Club] they would see the Lesleys and Callendars, the Turtons and the Burtons, and invite them and be invited by them, while the true India slid by unnoticed.[2]

Adela Quested's realization in E.M. Forster's *A Passage to India* that her social life as a married woman would revolve around this introduced European social institution, the limited company of her compatriots and the marginalization of, in her words, the 'true India', encapsulates the centrality of a domesticated but public or communal interior space – the club – to British social and cultural life within the Subcontinent.

Public space and pathways through the colony

As previously suggested, in many cases British experience of the colonial bungalow was as a flawed and unsettling space, a poor substitute for 'the English home', where India infiltrated and disrupted the most private spaces of British domestic life. The European club, on the other hand, was perhaps the most significant of a number of more public but domesticated locations within the civil settlements of India and Ceylon where Western social practices and cultural identity were respectively reproduced and reinforced. In fact, because Anglo-Indian domestic space was compromised by a number of local factors, for the British in India maintenance of a home culture (with its accompanying evocations of domesticity as well as communal belonging) was necessarily constituted within a series of separate but intersecting locations, both including and beyond the domestic sphere.

The existence of such a network was not particular to the colonial context and, indeed, related spaces were to be found within the home country. However, even by the late nineteenth century, the number of Europeans residing within the Subcontinent was insignificant, making their hold on power quite tenuous; as a consequence, in order that so few could continue to govern so many, it was deemed imperative to maintain and convey the appearance of prestige, authority and control in their life-styles. Therefore, the need for such Westernized public spaces was more pressing than in Europe.[3] These intersecting locations within the Subcontinent were intended to provide a series of demarcated routes or pathways for Europeans to navigate their way through the colonial city, settlement or rural district.

The intention of each of these routes was to bypass the local, as far as possible, and cumulatively to create a supra-colonial space within which Europeans could evoke the familiar and endeavour to reassert their national and cultural identity. These non-domestic spaces where the European passed leisure time, socialized with their compatriots and engaged, as far as possible, in the everyday practices of the homeland, served to reaffirm, in the words of Catherine Hall, an 'imperial identity', albeit an identity which, as she has argued, was 'ruptured, changed and differently articulated by place'.[4]

The architectural historian A. Srivathsan has suggested that the term 'public space' within an urban setting had different meanings in Europe and South Asia.[5] Public spaces in Europe, as he asserts, 'have identifiable expressions' such as urban squares, plazas and parks, as well as meeting places such as halls and theatres. Within the Subcontinent, there existed a different perception of public space. Some space was indeed defined by the local population as public (for example, temples, streets and riverfronts), but, as Srivathsan suggests, lack of an identifiable expression of public space in the Western sense did not reflect absence of public life, only a 'different cultural understanding'.[6] Anthony King and others have written about the creation, by Europeans, of 'modern' and 'healthy' public spaces within Indian cities during the colonial era and the envisioning of these spaces as arenas for the performance of 'civilized' (i.e. Westernized) public life. This entailed the creation of recognizable urban spaces such as parks, promenades and squares. It also engendered, within the Indian city, the creation of new social spaces such as theatres, clubs, race-courses and shopping malls.

By the late nineteenth century, whole areas of the colonial city within the Subcontinent had become zones where the British could map their own territory and where the local elite were also permitted to indulge in Westernized practices. An example of such a zone was Mount Road (now renamed Anna Salai) in Madras, which was constructed in 1795 as a wide route of communication linking Fort St George with St Thomas's Mount. This thoroughfare has been described as an important mall 'frequented by Europeans and the local elite, it was an Indian equivalent to the high streets of European cities'. By the early years of the twentieth century, the public spaces of Mount Road comprised a series of Europeanized locations or pathways through the colonial city, including

> many important hotels, such as the Hotel d'Angeli's ... with restaurants that offered European cuisine, impressive buildings that housed photographic studios, book stores, musical stores, automobile showrooms and department stores ... [in addition] By 1910 Mount Road had become the preferred location of cinema theatres, with the Electric Theatre, Elphinstone, Gaiety and Wellington being some of the earlier ones.[7]

Within this public space, both Europeans and the local elite could find
suitable (i.e. Western-style) accommodation, dine on 'European cuisine'
and indulge in the pleasures of modern city living by partaking in Western
cultural pursuits (at the book and musical stores), in addition to finding
more popular forms of entertainment offered by the newly-introduced
cinemas.

The recent secondary literature is limited in its discussion of these public
spaces of empire. The secondary literature briefly describes the physical
attributes or arrangements of such spaces as clubs and hotels within the
Subcontinent. However, little has been written about how these venues
reproduced an ambience of European domesticity within South Asia.
Secondary sources are also limited in their discussion of the functioning
of these and other public spaces in the colonial context (such as shops or
department stores, photographic studios or cinemas) as locations which
were intended to help the European persona within the colony to re-inscribe
its authority and counter its own internal instability. Furthermore, no study
to date discusses such spaces as locations for the construction of colonial
social relations and identity formation, both European and local.

The European club as a protected social and cultural space[8]

Anthony King indicated the significance of the club to the European
experience within the Subcontinent and its relative neglect in the literature
when he wrote that 'as the central social form of the colonial community,
acting as social gatekeeper and arbiter in questions of status and behaviour …
the club in the colonial society has not received the … attention it deserves'.[9]
Previous authors who have written about the European club within the
Indian Subcontinent have relied on the outputs of Charles Allen, in addition
to other works, and have described such aspects as the role of sports, issues of
status and club membership, and initiation of new members of the European
club into the colonial social code.[10] The main functions of the club in India
and Ceylon were social interaction between the British community and
reaffirmation, by this group, of both national and cultural identity.[11]

King has suggested that the club functioned in a number of ways:

> the colonial community lived separately, had separate kinds of behaviour
> and shared separate forms of knowledge. The very lack of privacy between
> them was essential in the maintenance of their collective identity. The club,
> with its familiar surroundings and established rituals, provided the setting
> for the exchange of this social knowledge, the place where community
> beliefs and sentiments were continuously reinforced and modified, the
> context in which newcomers were socialized into the folkways of the
> colonial culture.[12]

Many of the older clubs entered into reciprocal arrangements with clubs in different urban settlements in India. There existed, therefore, a network of such social institutions scattered throughout the Subcontinent where the physical surroundings, customary rituals and exchange of social knowledge were replicated with little alteration and where transient, but socially acceptable, members of the British community were welcomed into the extended 'family' of Anglo-Indian society.

For much of the nineteenth century, the main constituency of clubs in India, at least those reserved for members of the Indian Civil Service, to paraphrase the words of Bernard Cohn, was drawn from a restricted group within English society. This group was entirely male, was mostly London-based with its roots in banking and commercial families, or comprised land-owning families in Scotland as well as the south-east of England.[13] Most of this group had attended the East India Company's college at Haileybury in Hertfordshire, which equipped them with a shared set of values and a network of friendships when they arrived in India, and accustomed them to a collegial life.

During the nineteenth century, these shared experiences were expressed and constituted throughout the Subcontinent in a range of recently established clubs. In fact, it is arguable that the ambience of British clubs within the Subcontinent affirmed the domestic nature of colonial authority, and these venues reproduced the closely knit elite masculine communality of Haileybury, in the same way as did the colleges of Oxford and Cambridge, the Inns of Court and, of course, clubs in metropolitan centres of the homeland. Bernard Cohn has noted the social, cultural and economic cohesiveness among the Indian Civil Service during the middle decades of the nineteenth century:

> Cultural and economic ties of [this group] were very much buttressed by ties of descent and affinity. It is likely that from 1840 to 1860 fifty or sixty interconnected extended families contributed the vast majority of the civil servants who governed India. And these civil servants certainly had crucial administrative roles until the 1870s when those selected through open competition had enough seniority to begin to rise in the bureaucracy.[14]

In addition to reinforcing communal social rituals, the plan and interior spaces of most clubs within the Subcontinent replicated and amplified the interior spaces of the colonial domestic dwelling. In many cases, clubs were actually established within bungalows or houses which had previously been reserved for domestic use.[15] The majority of clubs presented such features as a verandah, a dining room, a smoking room, a reading room/library, a drawing room and a billiard room, all of which were features to be found within the domestic realm in India. Furthermore, the club was usually furnished in the

25 The standard furnishings of the Anglo-Indian bungalow transferred to the location of the club. 'The Drawing Room, [Mount] Abu Club' [N. India, *c.* 1900].

manner of an Anglo-Indian bungalow with standardized furnishings familiar to the British from the colonial domestic sphere, as the illustration of the drawing room of the Mount Abu Club shows (see figure 25).

Significantly, larger clubs also devoted a high proportion of their interior space to accommodation or 'chambers' for long-term or transient residents, which allowed the latter to inhabit club premises as they might inhabit the domestic dwelling. For example, the United Services Club, at its premises at 22 Chowringhee Road, Calcutta offered a suite of rooms to members 'consisting of sitting-room, bed-room and large bath' at 60 rupees per month. The club's premises next door at number 21 offered a 'large drawing room, bed-room and bath' and a series of other suites with different configurations of sitting, bed and bath-rooms.[16] The large numbers of Indian servants employed in the Anglo-Indian bungalow were equally well represented in the club. In a number of ways, however, the colonial club offered greater privacy to residents than the Anglo-Indian bungalow, as inhabiting a suite of rooms offered more control over the comings and goings of local servants.

There was also much correspondence between the physical appearance of the club and that of the colonial domestic interior. Often, the same suppliers who provided for the domestic interior furnished club premises. For example, the Ootacamund Club was supplied with household furnishings by both local suppliers as well as the foremost cabinetmakers and upholsterers in Madras, Deschamps and Co. of Mount Road.[17] In a similar fashion in Ceylon, H. Don Carolis and Sons, the principal furniture makers and 'complete house furnishers' of the island, advertised in 1908 that, in addition to supplying furniture for private households, 'Hotels, Clubs and Public Institutions [were] Furnished' also.[18] In fact, there was often little difference between the club drawing room and the hall room of an upper-roomed house or bungalow drawing room in terms of the range, variety and materials of furnishings supplied.

One area of the club which played a significant role in the reaffirmation of national and cultural identity was the club reading room or library. Here, members could remain informed about news from the homeland, in addition to news of the British community within the Subcontinent. Moreover, a variety of periodicals and journals from the homeland allowed knowledge of metropolitan fashions, social and cultural events, as well as the underlying assumptions and interests of the metropolitan elite, to be absorbed, transmitted and reinforced among the British community in India and Ceylon. Activities, such as field sports, which were culturally specific to the colonial elite were reaffirmed through the reading matter subscribed to by club reading rooms.

Publications subscribed to by the Reading Room of the United Services Club, Simla in 1911, for example, included *The Sportsman, The Financial Times, The Field, The Illustrated London News, Country Life, The Graphic, Punch, the Army and Navy Gazette*; Indian papers included *The Times of India, The Asian, The Empress*; and magazines and reviews included *The Tatler, The Queen, Ladies' Pictorial, Lady's Field*, and *Westminster Gazette*.[19] The most popular reading matter in the Reading Room of the Dalhousie Institute, Calcutta, in 1888 was not the staples of English literature: as the Institute's Librarian noted 'experience has shown that the writings of English classical authors lie altogether neglected on our shelves, and ... the great demand is for light literature'.[20]

In urban centres of India and Ceylon, when British clubs were first established, their entry requirements were based on very restricted social and racial criteria. They were exclusively for the use of those British men from approved sections of that community, such as middle- and high-ranking members of the colonial civil service or armed forces. Women were initially excluded, as were the Indian and Ceylonese elites (as indeed were socially inferior members of the European communities within India and Ceylon).

Every club adopted a set of rules, the first of which usually prescribed the process by which new members could be admitted. Almost without exception, new members were put up for election by existing club members through a ballot.[21] This process ensured that only those among the Anglo-Indian population who were socially acceptable to the majority of existing members were permitted to join the club; in other words, they were regarded by their peers as 'clubbable'.[22] These new members were therefore able to benefit from the amenities of the club and, more importantly, to make connection with its social and informational networks.

The rules of club membership ensured that the status of members was carefully policed. Usually club membership was dependent on occupation, at least within the main urban centres of India, and many of the discussions recorded in the minutes of club subcommittees dealt with negotiations about the status of aspirant groups seeking membership. One increasingly large group of British residents in India who were excluded from membership of the oldest clubs were those engaged in trade. Writing in the 1930s, Sir Ridgeby Foster noted that 'people who worked in shops were known as 'counter-jumpers' and even the general manager of one of the biggest stores in Calcutta could not get into the more select clubs'.[23] British women only gained access to membership of the more select clubs from the last decade of the nineteenth century, and club premises, in many cases, had to be modified in order to accommodate this new constituency, usually in a new building entirely separate from the main body of the club.[24]

In addition to concerns about restricting club membership to those Britons in approved occupations (usually in the Indian Civil or Military Service), the obsession of club committee members over whether ladies should be allowed to join was only matched by a related one, that of keeping the club white. The majority of clubs in metropolitan centres of India were bastions of racial segregation. This segregation lasted until the first decades of the twentieth century; however, with the increasing Indianization of the civil and military services and especially the immense contribution which Indian officers and soldiers had made to the Allied victory in the First World War, it was difficult for all but the largest and most prestigious clubs to preserve their racial exclusiveness and bar from membership suitable applicants from the local population.[25]

The club also served as a vital social institution for the Anglo-Indian community at large, which initiated new members into the colonial social code and acted as a venue where such a code could be carefully policed. In fact, the club was such a significant space within the colonial context because it functioned through the operation of a set of written regulations which, in theory, was intended to order the conduct of its members and at the same time reinforce the underlying assumptions and practices of the British community within the Subcontinent. As Elizabeth Collingham has noted, the club was a space where newcomers learnt the colonial social code and where those who transgressed that code were rebuked for allowing standards to slide.[26]

Toward the end of the nineteenth century, by virtue of the advances made by the temperance movement and the fact that clubs had begun to allow more women as members, drunken and rowdy behaviour by British club members was tolerated to a lesser and lesser degree. Club rules were framed to curtail this type of behaviour, but often with limited success. For example, in March 1898 the Sub-committee of the Bangalore Club minuted that

> it had been brought to [the club secretary's] notice that on the night of the 8th instant, Mr Hughes sat upon the Bar and when the notice from the committee requesting gentlemen not to do this was shown to him by the Havildar, he had taken it and after drawing and writing on the back of it had made the Barman hang it up with its face to the wall, but had declined to comply with the printed request of the Committee. Resolved that Mr Hughes be called upon for an explanation.[27]

Many accounts from club minutes record the boisterous and often violent behaviour of the English members, the violence usually directed at the local club servants. In April 1905, it was noted in the Bangalore Club minutes that

> On the night of the Hockey Dinner, Lieut. M.F. White I.M.S., had thrown a heavy match holder at one of the peons [local club servants], also that he had thrown a brass call bell at the bar waiter. The Committee directed that the Hon. Sec. write to Lieut. White and call upon him for any explanation he may care to make in the matter and inform him that under Para. 6 of Club Byelaws, he could be charged 5 times the cost of the bell in addition to his share of the cost of damage done to other articles.[28]

The apparel of club servants also became the subject of debate. Members expressed strong views about all aspects of the material and visual culture of the club, and the uniform of club servants was perceived as a significant aspect of this environment. In May 1902 it was recorded in Bangalore Club minutes that

> The Subcommittee were unanimously of the opinion that the present dress
> of the peons [local club servants] and 2nd and 3rd butlers is neither useful
> nor ornamental and that they be put into a national costume.[29]

In addition to policing minor transgressions of European behaviour,
in times of perceived crisis for the British community in India, the club
served as a rallying point for that community where the group's position on
contentious or hazardous issues could be expressed, negotiated and distilled
and where the group's consensus was validated by the club membership as
a whole.[30]

Significantly, the club also provided a suitable venue for the 'culturally-
preferred leisure activities' of British elite society within the Subcontinent,
such as cricket, tennis, polo and billiards.[31] Sport grew in significance
during the heyday of the Raj and had a central place within European
culture.[32] The increasing importance of sport to the British middle class
during the nineteenth and early twentieth centuries was closely connected
to the growth of empire. As the British empire expanded, the need for
recruits to the imperial civil service and the increasing cultural importance
of athleticism combined to promote the cause of the sportsman.[33] Sport
was not just a matter of inculcating the right spirit and training the body.
It also became a vital source of recreation and amusement for the British
colonist. Richard Holt has discussed the imperial aspects of sport and has
argued that the British elite in India, in addition to being a ruling class or
'colonial aristocracy', was also a leisure class. As he suggests, 'sport helped
both [to] relieve the tedium of a distant posting and to integrate new arrivals
into the small world of colonial society'.[34]

The practice of British sports within India was another important
element of the expression and enhancement of the communal solidarity
within Anglo-Indian society. Sport was an essential mediating activity
between members of the colonial elite, and the material culture of sporting
activity located within club premises – the lawn-tennis court, rackets and
balls, the badminton court, the billiards room, the cricket pitch, clubhouse
and cricketing paraphernalia, together with a shared knowledge of the arcane
rules of these activities – helped maintain British morale and 'a sense of
shared roots, of Britishness, of lawns and tea and things familiar'.[35] Sport
occupied such a central place within Anglo-Indian society that a number
of 'lawn sports' evolved into their modern form within the Subcontinent.
The laws of badminton, for example, were first codified at Poona in 1870,
and lawn tennis was an increasingly popular activity within the British
settlements in India, which served to unite not only British men but British
men and women. In addition, in the last decades of the nineteenth century
it forged cultural bridges across the race divide.

The game of billiards (played in elite houses in Britain since the seventeenth century) became increasingly popular as a form of sporting activity during the nineteenth century in the home country and was also played extensively by the British within India.[36] Most colonial clubs contained at least one billiards room. The game was recommended within Anglo-Indian society to the infirm as a way of recovering their strength, as a health-giving relaxation for the Anglo-Indian male and to offer appropriate exercise for women.[37] In April 1845, the Reverend Charles Acland, who was recuperating from an illness at Pooree in India, extolled the benefits of billiards when he wrote 'the doctor desires me to play [billiards] as much as I can everyday … The game of billiards is about the best exercise for India. It is not too violent, yet it gives a man about three miles walking in the hour and brings all the limbs into play'.[38] Even some women among the local elite played a version of billiards within the privacy of their homes.[39] Although the majority of clubs contained billiard rooms, such was the popularity of the game among Anglo-Indians that hotels, including the following in Calcutta, also advertised this facility: the Adelphi Hotel, Waterloo Street, the Chowinghee Hotel, Chowringhee Street, Esplanade Hotel, Bentinck Street and Hope Hall, Waterloo Street.[40]

Perhaps the most culturally significant sport associated with club life in the Subcontinent was cricket. From the late nineteenth century, this game had epitomized Englishness and played a vital role in how the English envisaged themselves. Cricket was regarded by the English elite, in both the home country and the colonies, as an expression of moral worth. The cricket club within the Subcontinent became for Anglo-Indians not simply a pleasant social space for relaxation but also a repository for what were imagined as the best characteristics of the English race. Jack Williams and others have written how cricket became the sport of empire and the connection of cricket with notions of white supremacy.[41] Cricket, as did the colonial club, enforced the colour bar; until 1892 the two most prestigious cricket clubs in India – the Bombay Gymkhana and the Poona Gymkhana – were formed of white, British players; and only in that year did they begin to play against a local team, the Bombay Parsees.[42] Williams also argues that involvement of the local population in the 'playing [of] cricket was also believed to encourage non-whites to accept the white English qualities of sportsmanship and fair-play, which in turn would convince them of the beneficence of British rule'.[43] In the early years of the twentieth century, when cricket had been adopted by many Indians, the cricket clubhouse became a meeting place for members of the Anglo-Indian community and suitable members of the local community.

Club culture was rooted in a particular set of notions about Englishness and was intended to perform a number of functions, both at home and in the colonies. In 1879, *the Club Directory* related the concept of the club to the historicist element within English culture, which imagined history and tradition as a source of moral authority, and opined that

> membership of a Club is now accepted as a guarantee of the position of gentlemen of various professions and tends to keep alive sympathies which might otherwise be lost; and as a bond of union, it is scarcely too much to say that Clubs preserve much of the virtue of the early chivalry in its cosmopolitan features.[44]

In 1927, H.R. Panckridge noted both the spiritual and the more pragmatic benefits of club membership for British men in the far-flung regions of the colonies:

> In the tropical possessions of the British Crown, the idea of the club makes a special appeal to the large number of men, who are compelled by circumstances to be separated from their wives and families for longer or shorter periods. To these, clubs afford some consolation for the pains of exile and loneliness, while at the same time they offer a welcome solution of a difficult problem to the many bachelors with a distaste for housekeeping.[45]

The earliest clubs established by the British in India were the Bengal Club in Calcutta (1827), the Madras Club (1832), the Byculla Club, Bombay (1833) and the Western India Turf Club, also Bombay (1837). These establishments were contemporaneous with similar organizations in London such as the Athenaeum (1824), the Garrick (1831), the Carlton (1832) and the Reform Club (1837), and the constitutions of British clubs established in India were modelled on those of the latter. European Clubs were also established in smaller 'stations' or civil settlements such as, for example, Ootacamund in southern India, Mount Abu, in northern India and Nuwara Eliya in the highlands of Ceylon.

The principal functions of the European Club within the Subcontinent were to exclude the local, facilitate social interaction among the British community and act as locations which reaffirmed, on a daily basis, that community's national and cultural identity. In 1923 Kate Platt described the usual activities of club members, and her account highlights the role of the material culture of club life:

> the Club, to which the whole European population belongs, provides a meeting place, and is a centre for all kinds of sports and games, as well as for dancing … the Club is the centre of social life … It is the recognised meeting place of the station [settlement]. Most people manage to drop in during the interval between tea and dinner … almost everyone is to be met there during [this interval]. Much talk and gossip are heard – in a small station any news is appreciated. Bridge enthusiasts gravitate to the card-room; the young and energetic play tennis; others, watching the game or

idly turning over the last illustrated paper from home, find it very pleasant to sit under the shady trees … Dinner parties and dances are frequent … Everybody knows everyone else, the amount of income of each is known, and extravagance in entertaining or dress is not approved.[46]

As the centre of British power within India, until the early twentieth century at least, the city of Calcutta boasted a wide range of clubs catering for different interests and constituencies. The Bengal Club was both the oldest and also the most prestigious club in British India; by the 1890s club membership exceeded 650, half of whom were elected by ballot. Like many of the larger and more prestigious clubs within the Subcontinent, a large portion of the club's premises was allocated as either permanent or temporary accommodation for members. This situation had arisen because so few suitable lodging houses and hotels existed in the first half of the nineteenth century for the large transient European population.

By the late nineteenth century, the Bengal Club premises consisted of five large houses in the fashionable area of Chowringhee Road, including the Club House, number 33 Chowringhee Road,[47] a large house in the same compound given over as an accommodation block, houses at number 1 Park Street and number 1 Russell Street, similarly divided into so-called 'chambers' or accommodation for long-term residence by club members, and finally a large house at number 2 Russell Street, also providing accommodation.[48]

Whereas the Bengal Club was the domain of senior members of the administration of the English East India Company and subsequently the Indian Civil Service, membership of the Bengal Military Club, established in Calcutta in 1845, comprised military officers; eight years later its name was changed to the Bengal United Services Club and the club acquired premises close to the Bengal Club at 30 Chowringhee Road, 1 Kyd Street and 55 and 56 Park Street. As with the practice of the Bengal Club, most members were elected by ballot, ensuring control by existing members over the creation of new ones. A number of rooms were allotted to resident members for permanent occupation; temporary accommodation was also made available to club members.

In addition to these two prestigious clubs, Calcutta also boasted a number of other clubs, such as the 'Saturday Club' (established in 1878) and the New Club (1884). After 1880, a range of other clubs had been established to offer facilities to the increasingly variegated British society within the Presidency cities of India. The 'Saturday Club', located at number 7 Wood Street, had been founded for the 'promotion of social intercourse and amusements of a rational kind, the pursuit of literature and the facilitation of study in languages and the arts'.[49] As with so many clubs, sporting activities such as lawn tennis also occupied a prominent part in the space allocation within the club grounds, and the 'Saturday Club' boasted 'several well-kept courts' for that purpose. In 1896, Eustace Kenyon, Assistant Superintendent at the Indian Telegraph Office, described in a letter to his mother the diversions offered at this club: 'on Friday evening we had the Simons to dinner and went on together to an entertainment at the Saturday Club; the first half music, only about 6 pieces and the second half amateur theatricals, a very short amusing piece, well acted and we thoroughly enjoyed it all which is more than I expected to'.[50]

With the expansion of the European population in India during the late nineteenth century, social institutions such as the New Club in Park Street were established to cater for a range of social backgrounds and interests, and it was noted that this club 'supplied a much needed want among a certain class of the community'. The New Club contained, among other facilities a 'carefully and judiciously tended' library, and 'the amusements consist[ed] of lawn tennis, billiards, smoking concerts, house dinners, dances & c'.[51] Many other clubs catered for different interest groups.[52]

Madras and Bombay, the other Presidency cities apart from Calcutta, also contained a range of clubs. One of the best-known clubs within the

26 Plentiful accommodation for itinerant Anglo-Indians within the Westernized environment of the club. The Madras Club, main building and accommodation wing, *c*. 1880.

Subcontinent as a whole was the Madras Club, founded in 1832 (see figure 26). This club evolved from the acquisition of a private house, together with twenty acres of land, off Mount Road (Anna Salai) which had formerly been owned by a J.D. White. At the present time unoccupied and in the possession of *the Indian Express* group of newspapers, much still remains of the club premises. The central structure, or White House, comprises a large, upper-roomed house fronted by a classical portico. A 'chamber block' or accommodation wing was added during the middle decades of the nineteenth century to the East of this house and a library and billiard room to the West. The club premises grew during the nineteenth century with the addition of an octagonal *divan* or smoking room and two further billiard rooms to the rear. The *divan* was fitted with stained-glass windows and possessed a Madras-tile roof. In 1855 a swimming bath was added to the club facilities and later in the century a ladies' pavilion was built (1898). In 1865, the architect Robert Chisholm redesigned the front of the club, the original portico was replaced and unifying verandahs were added to three sides of the building.[53] The interior spaces of the club and social activities enacted there were described in the late nineteenth century in the following manner:

> up above the bar was a dining room and the reading room; really one huge long room. On one side were rows and rows of chambers of residence and some married quarters. On the other side was a very good library and another small dining room. It had a large verandah, where people met and talked. Then the men generally drifted off to the billiard room or to the bridge room.[54]

In Bombay, the principal meeting places for Europeans were the Byculla Club (1833), the Bombay Turf Club, the Bombay Gymkhana Club, the Royal Bombay Yacht Club, and the Bombay Club. Although the Byculla Club (see figure 27) was initially the most prestigious of the city's clubs, by 1876 with the expansion of the cotton industry and rapid encroachment of mills, the club's hinterland changed its ambience from residential to semi–industrial, a process which led to its eventual decline.[55] Despite this decline, however, in the 1880s the Byculla Club possessed around a hundred members 'of the civil and military services, merchants, bankers, lawyers and others'.[56]

The most successful clubs of the late nineteenth century were all located near the Esplanade and Fort.[57] The Bombay Club, for instance, was located at new premises in Rampart Row. In the 1880s the Royal Bombay Yacht Club was constructed close to the Apollo Pier in 'a pleasing mixture of Swiss and Hindu styles'.[58] Close by the main club premises were ample 'chambers' for the accommodation of members, both permanent and transient. Many of the hill stations within the Subcontinent also supported

27 The premier club of Western India. The Byculla Club, Bombay, *c.* 1900.

European clubs, including, for example Ootacamund, in the south of India (see figure 28).[59]

During the nineteenth century, the notion of the club became increasingly attractive to members of the local elite. Barred from entry to many of the British clubs within the Subcontinent, this elite began to form their own. For example, in 1873 the Cosmopolitan Club was founded in Madras as an Indian club, since others at the time were only open to Europeans. In 1882 this club moved to Mount Road, the heartland of British public space within the city, and was described at the time as 'the best Indian Association in the whole of India'.[60] During the early years of the twentieth century, a number of local clubs were established in New Delhi, including the Madras Club (patronized by South Indians), the New Delhi Club and the Talkatora Club.[61] In Colombo, Ceylon, the Orient Sports Club was founded to provide facilities for members of the local elite and, as Arnold Wright noted, the 'club takes a prominent place amongst the social institutions of Colombo. Its membership includes many leading native gentlemen interested in sport'.[62] Other clubs for the local elite in Ceylon such as the Burgher Recreation Club, The Tamil Union and the Sinhalese Sports Club became, as Ismeth Raheem and Michael Roberts have suggested, important sites 'for the reproduction of solidarity across and within the [local] middle class'.[63]

As the British came later to Ceylon than to India, the majority of clubs on the island had been founded after 1850. The premier club in the capital

The "Club House", Ootacamund. 1852.

a splendid building; beautifully furnished, accommodation for about 30 members; with Library, Billiard rooms, &c. (worth a lac of rupees.). — = £10,000.

28 Club in one of the many Anglo-Indian hill stations. 'The "Club House", Ootacamund, 1852' [by H. Bellasis].

of the island was the Colombo Club, founded in 1871 'for the promotion of social intercourse among gentlemen residing in Ceylon'. It occupied a building that had acted as a grandstand for the race-course (the Race Bungalow), which existed on Galle Face Green until the 1850s. Membership was more mixed than that of the most prominent clubs in India and was not restricted to the Ceylon Civil Service alone. By 1900 the number of club members was around 700 and included 'the leading representatives of the official, commercial and social circles of Ceylon'.[64]

Many of the clubs in Ceylon (as in India) had their origins as venues for participation in various sporting activities. For example, the Colombo Rowing Club was founded in 1865 and the present boat-house was built on the shores of Beira Lake in 1900. The Colombo Cricket Club was most probably founded in 1876 and moved in 1894 to a new clubhouse adjoining the racecourse. The Colombo Golf Club was established in either 1879 or 1880 and moved from the Galle Face Green to Borella district of Colombo in

United Club, Nuwara Eliya.

29 Club for the planters of highland Ceylon. United Club, Nuwara Eliya, Ceylon, *c.* 1900.

1896. A new club-house or pavilion was built in 1905.[65] Outside Colombo, in the plantations of the central highlands, clubs were established from the third quarter of the nineteenth century to service the growing number of planters engaged in the tea industry (see figure 29). For example, a club was founded in 1876 at Nuwara Eliya; in 1885 it moved to new premises in that settlement and was designated the Hill Club, which still functions at the present time.[66]

Acquiring 'the hotel habit': new leisure space and the de-personalization of colonial hospitality

In addition to the club, the colonial hotel also functioned as a significant social space within the Subcontinent. There is a limited secondary literature discussing the development and importance of hotels within India and Ceylon during the colonial period and their role as locations where national and cultural identity could be affirmed.[67] Hotels or inns – designated in an Indian legal publication of 1902 as 'house[s] of public entertainment, where provisions and beds are furnished to persons who apply for them' – served as social meeting places and introduced to the Subcontinent the continuation of a function which public houses, inns or taverns had provided in the eighteenth century in Britain, but with changes in the scale of their operation, appearance and pretensions.[68]

Clubs within the metropolitan centres of the Subcontinent provided accommodation exclusively for their members, who were drawn from a self-defining male elite within the Anglo-Indian community. However, with the growth of metropolitan centres within the Subcontinent there was an increase in the number of itinerant Britons and other Europeans residing in India of a social or occupational status which barred them from club membership. This group still required places of temporary accommodation, and hotels satisfied the basic needs of subsistence and rest and offered venues where such Britons could socialize.

In addition to satisfying these needs, public rooms in the grander hotels built after 1850 in Calcutta, Bombay and Colombo became analogous to function-specific rooms both in middle-class houses in the home country and in some interior spaces within the Anglo-Indian domestic dwelling. An advertisement of 1899 for the Great Western Hotel, Bombay, described the types of interior spaces found in the hotel and these included 'single bed-rooms, bed-rooms with sitting-rooms attached, a spacious dining hall, drawing-room for ladies, smoking-room for gentlemen, reading-room, billiard-room'.[69]

A much vaunted feature of Anglo-Indian society, noted often by contemporary commentators, was the hospitality offered by Anglo-Indian residents to British travellers of their own class. Such acts of hospitality, which involved accommodating and feeding fellow Britons for considerable periods, most probably did take place during the late eighteenth and early nineteenth centuries, when the total number of European residents in India was small. However, a self-perpetuating myth developed within the Anglo-Indian community about the continuance of such acts of hospitality into the second half of the nineteenth century, when it had most probably ceased to be a widespread practice.[70] This informal mode of accommodation became more problematic with the growth Calcutta and Bombay and the increasing number of transient visitors from Britain passing through these cities, as well as a lack of certainty as to the social credentials of this group.

Initially boarding houses satisfied this demand for lodging. In Calcutta around 1840 a small number of boarding houses were situated at New China Bazaar, Waterloo Street and North Range. In addition, at this time, two 'hotel taverns' were recorded, W.H. Benton's Clarendon Hotel at Ranneemoody Gully and J. Spence's Calcutta Hotel at Loudon's Buildings, the latter achieving some renown and becoming one of the landmarks of Calcutta.[71]

Writing in 1837, Emma Roberts noted the changes in colonial society, which had necessitated the introduction and expansion of public accommodation within the Subcontinent:

Formerly, strangers visiting Calcutta were dependent upon the hospitality of the residents, or compelled to take large unfurnished houses, there being neither lodging-houses nor hotels for the reception of guests. But the capital of Bengal has become too large to admit of the continuance of old customs; boarding, and other houses of public entertainment have been opened, and conducted in so respectable a manner, that notwithstanding the great difficulty of subduing ancient prejudices, no person, however fastidious, can now scruple to become an inmate of them … An enterprising person by the name of Spence, who has set up a splendid establishment of the kind in Wellesley Place, seems to receive all of the patronage which he so justly merits.[72]

In 1854, Mrs Frances Janet Wells described her arrival in Calcutta and the few days she spent at Spence's before she moved into a rented bungalow at Barrackpore:

This hotel is an enormous place in the best situation in Calcutta being just opposite Government House; the board and lodging for two people in private rooms is 250 rupees a month inclusive of wine and beer; for that we get four meals a day on a most liberal scale, in fact the dinner is always enough for eight people instead of two. Each room has its own *khitmagar* [head waiter] who has nothing else to do but attend to it and he accompanies you if you go out to dinner.[73]

During the second and third quarters of the nineteenth century, boarding houses and also the earliest manifestations of hotels within the Subcontinent developed in an organic manner, often being located in pre-existing domestic dwellings such as bungalows. In view of the large scale of many Anglo-Indian bungalows, these dwellings offered ideal locations for the accommodation and entertainment of paying guests. The fact that the interior space of the colonial bungalow or house rarely conformed to the function-specific room organization of the house in Britain allowed for the easy transferability of Anglo-Indian domestic space into commercial accommodation. An example of such transferability is found in Lahore. All of the earliest hotels in the city, such as Milner's and Goose's (established in the 1860s and both situated on McLeod Road), occupied former bungalows. In a similar fashion, a Mrs Hillier also opened a hotel 'of a superior class' at a house called 'Caversham' at the junction of Ferozepore and Mozang Roads.[74]

By the 1850s Calcutta boasted a large number (34) of respectable 'Board and Lodging Establishments' in a central location around Chowringhee Road, Wellesley Street, Park Street and Dhurrumtollah Street. The number and variety of hotels had also grown and included such premises as G.F. Kellner and Co.'s Family Hotel, 11 Hare Street; Bodry's Waterloo Hotel, 13–14 Waterloo Street; Spence's, Loudon's Buildings, Government Place; and D. Wilson and Co.'s, Family Hotel, 1–3 Old Court House Street (later to become the Great Eastern Hotel). In addition to these family hotels which were situated at the heart of official and commercial Calcutta, other hotels were also recorded beyond the centre of the city in the suburbs at Garden Reach and Howrah.[75]

A decade later Calcutta presented the same number of boarding houses, but the number of establishments designated as hotels had increased. These hotels were mainly located in central Calcutta (Waterloo Street, Dacre's Lane, Dhurrumtollah Street) and also at Howrah and Garden Reach on the outskirts of the city. Among this number was the Great Eastern Hotel, situated at 1–3 Old Court House Street, which was to become one of the city's landmarks in the last decades of the nineteenth century.[76]

Kellners's Hotel was established in 1855 in 'capacious and airy premises' at Hare Street for guests seeking 'a respectable, quiet and centrical [*sic*] locality'. Most of the public rooms in such hotels as Kellner's were analogous to rooms in the homes of the Anglo-Indian elite and, for example, often included a reading room, one or more billiard rooms and drawing rooms. Kellner's Hotel advertised both 'private and public Tiffin Rooms' where light meals of curried dishes and fruit could be taken.[77]

However, even in the 1870s contemporary commentators were dismissive of many of the hotels which had been established within the urban centres of the Subcontinent, especially those owned by Indians. In 1858, John Beames of the Indian Civil Service wrote that the Grand Hotel, Calcutta, when it was known as D. Wilson's Hotel, was 'a large, stuffy, vulgar, noisy place permeated with a mixed odour of cooking and stale tobacco'.[78] Writing in 1874, Edmund Hull noted that

> hotel living ... possesses few recommendations in India. The hotels often belong to natives, who do not understand the comfort of us Englishmen ... These native hotel-keepers ... are ever anxious to seize upon an immediate profit ... such hotels are found lacking in order, quiet, cleanliness and comfort.[79]

One or two of the larger hotels in Calcutta, in addition to providing accommodation and sustenance for paying guests, created new forms of public space in the colonial context, which combined the traditional role of a hostelry with that of retail outlet or 'general provider'. As Chris Furedy has suggested, some of Calcutta's leading hotels developed into large and complex establishments which incorporated numerous lines of business. The Auckland Hotel, for example was described in late 1850s as an

> attempt to combine a tailor's, a milliner's, a dressmaker's, a haberdasher's, a confectioner's, a hardwareman's, a woollen merchant's, a perfumer's, a restauranteur's, a spirit and wine merchant's, a provision dealer's, a grocer's, a coffee-house keeper's establishment, with an hotel.[80]

Similarly, the Great Eastern Hotel, located in Old Court House Street at the epicentre of British commercial activity in Calcutta, in addition to providing the usual services of such an establishment, also offered itself as a millinery warehouse and dressmaker and described itself in promotional material as 'oilman's stores and Italian warehouse' (see figure 30).[81] By the late 1890s, advertisements described this establishment as the 'Great Eastern Hotel, Wine and General Purveying Co. Ltd.' and noted that the company manufactured 'all kinds of Indian condiments' and imported all descriptions of 'wines, stores cigars etc.', which were sold either on the premises or by mail order.[82]

Although only a few hotels in India spread their nets as wide as the Great Eastern in terms of business activity, such enterprises created new, hybrid social spaces for the British in which to meet, socialize and through their acts of consumption partake in and shape the material culture of Anglo-India. In addition, establishments such as the Great Eastern were novel and stimulating venues for Anglo-Indians. Rudyard Kipling recorded his excitement at finding hundreds of Europeans under one roof in this hotel, the majority of whom were strangers to one another, after the restricted Anglo-Indian society of a colonial city such as Lahore.[83]

Bombay and Madras also possessed a growing range and variety of accommodation for paying guests from the second half of the nineteenth century. In the 1870s the two best hotels in Bombay were Watson's Hotel and Pallonjee's.[84] By the 1890s the former had expanded its accommo-dation with the addition of Watson's Annexe Hotel, which was described in glowing terms as 'mostly patronized by the elite; facing the sea and opposite the Royal Yacht Club. It stands unrivalled for its situation, appointments, magnificent apartments and excellent cuisine'.[85] In Madras, the area around Mount Road contained those hotels which were recommended to Anglo-Indians in contemporary guidebooks, including the Albany, Dent's Garden, Elphinstone and Royal.[86] In the first decade of the twentieth century, the area around Mount Road still contained the favoured hotels, including the Connemara, the Buckingham, the Elphinstone and the Victoria.[87]

The British elite in India were carefully guided to those hotels at the heart of British commercial and administrative activity within the colonial metropolis and away from those hotels beyond the centre, in the 'Black Town', which as one guidebook noted were 'generally inferior and promis-cuously resorted to by all classes'.[88] This advice was offered in order that the British middle class could avoid mixing with the local population, but equally could avoid contact with the increasingly large numbers of itinerant Britons and other Europeans whose social credentials excluded them from the more prestigious venues such as the clubs and the grander hotels of British India.

30 Both hotel and general provider of Anglo-Indian provisions. The Great Eastern Hotel, Old Court House Street, Calcutta, *c.* 1880.

During the first half of the nineteenth century, while the British population in India remained small, suitable accommodation existed for modest numbers of that population who were in transit through India. The bungalows and houses of their compatriots offered shelter and succour. Club chambers also, although in a less personalized fashion, offered subsistence and shelter. In addition, traveller's or *dak* bungalows, erected by the British administration at strategic points throughout the country, provided rudimentary accommodation for itinerant Britons engaged on government business (although provisions and bedding materials were the responsibility of the traveller). Such bungalows were usually only provided with the most basic furnishings (which might often be broken or defective in other ways) and the dilapidated state of these dwellings became the stuff of Anglo-Indian folk lore.[89]

Before 1850, in metropolitan centres of India, a small number of lodging houses and hotels had been established to cater for paying members of the itinerant Anglo-Indian population. These first few establishments in India and Ceylon that were prepared to receive paying guests developed in a piecemeal or organic fashion and were often located in dwellings previously used for domestic purposes. However, by the third quarter of the nineteenth century, the premises in which these businesses were located and the facilities which they offered were becoming inadequate to the task of accommodating members of different social groups. These included British officials in transit on business but also, in addition, growing numbers of Anglo-Indians, as well as the first of many cohorts of Western tourists arriving from Europe.

A new type of building began to be erected within the Subcontinent to accommodate this expanding number and range of visitors, and this became the site of new activities and a significant aspect of the architecture of leisure which grew in importance during the first decades of the twentieth century. The notion of the 'palace hotel', or 'modern type of imposing hotel', as one such building was described in 1907, while not a phenomenon peculiar to India, took hold in many parts of the Subcontinent. With the erection of these structures, interior spaces were created where new types of social activity could take place on a scale unimagined in the older hotels of the region.[90] Writing in 1924 of the situation in Lahore (although his comments have relevance for the rest of the Subcontinent), H.R. Goulding described the background to the shift from smaller to larger hotels in India:

> In those days [the 1870s], as suggested in the old guidebooks, the hotels in Lahore had to depend on the patronage of 'birds of passage'. It was not until permanent or quasi-permanent residents of the station [British settlement] showed a preference for hotel life and acquired the hotel habit, that the demand for such accommodation grew sufficient to ensure the success of an up-to-date hotel on a large scale.[91]

In a similar vein, in 1907, Arnold Wright described how the recently built Grand Oriental Hotel in Colombo served the needs of the steamer trade as well as the internal tourist market when he wrote 'the hotel is … largely used by visitors to Colombo from various parts of the island, while it is [also] a favourite place of resort with the residents of the city'.[92]

A growing 'preference for hotel life' and acquisition of 'the hotel habit' among Anglo-Indians led to the creation of a number of modern and monumental hotels in key locations within the Subcontinent. One such establishment was the Galle Face Hotel, Colombo, Ceylon. Situated a short way beyond the perimeter of the old Dutch fort, set beside the Indian Ocean and overlooking a large, open expanse of grass which was formerly used as a racecourse, the Galle Face Hotel evolved from relatively humble origins. Photographs of the hotel taken before the 1880s depict a modest single-storied structure, on the scale of a domestic dwelling (see figure 31). Writing in 1908, Henry Cave described the limited and less than polite accommodation offered by the hotel at this time:

31 The hotel as a development of the domestic dwelling. The Galle Face Hotel, Colombo, Ceylon, *c.* 1880.

> Those, who like the author, were acquainted with Ceylon upwards of thirty years ago can best appreciate the change which has taken place in its hotel accommodation. The Galle Face Hotel of those days was a mere shanty compared to its present successor. Its bedrooms were merely divisions marked off by canvas screens. The remarks of occupants of several rooms on either side of one could be distinctly heard.[93]

The Galle Face Hotel was rebuilt and substantially enlarged in 1894 (see figure 32). The architecture of the new building was described as being 'in the Renaissance style' and the interior arrangements [were] on a scale befitting the imposing exterior'.[94] As with the internal arrangements of clubs established within the Subcontinent, hotels such as the Galle Face replicated the domestic spaces of the bungalow and lower-roomed house, but on a vast scale. An extended account of the public spaces of this hotel merits quotation in full, as much of the description could be applied to the majority of the new 'palace hotels' established in the Presidency cities of India and elsewhere in Ceylon.

In 1907, Arnold Wright provided a fulsome account of the hotel a few years after it had been rebuilt. In addition to a 'lofty reception hall [which] leads into the various wide verandahs' and a ball-room 'where weekly dances are held',

> the principal dining room … which has a verandah facing the sea … is fitted with electric fans. This is the largest hall in the island, the dimensions being,

32 The new 'palace' hotel of the late nineteenth century. The Galle Face Hotel, Colombo, Ceylon, *c.* 1895.

76 by 39 feet and 30 feet high … the reading room and library, which faces the sea, is the finest situated room in the hotel and is provided liberally with English and foreign newspapers. The drawing-room also with a verandah facing Galle Face Esplanade, is handsomely furnished and contains a Bechstein Grand piano; while the Public Billiard Room is equipped with four Burroughs and Watts tables and all the usual appointments in the best style. The dimensions of the room are 60 by 39 feet and 30 feet high … There is also a small private billiard room for the use of ladies … suites of rooms with private bathrooms attached and elaborately furnished apartments are provided on every floor.[95]

The sheer scale of these new 'palace hotels' (the refurbished Galle Face Hotel could accommodate more than 350 diners) and the lavishly appointed interiors 'in the best style', created new social spaces within the Subcontinent. Such spaces, which derived their inspiration from both the grand English country house and Indian princely interiors of the era, were accessible to anyone who had the means to pay the rate for a room (or even someone, who simply wished to make use of the public rooms), thus pandering to a notion of the British as successors to the Indian princely tradition and also the Western trope of the luxurious Orient, where indolence and comfort were unsurpassed.

Around 1900, the palace hotel, although making reference to the colonial domestic interior, created new interior spaces – although archaic in terms of their inspiration – where, in addition to white, middle-class Englishmen, less privileged groups within the colonial culture (in terms of their full participation in social life) could engage in the everyday practices of modernity. Because they were open to all comers who were dressed in appropriate manner, these hotels helped to obscure or disrupt the rigid lines of status in Anglo-Indian society, which could be strictly enforced within other venues such as the club. The ambience of the palace hotel created a series of public but domesticated interior spaces. Here, issues of status could more easily be negotiated and members of the colonial culture, whose background or employment excluded them from many of the social activities practiced by the colonial elite, could engage in the everyday activities of that elite and lay claim to a social status (or at least a simulacrum of that status) above that to which they could aspire in the home country. Even on a smaller scale, the public lobbies and circulation areas of many hotels in India built after 1900 evoked the middle-class drawing rooms and halls of the homeland (see figure 33).

33 Simulating the domestic environment in the Anglo-Indian hotel. Laurie's Hotel, Agra, Drawing Room, *c.* 1920.

In addition to the location of such hotels in the great colonial seaports of the Subcontinent, the growth in the number of hill stations (established in India and Ceylon throughout the last half of the nineteenth century) led to an increasing number of hotels being built at these cool, mountain sanatoria. The hill stations of the British Raj have been discussed in a wide range of previous publications.[96] However, few of these publications address the growth in the number of hotels which were built within these Anglo-Indian highland enclaves, and such publications are mostly concerned with the private domain of the rented house. The increase in the number of hotels built at Coonoor, Darjeeling, Mussoorie, Ootacamund and other hill stations supported an influx of Anglo-Indians as well as Indians into these resorts, and gradually contributed to the erosion of their principal function as locations that 'offered isolated, exclusive milieus, where [white, middle-class] sojourners could feel at home'.[97]

Hotels such as the Hillgrove and Gray's in Coonoor, and the Rockville in Darjeeling all offered accommodation which was promoted as being

Queen's Hotel, Kandy, Ceylon

34 Hotel for Western tourists on the Asian 'Grand Tour'. Queen's Hotel, Kandy, Ceylon, *c.* 1910.

35 A standard feature of the Anglo-Indian hotel. 'The Reading Room', Queen's Hotel, Kandy, Ceylon, *c.* 1920.

centrally located close to the main attractions of the hill station, as well as offering sporting activities such as tennis or badminton, and special suites for bachelors and families.[98] Further distinction was added by the announcement that a hotel was 'under European management'. Growing centres of cultural tourism within the Subcontinent, such as Kandy in Ceylon, also supported the development of new or refurbished hotels, many built around 1900, to cater for those Europeans engaged in an Asiatic 'Grand Tour' (see figures 34 and 35).

During the 1920s, many established hotels such as the Connemara in Madras underwent refurbishment and their interiors were transformed into local adaptations of the *moderne* or Art Deco style. The Connemara's bar area was converted into a cocktail bar with streamlined and metal-trimmed counter and mural behind the bar depicting a young, fashionable European woman in an athletic pose. The bedrooms were also furnished in a commercial version of the *moderne* style, supplied by local cabinetmakers in Madras; each suite was supplied with comfortable armchairs, low tables, each with rounded edges, and stepped bookcases.[99]

The larger hotels within the urban centres of the Subcontinent, in addition to creating new spaces for leisure and spectacle, may also be conceptualized within a colonial 'exhibitionary complex'. This point was made as early as 1926, when Aldous Huxley defined the Taj Mahal Hotel in Bombay, built by an Indian entrepreneur, in the following terms: 'the gigantic Taj …

combines the style of the South Kensington Natural History Museum with that of an Indian pavilion at the International Exhibition'.[100]

Envisioning the modern interior: photographic studios and cinemas

Two arenas where modernity and a sense of progress were constituted within the Subcontinent were, during the last half of the nineteenth century, the photographic studio and, from the second decade of the twentieth century, the cinema. In a similar fashion to that of the club and the hotel, these venues formed significant locales where both the European population and members of the local population could reaffirm their identities (or acquire new ones), both social and cultural.

After a faltering start in the 1840s, photography became more firmly established in both India and Ceylon in the following decade. Within India, as John Falconer has suggested, there was a 'remarkable efflorescence of photographic activity' which was typified especially by the output of amateur photographers, the establishment of photographic societies in the three presidencies and active government sponsorship of the medium.[101] Between the 1860s and the 1890s both British and Indian commercial photographers established studios in Calcutta, Bombay and Madras and produced increasing quantities of landscape views, representations of the local population and portraits.

Less attention in the secondary literature has been paid to local consumption of locally produced photographic outputs, including portrait work, than to the views of the ancient sites of the Subcontinent, depictions of local peoples and picturesque representations of majestic landscapes, largely commissioned by Europeans. However, photographic portraiture, especially after the development of technology which allowed for the reproduction of numerous prints from a single negative and the exponential growth in demand for *cartes-de-visite*, became the staple fare of many commercial photographers within the Subcontinent.

A number of commercial photographers of European origin established studios throughout India, and these included, for example, Bourne and Shepherd, with premises in Simla, Calcutta (1867) and Bombay (1870); Herzog and Higgins, Mhow (1894–1921); G.W. Lawrie and Co., Naini Tal (1883–1921); Robert Phillips, Darjeeling (1870–1880s); Thomas Rust, Calcutta and Allahabad (1860s–1910s); Wiele and Klein, Madras and Ootacamund (1882–1900s), among others.[102] Studios in the main urban settlements were also set up by local professional photographers such as the Bengal Photographers, Calcutta; P. Gomes and Co. and the Eos Photographic Company, both of Kalbadevi Road, Bombay.[103] One of the most prolific producers of local photographic portraits in Bombay was Hurrichand Chintamon, who sent a large number of *carte-de-visite* portraits to the Paris International Exhibition of 1867. Although a local photographer, Chintamon's portraits are ambivalent in their depiction of local people. They can be conceptualized as being produced within a Westernized visual discourse, and many of his portraits can be viewed as ethnographic representations of local people.[104] However, the setting within the studio, the physical props and the attributes such as books or other personal possessions reinforcing the subjectivity of the sitter tend to counteract this reading of the image. The figures within his *carte-de-visite* portraits, it could be argued, are caught in the process of negotiating their identity within colonial society.

The development of photography in Ceylon followed similar lines to that within the larger Indian settlements, although with a considerably smaller potential market the number of photographers able to make a living on the island was reduced. While the celebrated photographer Julia Margaret Cameron lived in Ceylon from 1875 until her death, British commercial photographers and photographic companies such as Charles T. Scowen, Skeen and Co., the Colombo Apothecaries Co., and Plâté and Co., in addition to a number of local photographers such as Joseph Lawton, Adolphus William André and Mme del Tufo, all established studios in Colombo and Kandy in the last quarter of the nineteenth century.[105]

A large part of the stock in trade of all these photographers was the portrait in cabinet card or *carte-de-visite* format. These studios became spaces where both European and local customers could acquire 'an elevated and intensified identity' and where the props, such as fashionable European-style pedestals, couches, davenports, low chairs and backcloths painted with classical or other scenes, recreated an idealized Western, middle-class space.[106] This space, in which members of the local population especially could represent themselves in the same surroundings and in the same attitudes or poses as the European elite, created locations which acclimatized the indigenous elite to modernity and its new social practices. Many of the more fashionable photographic studios within the Subcontinent were also venues where both local and European clients imbibed new styles of decoration. At the turn of the twentieth century, the 'New Art' style began to manifest itself in the material culture of everyday life within the Subcontinent, much to the dismay of astute observers such as Ananda and Ethel Coomaraswamy.[107] For example, this imported style appeared in the graphic design of photographic cabinet cards, on the painted backcloths and in the style of furniture used as props within the studio.

Following the development of photographic studios within metropolitan centres of the Subcontinent, and the emergence of theatres in the colonial city, another public space which communicated the concept of progress and modernity was the cinema.[108] Cinemas, or cinema theatres as they were described in the early years of the twentieth century, developed from the traditional form of the theatre. Victorian theatre evolved from a period of neglect to become one of the most powerful forms of entertainment in the late nineteenth century. The domestication of the Victorian theatre, in order to encourage attendance through the presentation of a 'respectable' front, has been discussed elsewhere and it has been argued that

> rather than creating a venue, which through its décor challenged the spectator, the theatre instead encouraged reassurance. It employed a decorative idiom in keeping with the most fashionable tastes. The lobbies and circulation spaces became extensions of the home environment and bridged the gap between the comfort of the home environment and the possible threat of a public venue.[109]

In a similar fashion, cinemas followed the trend set by the theatre and 'employed a decorative idiom in keeping with the most fashionable tastes'. This trend culminated in the great Art Deco cinema interiors of the Subcontinent. Early examples of cinemas within a colonial city such as Madras included the Bioscope, Popham's Broadway, The Globe (renamed The Roxy), Purasawalkam High Road, which was built in 1918, and the Electric Theatre, Mount Road, constructed in 1913 by Warwick Major and Reginald Eyre for the express purpose of screening silent films. These early structures were fairly basic in terms of their construction. The Electric Theatre, for example, was built with a corrugated and galvanised iron roof and a gabled front of plastered brick. The theatre was, however, tastefully decorated inside with blue and red drapes, the former covered with stars. Seating within the Electric Theatre was divided into five classes including a specially screened-off area for local women in *purdah*.[110]

The first such building expressly built to show films in Bombay was the Regal, which was constructed in 1933.[111] The British-trained architect Charles F. Stevens designed this structure, with interior decoration by the Czech designer Karl Schara. In addition to its *moderne* or Art Deco façade, the Regal's interiors presented modern social spaces such as a café, soda fountain and grand balcony, all of which were much influenced by the Hollywood film sets of the day. The interior spaces of the cinema, such as lobbies and foyers, were locations where the film-goer could enact a new and imagined persona by (momentarily) inhabiting the modern, glamorous and filmic interior spaces of the cinema.[112]

Other cinemas such as the Eros and the Metro, built in Bombay in 1938, recreated similarly modern and glamorous interior spaces, especially by the inclusion of strikingly decorated foyers. As Arthur Marwick has argued in the European context,

[a] crucial element of 'modern', 'mass' society [in the 1920s and 30s] was the way technology was exploited, particularly in the development of mass communications ... film [increasingly] gained prestige among middle class and respectable upper-working class audiences.[113]

Within the Indian context, the advent of cinema offered an alternative vision of the West that was not filtered through a British perspective. Images of a modern and glamorous West were presented to local audiences where the role models were no longer the British elite but the stars of Hollywood, in addition to the home-grown stars of the nascent Indian film industry. American film actors such as Joan Crawford, Anita Page, Jean Harlow and Norma Shearer offered Indian cinema audiences visions of emancipated, modern and glamorous women.[114] As Marwick suggests, at the end of the 1920s 'sound films ... forcefully established fashions, set agendas and reinforced the position of America as both a prototype of everything modern ... and yet a place ... different and distant from Europe'.[115] Cinemas also manifested a new feature of urban life within Bombay and other metropolitan centres in India, namely the transition from private enjoyment for the affluent family to mass leisure activities for the ordinary man and woman, in fact 'cinemas sprang up everywhere: palaces of democracy and of dreams'.[116]

The period after 1920 in India was one of economic growth from which both local businessmen and manufacturers benefited, particularly within the textile sector of Bombay and its hinterland.[117] This period witnessed the growth of a new indigenous urban elite, who were beginning to turn their backs on the outward manifestations of tradition. In both its external and internal arrangements, its visual culture (such as film posters and magazines), together with the *mise-en-scène* of the films on the screen, the cinema introduced local mass audiences to a vibrant and modern new style, later termed 'Art Deco'.[118] The local urban middle class also formed a growing section of the cinema-going public, and were enthralled by big-budget films such as *Fashionable India*, directed by Mohan Sinha in 1935, about living in a modern age. Divia Patel notes that such films reflected 'the ethos of the time and the life-style that the new urban elite of Bombay aspired to'.[119] These new social spaces of the modern age also provided the local middle class with a new visual vocabulary which could be applied as appropriate in the furnishing of their own homes.

In addition to the dream-like spaces which the physical structure of the cinema presented to Indian audiences, idealized domestic interiors were also portrayed on the cinema screen. Indian films of the 1930s and 1940s usually depicted the domestic interior in a realistic if glamorized manner. Elite houses on screen were usually depicted as an amalgam of Western and Eastern elements, containing such domestic spaces as a staircase, library, bedrooms, hall, music room, garden and *pooja* (worship) room.[120] Rachel Dwyer has discussed the variety of meanings associated with the staircase within the Indian film, including its representation as a liminal space, a boundary between the private and public zones of the interior, and as a replacement for the courtyard in the traditional Indian *haveli* or elite urban house.[121] Indian audiences could assimilate the style of decoration of the room settings in these films as well as the manner in which the actors inhabited the fictive spaces on screen.

Shopping in the Raj: consumption and colonial material culture

Shopping, as an Anglo-Indian activity, began to converge with practice in Europe during the last decade of the nineteenth century, although with some fundamental differences. Shops for Europeans within the colonial urban environment were not isolated phenomena or islands of Anglicization, but can usefully be assessed as integral parts of a network of routes followed by the British elite through the Indian city. Within metropolitan centres of the Subcontinent, palace hotels, large shops and the emergent department stores of the late nineteenth and early twentieth centuries could be defined as part of a network of intersecting sites which Tony Bennett, in a different context, has described as an 'exhibitionary complex'.[122]

However, it is over-deterministic simply to map the activity of shopping in the department stores of the European metropolis onto the India Subcontinent. By virtue of the relative homogeneity of the small Anglo-Indian middle-class population and also the absence of a white industrial working class, 'European shops' within Indian urban centres catered exclusively for the luxury end of the market.[123] The act of looking, initially by obtaining visual pleasure from shop-window displays, it has been argued, was an increasingly significant aspect of the activity of shopping in late nineteenth-century Europe. Window displays devised by the department stores in Europe were intended to stimulate unsatisfied desire, attract attention of the – usually female – passer-by and entice her to enter the store.[124] This casual browsing was less feasible within the Indian climate, and shoppers tended to go straight to the shop they had selected. By the early twentieth century, however, some of the larger European shops within Calcutta and Madras had addressed this issue, and new shop developments often incorporated colonnaded arcades as part of their frontage. These arcades sheltered the passer-by from the sultry climate and also created a zone of transition between the Indian street and the shop.

By the mid-nineteenth century, retailing within the urban settlements of India was divided into a number of sectors, the main components of which comprised the European retail trade, Indian-owned modern retail companies and the bazaar sector of the city's markets. The top end of the European retail trade in the early nineteenth century was exemplified by shops such as Taylor and Co., Calcutta where Anglo-Indians could buy fine imported European porcelains, glassware, books, paintings and other articles at a high cost.[125] Such shops were not simply locations to purchase goods, but were also becoming arenas of spectacle where the jaded eye of the British resident within India could contemplate the visual delights of an array of European goods and, through their consumption of these products from the homeland, distance themselves from local material culture.

In 1837, Emma Roberts described how European shops in Calcutta attracted custom:

> the only shops in Calcutta to make a shew [*sic*] on the outside are those chemists and druggists, who bring all the London passion for display to a foreign country ... the European jeweller's shops are large and handsome; they do not make shew on the outside but the interiors are splendid [with marble floors and glass display cases].[126]

During the first half of the nineteenth century, shopping in a locally-owned establishment provided access to a wide range of goods (many of which were imported from Europe). However, this experience was recorded in the accounts of contemporary commentators less as an enticing or soothing activity than as an unusual and slightly disturbing one. Writing in 1838, Mrs Postans described the interior of a Parsi-owned shop in the Fort, Bombay in the following manner:

> the Parsee shops [within the Fort] are innumerable. The best is kept by Jangerjee Nasserawanjee, who vends goods of all descriptions ... On either side of [the] open door are fixed benches, where may usually be seen, couchant a pair of ... Parsees ... The shop is large and dark; the walls surrounded with glass cases, filled with fine French china, bijouterie, gold, lace, sauces, brandied fruits, riding whips and other European superfluities. The central avenue is flanked with cases of jewellery, French clocks and all descriptions of nicknackery.[127]

On the floor of the shop were stacked hams, cheeses, cases of sardines; and hanging from the ceiling and walls were bird-cages, lamps and 'coloured French lithographs'. Despite the fact that most of the goods were of European origin, the recumbent figures of the shop staff, as well as the darkened and crowded nature of the interior, were presented as elements which counteracted the activity of shopping as a pleasant and leisurely experience. Furthermore, the material culture of the shop interior insistently reminded Anglo-Indian customers that they were engaged in a familiar yet alien experience. Recent scholarship has noted a shift, in the early years of the nineteenth century, away from the consumption of local products toward a marked preference for 'Europe goods'.[128] By 1850, to satisfy this demand, local bazaar traders were able to supply a range of European goods which had previously been imported by European shopkeepers. However, in order to obtain these goods, one had to venture into the insalubrious local bazaars.

Since the 1860s in Europe, department stores such as Bon Marché and Magasin du Louvre in Paris, as Michelle Henning has suggested, took inspiration for their interior décor from the museum.[129] It has been argued that the museum and the exhibition were central to the development of nineteenth-century visual and material culture. Erica Rappaport has discussed the influence of the Great Exhibition on nineteenth-century capitalism and consumer culture and how theorists such as Walter Benjamin characterized the way in which exhibitions 'built up' commodities 'glorifying' their exchange values.[130] As she notes,

> department stores and exhibition halls certainly share similarities. In both locales, new glass and iron technology, special lighting, grandiose architecture and [display] of diverse products created 'theatrical excess' intended to overwhelm if also delight the spectator.

The development of the department store within the Subcontinent was also linked to the exhibition. Exhibitions had been staged in India since the 1850s in such locations as Jaipur, Madras, Nagpur and Calcutta. The first international exhibition took place in Calcutta in 1883. As Peter Hoffenberg has suggested, the six thousand visitors each day who saw the exhibition between December 1883 and March 1884 experienced an event that was 'part museum, carnival, department store and bazaar (since some exhibits could be purchased in the sales area), the popular nineteenth century exhibition as a whole was far greater than the sum of its parts'.[131]

As discussed earlier, a few European retail outlets were located within the grand Anglo-Indian hotels, such as the Great Eastern in Calcutta. These venues offered a hybrid consumer experience, combining as they did a haven from the Indian street, visual spectacle, novelty in terms of goods on display and encounters with other members of the Anglo-Indian community. During the middle decades of the nineteenth century the most prestigious shopping street in Calcutta was Old Court House Street and, after 1860, both Bentinck Street and Park Street also became fashionable retail zones (see figure 36).[132] This illustration depicts the premises at number 12, Old Court House Street of F. & C. Osler, Birmingham-based retailers of glassware, including chandeliers and glass furniture. The façade of the shop owes more to a grand Anglo-Indian domestic dwelling than to a retail outlet. The interior of Osler's premises was filled with display cabinets and arrays of hanging chandeliers and other forms of lighting.[133] Old Court House Street

36 One of the main European retail establishments in late nineteenth-century India, F. & C. Osler's Glassware Showrooms, 12 Old Court House Street, Calcutta, *c*. 1875.

was gradually superseded by more fashionable areas and, as Chris Furedy has noted, 'Park Street came into its own when the large department stores located there, taking advantage of the space to design large and impressive premises'.[134]

The first department store proper in Calcutta was the outlet of Francis, Harrison, Hathaway & Co., established in 1864. Hall and Anderson's premises on the Esplanade, Calcutta also described itself as a 'general departmental store' with special departments in 'furniture, china and glass, cutlery, stationery, outfitting and dress making, millinery, drapery and footwear'.[135]

Although Colombo in Ceylon was smaller than the Presidency cities of India, it boasted a number of department stores in the commercial hub of the Fort by the turn of the twentieth century. One of the largest of such stores was Cargill's Ltd., founded in Kandy in 1844. Between 1902 and 1906, the firm built a new department store in York Street, Colombo which contained the following departments: ladies' drapery, dressmaking, millinery,

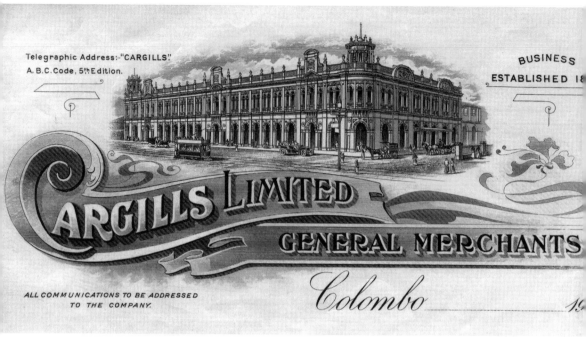

Telegraphic Address:-"CARGILLS",
A.B.C.Code, 5th Edition.

BUSINESS
ESTABLISHED 18

CARGILLS LIMITED
GENERAL MERCHANTS

ALL COMMUNICATIONS TO BE ADDRESSED
TO THE COMPANY.

Colombo   19

37 One of the new department stores of colonial South Asia. Cargill's Limited, General Merchants, Colombo [*c.* 1905].

household furnishings, wines and spirits, groceries, horse-feed, gentlemens' tailoring and outfitting, and drugs and dispensary (see figure 37).[136] The bewildering range and variety of goods and services available within such stores is illustrated by the list of departments recorded in H.W. Cave and Co., Chatham Street. As a contemporary commentator noted,

> the firm have large stocks of pianos and American organs of various sizes; they have a fancy goods department, where perfumery, smokers' requisites and all the usual articles in this line can be obtained; [an] up-to-date stock of pictures which may be framed in any style on the premises; silver and leather goods … a large stock of books and stationery is kept; in the Sporting Goods department, rickshaws, billiard-tables, Singer and Alldays' cycles and appliances for every sport and pastime are to be found … printing and bookbinding … cycle repairs, racquet stringing and cabinet work are executed on the premises.[137]

The growth of department stores within the Subcontinent was supported not only by middle-class European consumers. From the 1860s, growing amounts of business were done with the increasingly Westernized local middle class.[138] Shopping for European goods within the new and Westernized environments of the colonial department store aided assimilation of the local middle class into Western modes of consumption. Both the material goods purchased and the practices enacted during the process of shopping inflected the manner in which this group defined themselves. In addition to patronizing the local bazaar, the Bengali, Ceylonese and Bombay middle class acquired new habits of consumption within the increasing numbers of 'universal providers' established at the heart of the colonial city.

Public space within urban centres of the Subcontinent has been discussed in this chapter as an arena where the Anglo-Indian could navigate routes through the colonial city which mitigated or avoided the local. Such spaces offered reassuring and supportive havens where the local was circumvented and Europeans could re-affirm their national and cultural identity. Colonial public space was so significant to Anglo-Indians because the domestic sphere within India and Ceylon was compromised by local factors, resulting in the creation of what has been termed in another context 'anxious homes'.[139] The material culture of the club and the hotel, the arrays of Western goods in the department store connected British residents in India to the ordinary things of home. The design of colonial public space and its contents evoked sense memories of similar spaces in Europe and helped stabilize Anglo-Indian personhood. Rather than distinguishing between the private domestic sphere of the colonial home and the public space of empire, this chapter has sought to interpret the latter within a single analytic frame, as an integral part of a supra-colonial space which encompasses both the bungalow and that public space beyond. Many colonial public spaces discussed above were treated by Anglo-Indians as extensions of the home environment and served to mitigate the strange and troubling qualities of the local environment. It helped them connect with their small exiled community and that larger community in the homeland. However, it is argued here that these connections were evoked less through discourses than through the material culture of such public space and by, for example, such tangible things in the European club as 'the comfortable old smoking-room that has club chairs, potted palms, fly-blown hunting prints and … an air somehow evocative of warmed-up gravy and cold mutton'.[140]

Notes

1 T. Bennett, *The Birth of the Museum: history, theory, politics* (London, 1995), cited in D. Boswell and J. Evans (eds), *Representing the Nation: histories, heritage and museums* (London and New York, 1999), pp. 332–61.

2 E.M. Forster, *A Passage to India* (London, 1924, republished, 1987), p. 60.

3 For example, *The Imperial Census of 1881; operations and results in the Presidency of Bombay, including Sind*, vol. 1 (Bombay, 1882), the total population of Bombay City was recorded as 748,309. Of this number, 3,910 are recorded as having been born in Great Britain.

4 Catherine Hall, *Civilising Subjects: metropole and colony in the English imagination, 1830–1867* (Cambridge, 2002), p. 65.

5 A. Srivathsan, 'City and public life: history of public spaces in Chennai', in K. Kalpana and F. Schiffer (eds), *Madras: the architectural heritage* (Chennai, 2003), p. 207.

6 Srivathsan, 'City and public life', p. 207.

7 Srivathsan, 'City and public life', pp. 214–15.

8 This phrase is Anthony King's.

9 A.D. King, *Colonial Urban Development: culture, social power and environment* (London and Boston, 1976), p. 175.

10 Charles Allen (ed.), *Plain Tales from the Raj: images of British India in the twentieth century* (London, 1975); the same author, *Raj: a scrapbook of British India, 1877–1947* (London, 1977). Both Anthony King and Elizabeth Collingham have briefly discussed the European club within the Subcontinent. See the latter's *Imperial Bodies: the physical experience of the Raj, c. 1800–1947* (Cambridge, 2001), pp. 162, 190–3.

11 King, *Colonial Urban Development*, p. 87. See also Mrinalini Sinha, 'Britishness, clubbability and the colonial public sphere', in Tony Ballantyne and Antoinette Burton (eds), *Bodies in Contact: re-thinking colonial encounters in world history* (Durham, NC and London, 2005), pp. 183–200.

12 King, *Colonial Urban Development*, p. 173.

13 Bernard Cohn, *An Anthropologist among the Historians and Other Essays* (New Delhi, 1998), p. 520–1.

14 Cohn, *An Anthropologist among the Historians*, pp. 520–1. In Ceylon a similar situation arose, although on a smaller scale. Throughout the nineteenth century, the higher ranks of the Ceylon Civil Service were dominated by a small number of families whose members had intermarried. Chief among the members of the so-called 'Family Compact' on the island were the Templers and the Layards. See K.M. de Silva, 'Sir James Emerson Tennent: colonial administrator and historian', *Journal of the Royal Asiatic Society of Sri Lanka*, vol. 41 (1998), pp. 15–16.

15 The Madras Club was established in the house of a Mr White.

16 *The New Calcutta Directory for 1856* (Calcutta, 1856), p. 91.

17 *Annual Report of the Ootacamund Club for 1866* (Ootacamund, 1866), n.p.

18 *H. Don Carolis and Sons, Upholsterers, the Largest and Most Experienced Manufacturers in Asia of Furniture for the House, Office, Club, Hotel, Showroom …* (Colombo, 1908), p. V. The firm listed some of the social institutions it had supplied including Prince's Club, Colombo, Monk's Hotel, Calcutta, The Darrawella Club, Grand Central Hotel, Nuwara Eliya, Hill Club, Nuwara Eliya, Colombo Club and the Kandy Club. I am grateful to Mala Weerasekera for allowing me access to this publication.

19 London, British Library: Mss. Eur. D 1236/4, Headlam papers.

20 *Dalhousie Institute, Calcutta; report for the year ending 31 October 1888* (Calcutta, 1888), p. 2. Periodicals subscribed to included *The Graphic, The Illustrated London News, Punch, Home News, Sporting and Dramatic News, The Queen, The World, The Field, The Scotsman, Harper's Magazine, Fortnightly Review*; Newspapers included *The Englishman, Indian Daily News, Madras Times, Indigo Planter's Gazette, The Empress, Times of India (Bombay)* and *Calcutta Gazette*.

21 London, British Library: Mss.Eur. A225, *NAGPUR, NAGPUR HUNT CLUB*, (Nagpur, no date but *c.* 1922), 'Rules of the Nagpur Hunt Club', no. 2 'In order to become a

member of the … Club, a candidate must be proposed by one member and seconded by another … 4. Election of candidates for full and temporary membership shall be by ballot of members; one black ball in five to exclude'.

22 Sinha, 'Britishness, clubbability and the colonial public sphere', pp. 183–200.

23 Allen (ed.), *Plain Tales from the Raj*, pp. 118–19.

24 For example, in 1898, a Ladies' Pavilion was built as an annexe to the Madras Club. This was known by the derogatory term of 'Moorghi-Khana [hen-room]. In 1907, after the construction of an annexe to the Bangalore Club, women were finally elected as members, but as members of the annexe rather than of the club proper.

25 The rules of the Bangalore Club were amended in 1915 to allow for the admission of Indian officers. The rules of many clubs did not state that Indians were not permitted to join, but the process of election ensured the operation of this tacit form of exclusion. Although defeated at a general meeting of Bangalore Club members in 1897, a resolution to amend club rule number III was put to the membership, which stated that 'with the exception of His Highness the Maharaja of Mysore, no native of India shall be qualified to become a member of the club'.

26 Collingham, *Imperial Bodies*, p. 162.

27 M. Bhaktavatsala (ed.), *Bangalore Club: a club's world* (Bangalore, 1993), 'Minutes of the Subcommittee', 11 March 1898.

28 *Bangalore Club*, 'Minutes of the Subcommittee', 27 April 1905. No mention is made of compensation for injury to any of the local servants on the receiving end of Lieut. White's high jinks.

29 *Bangalore Club*, 'Minutes of the Subcommittee', 15 May 1902. If the uniforms of local servants were perceived as not Indian enough, then other aspects of the material culture of the club with which the British came into contact were often emphatically English. In February 1901, the Subcommittee of Bangalore Club ordered, at great cost, from the Army & Navy Stores, London extensive sets of electro-plated crockery and glassware.

30 Forster, *A Passage to India*, pp. 171–80. After the alleged assault on Adela Quested, the British community in Chandrapore gather at the club to exchange information and receive reassurance from the most senior British administrator in the district. 'The club was fuller than usual, and several parents had brought their children into the rooms reserved for adults, which gave the air of the Residency at Lucknow'.

31 King, *Colonial Urban Development*, p. 87.

32 See C. Wilk, 'The healthy body culture', in C. Wilk (ed.), *Modernism: designing a new world 1914–39* (London, 2006), pp. 250–66. One of the iconic European sporting figures of the 1920s was the French tennis champion Suzanne Lenglen.

33 R. Holt, *Sport and the British: a modern history* (Oxford, 1989), p. 206. See also J.A. Mangan, *The Games Ethic and Imperialism: aspects of the diffusion of an ideal* (London, 1998).

34 Holt, *Sport and the British*, p. 206.

35 Holt, *Sport and the British*, p. 208.

36 M. Girouard, *Life in the English Country House: a social and architectural history* (London, 1978), pp. 235–6 and 297. Trade directories of British firms within the Presidency towns of India separately listed billiard-table makers. See *The Madras New Almanac for 1852* (Madras, 1852), p. 177.

37 A photograph by Roger Fenton in the J. Paul Getty Collection depicts the interior of

'the Billiard Room at Mentmore [House, Bucks.]' in 1858, catalogue number 72. In this image, a group of women are shown playing billiards.

38 Rev. C. Acland, *A Popular Account of the Manners and Customs of India* (London, 1847), p. 155.

39 University of Cambridge, Centre of South Asian Studies: Scott papers, 20 April 1885.

40 *The Bengal Directory, 1875* (Calcutta, Bombay and London, 1875), p. 409.

41 J. Williams, *Cricket and Race* (Oxford and New York, 2001), pp. 16–28.

42 The Madras Cricket Club (the MCC) was founded in 1846 and moved to Chepauk, Madras in 1865. The MCC clubhouse, which was built shortly after the move to Chepauk, was constructed in the form of a colonial bungalow with low-hipped, tiled roof and verandah.

43 Williams, *Cricket and Race*, p. 28.

44 Lt. Col. G.J. Ivey, *The Club Directory; a general guide or index to the London and County clubs and those of … British colonial possessions* (London, 1879), p. iii.

45 H.R. Pankridge, *A Short History of the Bengal Club (1827–1927)* (Calcutta, 1927), p. 1, cited in Sinha, 'Britishness, clubbability and the colonial public sphere', p. 184.

46 Kate Platt, *The Home and Health in India and the Tropical Colonies* (London, 1923), pp. 27 and 53, cited in King, *Colonial Urban Development*, pp. 87–8.

47 The Bengal Club House, at 33 Chowringhee Road, was the residence of Thomas Babington Macaulay between 1834 and 1838.

48 *W. Newman and Co.'s Handbook to Calcutta; historical and descriptive with a plan of the city* (Calcutta, 1892), p. 307.

49 *W. Newman and Co.'s Handbook to Calcutta*, p. 310.

50 Cambridge, Centre of South Asian Studies: E.A. Kenyon papers, 15 November 1896.

51 *W. Newman and Co.'s Handbook to Calcutta*, p. 311.

52 Such as, for example, the Calcutta Gun Club (1881), the Calcutta Turf Club (1861), the Calcutta Golf Club (1829), the Calcutta Rowing Club (1891) and the Photographic Society of India.

53 Kalpana and Schiffer (eds), *Madras*, p. 177.

54 Allen (ed.), *Plain Tales from the Raj*, p. 124.

55 James Mackenzie Maclean, *A Guide to Bombay; historical, statistical and descriptive* (Bombay, 1876), p. 246. 'The Byculla Club has had great prestige, but its situation is very much against it. It is now nearly surrounded by mills and other buildings'.

56 Maclean, *A Guide to Bombay*, p. 246.

57 *Bombay through the Camera* (Bombay, c. 1904) illustrates the main clubs of the era together with their 'chambers' or accommodation blocks. Plate 4 of this publication is devoted to the Royal Bombay Yacht Club.

58 Gillian Tindall, *City of Gold: the biography of Bombay* (London, 1982), p. 25.

59 The watercolour of the Ootacamund club is inscribed 'The "Club House"; Ootacamund, 1852, a splendid building; beautifully furnished; accommodation for about 30 members; with library; Billiard Rooms …'

60 Kalpana and Schiffer (eds), *Madras*, p. 167.

61 King, *Colonial Urban Development*, p. 260.

62 A. Wright (ed.), *Twentieth Century Impressions of Ceylon* (London, Durban.and Colombo, 1907), p. 913.

63 I. Raheem and P. Colin Thomé, *Images of British Ceylon: nineteenth century photography of Sri Lanka* (Singapore, 2000), p. 123.

64 Wright (ed.), *Twentieth Century Impressions*, p. 419.

65 Wright (ed.), *Twentieth Century Impressions*, p. 261.

66 J.D.N. Banks, *The History of the Hill Club* (Colombo, 1988), prologue and p. 3.

67 Anthony King briefly discusses Indian hotels, as does Jan Morris. Ismeth Raheem and Michael Roberts touch on the hotels of colonial Ceylon.

68 Beni Pershad, *Law of Landlord and Tenant and of Hotel-Keeper and Guest* (Lahore, 1902), p. 145. Katherine Grier, *Culture and Comfort: parlor making and middle class identity, 1850–1930* (Washington, D.C. and London, 1997), p. 32.

69 G. Hutton-Taylor, *An Illustrated Guide to India and its Hotels* (Calcutta, 1899), p. lv.

70 Even as late as 1909, Maud Diver reiterated this mythical Anglo-Indian hospitality when she wrote that 'it is part of the immemorial order of things, in the land of the open door, where the wandering bachelor drops into any meal … where a guest may come for a week, and stay for a month'. Maud Diver, *The Englishwoman in India* (Edinburgh and London, 1909), p. 49.

71 *The Bengal Directory and Annual Register for the Year 1840* (Calcutta, 1840), p. 333. One of the earliest sets of photographs of Calcutta, produced by Frederick Fiebig around 1851, includes an image of Spence's Hotel.

72 Emma Roberts, *Scenes and Characteristics of Hindoostan; with sketches of Anglo-Indian society* (London, 1837), cited in J. Losty, *Calcutta: city of palaces* (London, 1990), p. 118.

73 University of Cambridge, Centre of South Asian Studies: Berners Papers, Frances Janet Wells, letter 14 January 1854.

74 Col. H.R. Goulding, *Old Lahore; reminiscences of a resident* (Lahore, 1924), p. 51. 'Another hotel which did fairly good business was owned and managed by Mrs Cunningham. It was accommodated in a large bungalow on the Lower Mall'.

75 *The New Calcutta Directory for 1856*, p. 183. These hotels in the suburbs included, for example, Aguilar's Oriental Hotel, W. Dowley's Oriental Family Hotel, and W. Carpenter's Hotel.

76 *Thacker's Directory for Bengal, the North Western Provinces and the Punjab … for 1865* (London, Allahabad and Bombay, 1865), p. 345.

77 *The New Calcutta Directory for 1856*, p. 25.

78 John Beames, *Memoirs of Bengal Civilian* (London, 1896 and 2003), p. 79.

79 Edmund Hull, *The European in India; or Anglo-Indian's Vade-Mecum* (London, 1874), p. 77.

80 C. Furedy, *British Tradesmen and Shopkeepers of Calcutta, 1830–1900* (Quebec, Canadian Society for Asian Studies, May 1976), p. 6, cites William Howard Russell, *My Diary in India*, 2 vols (London, 1860), vol. 1, p. 107. Russell described the hotel in 1858.

81 *The Bengal Directory, 1875* (Calcutta, Bombay and London, 1875), pp. 414–15.

82 Hutton-Taylor, *An Illustrated Guide*, p. 45.

83 Jan Morris, *Stones of Empire: the buildings of the Raj* (Oxford, 1983, reprinted 2005), p. 147.

84 Maclean, *Guide to Bombay*, p. 246.

85 Hutton-Taylor, *An Illustrated Guide*, p. 37.

86 *A Guide to the City of Madras and its Suburbs* (Madras, 1889), p. 167.

87 *A Handbook for Travellers in India, Burma and Ceylon* (London, 1909), p. 519.

88 *A Guide to the City of Madras*, p. 167.

89 London, British Library: Mss.Eur C650, *Travellers' Bungalows in Sikkim and the Darjeeling District* (1935), pp. 1–3. See also George F. Atkinson, *Curry and Rice on Forty Plates; or the ingredients of social life at 'our station' in India* (London, 1859). This work includes a chapter and illustration entitled 'Our Traveller's Bungalow'. The illustration depicts the meagre interior of the bungalow, with shabby and bare walls, simple table, basic cot, torn punkah cloth and chair with three legs and broken arms.

90 Wright (ed.), *Twentieth Century Impressions*, p. 452.

91 Goulding, *Old Lahore*, p. 51.

92 Wright (ed.), *Twentieth Century Impressions*, p. 452.

93 Henry Cave, *The Book of Ceylon* (London, Paris and New York, 1908), p. 57.

94 Wright (ed.), *Twentieth Century Impressions*, p. 466.

95 Wright (ed.), *Twentieth Century Impressions*, p. 466.

96 See Dane Kennedy, *The Magic Mountains: hill stations and the British Raj* (Berkeley, Los Angeles and London, 1996), p. 2 for a review of other works on the hill station.

97 S. Robert Aiken, 'Early Penang hill stations', *Geographical Review*, vol. 77, no. 4 (October, 1987), p. 421, cited in D. Kennedy, *The Magic Mountains*, p. 3.

98 Hutton-Taylor, *An Illustrated Guide*, pp. 59, 60, 65, and 131.

99 Photographs owned by the Connemara Hotel, Chennai.

100 Morris, *Stones of Empire*, p. 149.

101 *A Shifting Focus: photography in India, 1850–1900* (London, 1995), p. 9.

102 John Falconer, *India: pioneering photographers, 1850–1900* (London, 2001), pp. 137–41.

103 Christopher Pinney, *Camera Indica: the social life of Indian photographs* (London, 1997), pp. 72–6.

104 London, British Library: PDP photo 1000/42 (4349). Studio portrait by Hurrichand Chintamon of three Parsees and a Parbhu (Prabhu), Bombay, *c.* 1865. This group is seated around a locally produced occasional table in European style which is used as a studio prop. On this table are placed books and other items which emphasize the intellectual interests and attributes of individual group members. The print was shown at the Paris Exhibition of 1867.

105 *Regeneration: a reappraisal of photography in Ceylon, 1850–1900* (exhib. cat., London, 2000), pp. 93–5; Raheem and Colin Thomé, *Images of British Ceylon*, pp. 137–54

106 Pinney, *Camera Indica*, p. 74.

107 Cambridge University Library, Raja Durai Singham papers, Ethel Coomaraswamy, 'Notes made in Ceylon (from 7 March 1903), Book 1'. In October 1903, Ethel Coomaraswamy noted with distaste the spread of the 'New Art' style even into the rural areas of Ceylon.

108 The first theatres were built within Indian cities from the 1880s. The Museum Theatre, Pantheon Road, Madras was constructed around 1890 – as the name implies, within

the cultural zone which comprised the museum and Connemara library complex. The exterior of the Museum Theatre was built in an Italianate style and the interior was lavishly decorated with Renaissance-style plasterwork and Corinthian capitals. The Victoria Public Hall, Poonamallee High Road, Madras, designed by R.F. Chisholm in the Romanesque style, was constructed in 1887 and used for stage performances and lectures and as a ballroom. Kalpana and Schiffer (ed.), *Madras*, pp. 124 and 190.

109 H. Maguire, 'The Victorian theatre as a home from home', *Journal of Design History*, vol. 13, no. 2 (2000), p. 107.

110 Kalpana and Schiffer (eds), *Madras*, pp. 138 and 168.

111 Rachel Dwyer and Divia Patel, *Cinema India: the visual culture of Hindi film* (London, 2002), p. 124.

112 On the influence of Hollywood films on the material culture of Britain during the early twentieth century see Anne Massey, *Hollywood Beyond the Screen: design and material culture* (Oxford and New York, 2000).

113 Arthur Marwick, 'The Great War, mass society and "modernity"', in C. Benton et al., *Art Deco, 1910–1939* (exhib. cat., London, 2003), p. 30.

114 In relation to the factors which led to Indian independence, Collingham discusses the effect of the mass presence of American troops on Indian soil during the Second World War and suggests that this undermined the traditional prestige inscribed on the body of the British within India. In a similar manner, the viewing of Hollywood films by Indian mass audiences offered an alternative vision of the West which contrasted with that presented by the British in India. See Collingham, *Imperial Bodies*, pp. 196–7.

115 Marwick, 'The Great War, mass society and "modernity"', p. 30.

116 Marwick, 'The Great War, mass society and "modernity"', p. 31.

117 Dwyer and Patel, *Cinema India*, p. 122.

118 C. Benton et al., *Art Deco*, p. 16. The term Art Deco was coined as part of the title of an exhibition held in Paris in 1966, and two years later this style label was taken up by Bevis Hillier as the title for a book on the decorative arts and design of the 1920s.

119 Dwyer and Patel, *Cinema India*, p. 124.

120 Dwyer and Patel, *Cinema India*, pp. 71–2.

121 Dwyer and Patel, *Cinema India*, pp. 72–3.

122 Bennett, *The Birth of the Museum*, cited in Boswell and Evans (eds), *Representing the Nation*, pp. 332–61.

123 For late nineteenth-century Calcutta, this is evidenced in an album of photographs at the Royal Commonwealth Society Archive, University of Cambridge, depicting the ornate and imposing premises of most of the luxury providers within the city, such as Hamilton and Co., silversmiths and jewellers, Francis, Harrison & Hathaway, general department store and Smith & Stanistreet, chemists and druggists. University of Cambridge, Royal Commonwealth Society Archive: Y3022AA, 'Original Photographic Views of Calcutta, Old and New, used in illustrating Mr Montague Massey's "Recollections of Calcutta for over half a century"', (1864–1918).

124 E. Abelson, *When Ladies Go A-Thieving: middle class shoplifters in the Victorian department store* (New York and Oxford, 1989), p. 68.

125 Jaffer, *Furniture*, pp. 44–5.

126 Roberts, *Scenes and Characteristics of Hindoostan*, cited in Losty, *Calcutta*, p. 122. In 1862, Colesworthy Grant described the variety of 'European shops' that had been established in Calcutta. Colesworthy Grant, *Anglo-Indian Domestic Life; a letter from an artist in India to his mother in England* (Calcutta, 1862), p. 39.

127 Mrs Postans, *Western India in 1838* (London, 1839), pp. 22–3.

128 Jaffer, *Furniture*, pp. 43–6.

129 M. Henning, *Museums, Media and Cultural Theory* (Maidenhead, 2006), p. 30.

130 E. Rappaport, *Shopping for Pleasure: women and the making of London's West End* (Princeton and Oxford, 2001), p. 28 and the quotation in the next sentence.

131 P.H. Hoffenberg, 'Photography and Architecture at the Calcutta International Exhibition', in M.A. Pelizzari (ed.), *Traces of India: photography, architecture and the politics of representation, 1850–1900* (New Haven and London, 2003), pp. 176–7.

132 C. Furedy, 'Development of modern elite retailing in Calcutta, 1880–1920', *Indian Economic and Social History Review*, vol. 16, no. 4 (1979), p. 380.

133 Birmingham Museum and Art Gallery Archives holds two catalogues of the stock-in-trade at Osler's Calcutta premises of 1883 and 1894 respectively. These catalogues provide a sense of the range of objects which were on display in the company's shop. An impression of the interior of Osler's Calcutta shop display can be gained from an illustration of the company's premises in Oxford Street, London in 'A Visit to Messrs. F. & C. Osler's Birmingham factories', *British Trade Review*, 1 January 1904, p. 7. See Mark Poulson, 'The glass furniture of Messrs. F. & C. Osler: an investigation of the firm's international marketing and consumption of its products within the Indian Subcontinent, *c.* 1875–1900', unpublished MA dissertation, Southampton Institute, 2003, pp. 35–6 and figs 12, 17 and 18; and J. Smith, *Osler's Crystal for Royalty and Rajahs* (London, 1991).

134 Furedy, 'Development of Modern Elite Retailing', p. 380.

135 Furedy, 'Development of Modern Elite Retailing', p. 388.

136 Wright (ed.), *Twentieth Century Impressions*, p. 457. Other European department stores in Colombo included Whiteway and Laidlaw, Colombo Apothecaries Co. Ltd., and H.W. Cave and Co.

137 Wright (ed.), *Twentieth Century Impressions*, p. 456.

138 Furedy, *British Tradesmen and Shopkeepers*, p. 10. For example, in 1874, John Davis and Co., milliners of Calcutta, advertised English-made patent-leather shoes 'for Native gentlemen and boys'.

139 This phrase is taken from the title of a special issue of the *Journal of Design History*, vol. 16, no. 3 (2003).

140 P. Scott, *The Jewel in the Crown* (London, 1973, reprinted 1983), p. 177.

Conclusion

URING the colonial period, the domestic sphere and public space within the Indian Subcontinent, together with their constellations of objects, not only served a utilitarian function but also performed important ideological and cultural work. These often unsatisfactorily furnished spaces played a significant role in the affirmation of identity, in social self-creation and, cumulatively, in the production of colonial social practices intended to sustain the Anglo-Indian persona. It has also been argued that these spaces and their furnishings objectified colonial social relations. Europeans living in South Asia inhabited an unfamiliar and disquieting environment, however superficially their immediate surroundings may have appeared to share common aspects of the homeland. The physical character of the colonial built environment and modifications to their lifestyle necessitated by local climatic conditions incessantly undermined the colonizers' sense of their East Indian home as a protected and familiar haven, as a space to shield them from the alien surroundings of the colonial city, enclave or plantation.

Although many Anglo-Indian domestic interiors were filled with objects, contemporary commentators including the authors of household-management advice literature represented this space as 'unfurnished' and lacking in comfort. In a nineteenth-century semantic sense, the word 'unfurnished' indicated certain specific wants within the interior, such as a lack of the 'polite' or softening effects of curtains and wall-paper (both of which were impractical within the Indian context). However, on another level, those commentators also alluded to a psychological need. It has been argued that one way in which objects serve memory is to 'stimulate remembering'.[1] Through their sense experiences of objects as well as particular environments and consequent evocation of memories, Anglo-Indians often vividly recalled sensations of their previous lives in England. Objects and images, it has recently been suggested, are an important part of a process termed 'priming', or 'the making of associations, some of them unconscious, by which the brain gains access to its own memory banks'.[2] These sensory experiences and the evocations that they provoked were occasionally so powerful that they effectively obliterated the present and briefly substituted a memory of home. A record of such an instance occurs in the diaries of Lady Nora Scott. In 1884, while seeking rest in the hills away from the heat of Bombay, she describes the arrival of a gift of a covered dish from an Indian neighbour: 'we took off the cloth, and there, between two pieces of banana leaf, was a little heap of strawberries, real English strawberries, with the proper English smell. *We forgot the heat and India and everything* ... We had them for lunch ... it was *so* English' (emphasis added).[3] While this memory of home was of unusual forcefulness (olfactory sensations having a particular power of evocation), related sense-provoked memories of the homeland occurred at lower levels of intensity, prompted by the material culture of the colony. This could include the Anglo-Indian room furnished with European-style furniture or with some other specific 'primer' which signified an aspect of the homeland. The dramatic intensity of the sensation experienced by Lady Scott when she saw and smelled the strawberries could not be repeated each time an Anglo-Indian entered the Westernized domestic sphere within the Subcontinent. However, in addition to their use value, the intended role of Westernized furnishings within this space was to act as both visual and bodily 'primers' which evoked associations of home. The variety, quantities, quality and arrangement of Anglo-Indian domestic material culture examined in this work presents evidence that there were many different ways in which colonial domestic space could be inhabited. Furthermore, this evidence also infers that the rhetoric of Anglo-Indian household-management advice literature was mediated by individuals in a number of ways.

Domestic space and its associated furnishings were used in different ways and had different meanings for the local and European middle class within the Subcontinent. As V.S. Pramar has suggested, at least during the nineteenth century, the local middle class, both Hindu and Muslim, conceptualized the domestic sphere as a polyvalent space. Due to the functioning of kinship arrangements within the local home, there rarely existed any concept of individual ownership of household possessions (with the exception of jewellery) within that space. Members of the family shared both space and things, with little or no personalization. Local elite houses were mostly inhabited by family members of different ages and kinship connections living under one roof, and a notion of privacy (and also comfort or being at ease in the Western sense) was largely unknown. A person's sense of identity was expressed within a local traditional household, not through material culture and a sense of interiority but through the relationship between one family member and another and that individual's place within the broader family structure. Visitors to the local house were, for the most part, other members of the family and it was less common for strangers to be admitted.

Within the European experience since the eighteenth century, personhood was to a great extent constituted and expressed through things. By the early nineteenth century, domestic space within the British middle-class home had become function-specific. This fixing of function was effected and communicated by the placement of specific objects within those interior spaces – i.e., a dining table and a set of chairs indicating a space for taking meals. Individual members of the household were also assigned their own space (usually dependent on their sex) such as the library (masculine) or drawing room (feminine) (as well as their sleeping accommodation).[4] As has been suggested, contemporary commentators articulated the connection between household possessions and the persona of the householder and the role that domestic objects played in the formation of identity and social self-creation. In fact, contemporary domestic discourse during the nineteenth century repeatedly asserted that household furnishings embodied and marked the character and taste of their owner. Furthermore, visitors to the middle-class home in Britain were, in many cases, social acquaintances. This factor emphasized the significance of domestic space and the array of objects in that space. These became social agents for the householder's persona and physical extensions of the intangible and encoded attributes of the household as a whole, such as its status, moral climate and taste.

Within the Subcontinent, despite endeavours to create insulated pockets of Westernization, the British inhabited essentially Indianized domestic spaces. As Swati Chattopadhyay has argued in relation to the arrangement of space within the British home in India, the 'open-endedness of spatial meaning unsettled … ideas of public and private, self and other by refusing to grant the colonizers a sense of interiority within the safe confines of which to construct an imperial self'.[5] Although the British in India could do little to mitigate the spatial arrangements of their dwellings, attempts were made to modify that space through objects and the enactment of familiar social practices through the placement and use of those objects.

The furnishings of the Anglo-Indian bungalow or lower-roomed house could be viewed, in the words of Pierre Nora, as 'sites of memory' intended to evoke cultural memories of home and anchor the British imperial persona within India. The British had both a physical and a sensory need for furniture in South Asia. The arrangements of furnishings within the domestic interior, however scant and unsatisfactory by European standards, were intended to enable the British within the Subcontinent to operate socially and culturally as Westerners but also, more significantly, to allow their senses to experience familiar forms, materials and bodily postures. The physical surroundings of the Anglo-Indian home were intended, however imperfectly, to evoke the space of 'home' (domicile, region and nation). As argued elsewhere, however, there was a disjunction between this intention and its actualization.[6]

Within the Anglo-Indian home, domestic material culture and the everyday practices of home were problematized. Attempts by Anglo-Indians to secure the marks of difference between themselves and the local population in order to fend off the emergence of a hybrid culture were continually undercut by the plan of, and domestic arrangements within, the British dwelling within the Subcontinent. In fact, the spatial arrangements and furnishings of the British domestic interior in India rarely soothed their inhabitants, and unease about this state of affairs was the sub-text to many Anglo-Indian accounts of domestic life in India.

In the early decades of the twentieth century, British perception of their Indian home began to change, following publication of the Lee Commission report. As a result of recommendations from this commission, after 1925 British military and civilian officers within the Subcontinent were 'entitled to four first class return passages between England and India'.[7] As Alison Blunt has suggested, this new entitlement to more regular contact between the home country and India changed the relationship that Britons had with their colonial homes. It is arguable that this shift began to occur before this date. Writing in 1912, Alice Perrin characterized the relationship that many Anglo-Indians had with the homeland '"home" had always stood for ready money, long visits to relations (hospitable enough to birds of passage), new clothes, all the theatres, the delightful companionship of the children in the holidays'.[8] This set of experiences was contrasted with the domestic compensations of return to India after a long visit and 're-settlement in a roomy bungalow with willing servants, good living, good horses, none of which, it must be noted cost more in India than the upkeep of a very moderate household in England'.

Anglicization of local middle-class life-styles, incremental absorption of Western objects and taste as well as relegation of local and customary social practices to the background of the local domestic sphere were not processes, it has been argued, that were 'value neutral in a political sense'.[9] Indeed, many Anglo-Indians understood the non-functional role that European domestic material culture performed within the Subcontinent, its acquisition of symbolic value and its transformation into a marker of Western cultural superiority. As H.B. Henderson asserted in *The Bengalee* of 1829, 'in the first place, is it nothing that a Chair is a visible sign of our civilisation and our superiority over the barbarous nations we have conquered? [It is] an outward symbol of our proud distinction from among the enslaved millions of the East'.[10]

   It has been argued that colonialism was not only facilitated by superior military and economic power but also by culture.[11] Not culture in the sense of a coherent, monolithic system but as varied sets of practices. In this work it has been suggested that sets of Western cultural practices associated with the domestic sphere and public space within the Subcontinent, from the second half of the nineteenth century, were intended to mediate those spaces and to shape and regulate the local physical environment. This process was, however, rarely fully realized. Although a by-product of British colonial rule, the introduction of European material culture and reproduction of a Westernized life-style within the homes of the local middle class could be discussed in political terms, as they were both constitutive and expressive of one aspect of the colonial relationship between Britain and the Subcontinent.[12] Nationalists in both India and Ceylon (although at different times) perceived the corrosive effect of Western cultural forms on local culture. Although they did not specifically excoriate the use of Western-style furnishings within the local domestic sphere, Buddhist nationalists within Ceylon toward the end of the nineteenth century, for example, did attack other Western 'things', including Western dress, women's hats, honeymoons and even lavatory paper; these and other aspects of Western material culture were perceived as powerful promoters of alien values.[13]

   What of the legacy of colonial domesticity both within Britain and the Indian Subcontinent in the post-Independence period? Although, as suggested elsewhere, Anglo-Indians returning to the 'Motherland' 'sunk into insignificance after 1947', many attempted to bolster their identities in the cold, northern climes by creating 'little Anglo-Indias in their British homes'.[14] They surrounded themselves in their Cheltenham, Brighton or Tunbridge Wells houses and flats with souvenirs of their former colonial lives, including carved Bombay rosewood furniture, Ceylonese ebony and porcupine-quill boxes, *shikar* or hunting trophies, Benares brassware, Indian jail-made rugs and photographs.

   The domestic interiors of the Subcontinent could not, of course, be transplanted to Europe. However, the artefacts which those interiors contained could be, and many such objects were shipped to Europe before the end of empire. These objects range from the ordinary, everyday items found within the Anglo-Indian bungalow to the rare and costly bespoke objects, formerly located in grander dwellings within the Subcontinent. The post-Independence generation of returned Anglo-Indians is now dwindling in number, but as the direct connection with and memory of empire dies away a resurgence of interest in the furnishings of the Indian colonial domestic interior is, paradoxically, now taking place. A colonial 'look' has been promoted in recent years in numerous interior-decoration magazines. The main London auction houses (those sensitively attuned interpreters of shifts in consumer taste) now devote whole sections of their best/most expensive furniture sales to colonial furnishings from the Indian Subcontinent. Wealthy collectors avidly seek out the finest examples in ivory and ebony. The national museum of design and the decorative arts in the UK, the Victoria and Albert Museum, has also played its part in this revival by validating and at the same time (although unintentionally) fostering an interest in these objects through the production of a scholarly catalogue of its holdings of Anglo-Indian furniture.[15] The power of these colonial domestic objects at the present time resides in their status as tokens or material vestiges of historic contacts between Europe and South Asia in the pre-globalized age. They reify a brief and exotic moment in world history in a way that only domestic objects, inscribed with the marks of previous ownership and usage, can. Their histories as three-dimensional signifiers of the colonial domestic interior are now overlaid with other, more recent histories as they pass into private collections, are traded, displayed with other non-Asian objects and used in ways for which they were never intended in Western European and American interiors.

Domestic and more public space within the Indian Subcontinent in the post-Independence period, including the present time, also bears the imprint of the colonial domestic interior. The Anglo-Indian club survives and has now become a thriving social and sporting centre for the growing Indian and Sri Lankan elite. Strangely, in these architectural spaces created by English colonizers to exclude the local population, a version of Anglo-Indian material and visual culture still survives – in fact, is recast to serve the needs of new constituencies, new status groups within the burgeoning middle class of the Subcontinent within the global era. The new Indian elites use the club in different ways to those of their British predecessors. Although used as a social hub for networking, the club is also a locale for status competition between different groups; elite women are also more prominent in their use of the club than their forebears in the colonial era. Many of the peculiar practices of the Anglo-Indian club, such as the use of 'chits' instead of cash, the 'signing-in' of guests, the description of sleeping accommodation as 'chambers', the careful preservation of old club armchairs, rosewood tables, sporting trophies and photographs, persists in the clubs of Bangalore, Chennai, Colombo and Nuwara Eliya.

Former domestic dwellings and their interiors from the colonial era now have new uses. For example, in the Jeypore Colony or district of Chennai at the present time a large, two storey house with classical façade now functions as an up-market meeting place with bar, restaurant, gallery and shop (see figure 38). The main room on the ground floor, with its marble tiles, multiple door openings, high, bare ceiling with rotating electric fans, is furnished in a re-creation of a local middle-class interior of the colonial

38 Local elite interior of the colonial era re-created in the present day. Interior, late nineteenth-century house, Jeypore Colony or district, Chennai, c. 2003.

period, with occasional tables and comfortable armchairs arranged around the outside of the room. The arrangement of this room reflects the influence of Anglo-India modified by inclusion of traces of the local, such as 1930s photographs of Indian elders and oleographs of Hindu deities. The house is well used by the affluent youth of Chennai and the occasional Western tourist.

The imprint of the colonial interior is also found in many of the homes of the local elite within India and Sri Lanka at the present time. Although perhaps an unusual example, the home of the Sri Lankan architect Geoffrey Bawa, located in a bylane off Bagatelle Road in Colombo, is at least represented in the public domain by a series of photographs.[16] Bawa's interior straddled two worlds and acted as a model for the Sri Lankan elite in the development of appropriate furnishing schemes for the post-Independence era. It is a modern interior, but not in the conventional, Western sense of this term. Through the furnishing of his home, Bawa negotiated both local traditions and those of the modern West. He incorporated an eclectic mixture within his domestic interiors, including local architectural salvage and Dutch- and English-period colonial furniture produced in Sri Lanka, as well as examples of modern Western furniture, especially models of Eero Saarinen's 'Tulip' chair. The underlying architectural structure reflects a knowledge and understanding of local, pre-colonial conventions. These are skilfully combined with colonial elements. In fact, his interiors contain allusions to the colonial past, an interrupted but continuous Sri Lankan vernacular and the modern West.

This book offers a material-culture analysis of British interventions within India and Ceylon using the colonial domestic sphere and public space of empire as a series of case studies. By deploying the methods of material culture, it has been argued that the acquisition and use of a range of furnishings within the domestic interior, as well as practices engendered in the new public spaces of the colony, had profound effects on the affirmation of identity, both national and cultural, within the Subcontinent during the colonial era. The object-world of nineteenth- and early twentieth-century India and Ceylon was not simply a neutral backdrop against which life was played out. Instead, the material culture of home, mediation of domestic discourse and the everyday practices engendered within the domestic interior re-presented, re-produced and shaped the material as well as the cultural lives of both the British and local elite.[17] The present analysis of a range of objects located within the colonial domestic and public sphere has sought to interpret these clusters of things as materializations of human behaviour and expressive, but formerly neglected, aspects of colonial culture.

Notes

1 Marius Kwint, 'Introduction', in M. Kwint, C. Breward and J. Aynsley (eds), *Material Memories: design and evocation* (Oxford and New York, 1999), p. 2.

2 Summary of a paper by Chris Frith delivered to the Material Memories conference, Victoria and Albert Museum, 1998. Kwint et al, *Material Memories*, p. 3.

3 University of Cambridge, Centre of South Asian Studies: Scott papers, Khandalla, 12 April 1884.

4 Juliet Kinchin, 'Interiors: nineteenth-century essays on the "masculine" and the "feminine" room', in P. Kirkham (ed.), *The Gendered Object* (Manchester and New York, 1996), pp. 12–29.

5 Swati Chattopadhyay, 'Blurring Boundaries: the limits of "white town" in colonial Calcutta', *Journal of the Society of Architectural Historians*, vol. 59, no. 2 (June 2000), p. 177.

6 Will Glover, '"A feeling of absence from Old England": the colonial bungalow', *Home Cultures*, vol. 1, no. 1 (2004), p. 79.

7 Alison Blunt, 'Imperial geographies of home: British domesticity in India, 1886–1925', *Transactions of the Institute of British Geographers*, vol. 24, no. 4 (1999), p. 422.

8 Alice Perrin, *The Anglo-Indians* (London, 1912), p. 19.

9 James Duncan, 'The Power of Place in Kandy, Sri Lanka, 1780–1980', in J. Duncan and J. Agnew (eds), *The Power of Place: bringing together geographical and sociological imaginations* (Cambridge, 1989), p. 195.

10 H.B. Henderson, *The Bengalee; or sketches of society and manners in the East* (London, 1829), p. 329.

11 Nicholas Dirks, *Colonialism and Culture* (Ann Arbor, 1992), p. 3.

12 Nicholas Thomas, *Colonialism's Culture: anthropology, travel and government* (Cambridge, 1994), p. 2.

13 One of the leading figures in the Buddhist nationalist movement in Ceylon was the Anagarika (Hewavitarne) Dharmapala, who founded the Maha Bodhi Society in 1891. A. Wright (ed.), *Twentieth Century Impressions of Ceylon* (London, Durban and Colombo, 1907), p. 119.

14 Elizabeth Collingham, *Imperial Bodies: the physical experience of the Raj, c. 1800–1947* (Cambridge, 2001), p. 201.

15 Amin Jaffer, *Furniture from British India and Ceylon: a catalogue of the collections in the Victoria and Albert Museum and the Peabody Essex Museum* (London, 2001).

16 Brian Brace Taylor, *Geoffrey Bawa* (New York, 1995), pp. 52–7, 114–19. Since his death, Bawa's home has been converted into an upmarket retail outlet called Paradise Road.

17 Nicholas Saunders, 'You are what you own and inhabit', *Times Higher Education Supplement*, no. 3 (November 2000), p. 34.

Bibliography

Primary sources

Private papers

University of Cambridge, Centre of South Asian Studies
Allan papers
Berners papers
Campbell Metcalfe papers
Kenyon papers
Plowden papers
Scott papers
Stokes papers
Thatcher papers
Thompson papers
Wentworth Reeve papers

Photographic material:
Cumming collection
D'Arcy Waters collection
Hyde collection
Jardine collection
Macleod collection
Mansfield collection
Montgomery collection
Thompson collection
Wildeblood collection

Cambridge University Library, Royal Commonwealth Society Archive – Photographs
Y3011B (LS) 354, Ceylon, Watagoda, Maude (1900).

Y303B/42, Queen's House, Colombo (1875).

Y3022AA, 'Original Photographic Views of Calcutta, Old and New, used in illustrating Mr Montague Massey's "Recollections of Calcutta for over half a century"' (1864–1918).

Y3022G (27), Tea estate bungalow, Ceylon, by Charles Scowen (1870).

Y303E/104, Beckington Bungalow, Colombo, Ceylon (1880).

Cambridge University Library, Special Collections

Raja Durai Singham papers

London, British Library, Oriental and India Office Collections

Add.Or. 2515, Plan of Lieut. Col. Gilbert's bungalow at Hazaribagh.

Add.Or. 3204, Plan and elevation of house, Calcutta, by Shadwell and Goss.

Mss.Eur. A225, Nagpur Hunt Club.

Mss.Eur. B369/5 (53), Journals of Thomas Machell.

Mss.Eur. C650, *Travellers' Bungalows in Sikkim and the Darjeeling District* (1935).

Mss.Eur. C725, Elphinstone papers.

Mss.Eur. D898, Ironside-Smith papers.

Mss.Eur. D1236/4, Headlam papers, United Services Club, Simla.

Mss.Eur. F197/37, Younghusband Collection.

WD 2301 'The "Club house", Ootacamund, 1852'.

London, British Library, Oriental and India Office Collections: photographs

PDP 332/1 Plate 27 'The drawing room, [Mount] Abu Club' [*c.* 1900].

PDP 559, Image 8 'Laurie's Hotel, Agra, drawing room'.

PDP 1000/ (4983), Frederick Fiebig: 'Singhalese woman'.

PDP 1000/ (4986), Frederick Fiebig: 'Singhalese gentleman in office'.

PDP 1000/ (5006), Frederick Fiebig: 'Singhalese gentleman in office'.

PDP 1000/42 (4349), Hurrichand Chintamon, 'Portrait of three Parsees and a Parbhu (or Prabhu), Bombay'.

PDP 1081/1 (3), *Album of architectural and topographical views in Calcutta*, 'F. & C. Ostler's glassware showrooms, 12 Old Court House Street, Calcutta'.

London, Church Mission Society

Missionary photographs: 'photograph of coffee planter's bungalow in Ceylon, 1874'.

Matlock, Derbyshire Record Office

Coke of Brookhill Collection, D/1881/L2, private and official papers, Sir William Coke.

University of Oxford, Rhodes House Library

Mss.Ind.Ocn.t.5: Sir Edward Creasy papers, letter to Emma Cottam, 1861.

Mss.Ind.Ocn.t.6: 'Plans of Coffee Estates in Ceylon and of Polwatte Mills and Coffee Store, Colombo', Colombo, 1865.

University of Peradeniya, Sri Lanka, Special Collections

Journal of Major and Mrs J. Darby Griffiths, 'Ceylon during a Residence in the Years 1841–2', 4 vols.

Unpublished government records

London, National Archives

CO (Colonial Office) 54/71: 'Schedule of the Goods, Chattels, Credit and Effects of the Honble. Sir William Coke', 6 October 1818.

CO 54/101: 'Inventory of the Queen's House, Colombo', 6 December 1839.

CO 54/104: 'List of Property belonging to Eheylepola Maha Nillame sold by Public Auction … January, 1825'.

CO 54/127: 'List of Furniture in the King's House' [Colombo], 18 January 1833.

CO 54/136: 'Inventory of furniture in the King's House, Colombo', 31 December 1834.

CO 54/156: 'Inventory of Furniture in the King's House, Colombo' and 'Inventory of Furniture in the Public Rooms of the Pavilion, Kandy', 29 September 1837.

CO 54/163: 'Plan Section's and Elevations of a Residence for the Assistant Agent and District Judge … built at Kaygalle … Colombo', 28 April 1838.

CO 54/173: 'Return of the Furniture in the Public Rooms in the Queen's House, Colombo', 6 December 1839.

CO 54/291: 'Supplementary Estimate … for Completing Repairs & c. to the Queen's House, Colombo', 9 October 1852.

CO 54/298: 'Lamps for the Queen's House, Colombo', 22 January 1853.

CO 54/316: 'Dispatch from the Governor', 29 September 1855.

CO 54/317: 'Dispatch from the Governor', 11 October 1855.

CO 54/359: 'Report by the Deputy Commissary General's Office', 28 February 1861.

CO 54/415: 'Report on the Queen's Houses: Report on the Public Furniture', 15 October 1866.

CO 59/3: *The Ceylon Times*, 29 December 1846.

MPH 864: 'Plan, Section and Elevation of the Court House, Galle', 26 June 1834.

MPHH 3 (4): 'Plan of the Square within the Fort of Colombo bounded by the four streets, King Street, Chatham Street, Galle Street, Flagstaff Row', 15 November 1833.

MR 1/522: 'Map of the Fort of Colombo exhibiting the figure of the ground appertaining to each house … Colombo, 10 July 1839'.

CUST 13: Goods imported into Ceylon.

Colombo, Sri Lanka, National Archives

NA 5/153: 'A Probable Estimate of the Expense Required to King's House, Colombo', 21 November 1831.

London, British Library, Oriental and India Office Collections

Wills, probates, inventories and administrations

L/AG/34/27/120, Bengal Wills, H. Martindell, 1840, Thomas Clarke, 1840.

L/AG/34/27/133, Bengal Wills, Maj. Fitzgerald, Calcutta, 1845.

L/AG/34/27/156, Bengal Wills, Muddenmohun Ruckhut, 1855, and Mrs Hutteman, 1855.

L/AG/34/27/163, Bengal Wills, Elizabeth J. Sarkies, Calcutta, 1859, Robert Dunlop, 1859, Mary Shillingford, Purneah, 1859, Amun Ali Khan, 1859.

L/AG/34/27/167, Bengal Wills, Ellahy Bux, 1861.

L/AG/34/27/170, Bengal Wills, G.M. Gasper, 1863, P. Delmar, 1863, C.B. Harris, 1863, and Sree Mutty Joypeary Dossee, 1863.

L/AG/34/27/174, Bengal Wills, G. Williamson, Sibsagar, 1867, and Puddolochan Singhee, 1867.

L/AG/34/27/177, Bengal Wills, Capt. J. Paterson, 1869.

L/AG/34/27/184, Bengal Wills, G.A. Atkinson, Monghyr, 1877.

L/AG/34/27/187, Bengal Wills, W. Smith, Jogapore, 1880, and Sreemutty Roymoney, 1880.

L/AG/34/27/190, Bengal Wills, R. Tilbury, 1883, and Gooroo Churn Singh, 1883, Abinash Chunder Dutt, 1883.

L/AG/34/27/261, Madras Wills, J. Dacre, 1829.

L/AG/34/27/397, Bombay Wills, J. Dwyer, 1846–50, William Wise, 1846–50.

Worcester, Record Office

Register of Wills, vol. 6, part 3, Steuart, J., 30 April 1870, last Will and Testament of James Steuart.

Published government records

Map of the Municipality of Colombo (Colombo, 1899).

Contemporary works

All books published in London unless otherwise stated.

Acland, Rev. C., *A Popular Account of the Manners and Customs of India* (1847).

Aitken, E.H., *Behind the Bungalow* (Calcutta and Bombay, 1895).

Annual Report of the Ootacamund Club for 1866 (Ootacamund, 1866).

Atkinson, G.F., *Curry and Rice on Forty Plates; or the ingredients of social life at 'our station' in India* (1859).

Beames, J., *Memoirs of a Bengal Civilian* (1896, reprinted 2003).

Bellew, Capt., *Memoirs of a Griffin; or a cadet's first year in India* (1880).

The Bengal Directory and Annual Register for 1839 (Calcutta, 1839).

The Bengal Directory and Annual Register for the Year 1840 (Calcutta, 1840).

The Bengal and Agra Directory and Annual Register for the Year 1844 (Calcutta, 1844).

The Bengal Directory, 1875 (Calcutta, Bombay and London, 1875).

The Bengal Directory, 1880 (Calcutta, Bombay and London, 1880).

The Bengal Directory, 1881 (Calcutta, Bombay and London, 1881).

Bennett, J.W., *Ceylon and its Capabilities* (1843).

Birdwood, G.C.M., *The Arts of India* (1880).

The Bombay Calendar and General Directory containing Civil, Army and Navy Lists for 1850 (Bombay, 1850).

Bombay through the camera (Bombay, 1904).

Bose, S.C., *The Hindoos as They Are; a description of the manners, customs and inner life of Hindoo society in Bengal* (London and Calcutta, 1881).

Braddon, E., *Life in India; a series of sketches showing something of the Anglo-Indian* (1872).

Buckland, C.T., *Sketches of Social Life in India* (1884).

The Bungalow; a paper for Anglo-Indian homes, vol. 1, no. 1 (Bombay, 1896).

The Calcutta Review, vol. 1, no. 1 (May 1844).

Capper, J., *The Duke of Edinburgh in Ceylon* (1871).

H. Don Carolis and Sons, Upholsterers, the Largest and Most Experienced Manufacturers in Asia of Furniture for the House, Office, Club, Hotel, Showroom … (Colombo, 1908).

Cave, H., *The Book of Ceylon* (London, Paris and New York, 1908).

The Census of India, 1901, vol. 7, part 3, *Calcutta: town and suburbs* (Calcutta, 1901).

Chichele Plowden, W., *Report on the Census of British India taken on the 17 February 1881* (1883).

Chota Mem, *The English Bride in India; hints on Indian housekeeping* (Madras, 1909).

Clemons, Mrs, *The Manners and Customs of Society in India* (1841).

Compton, H., *Indian Life in Town and Country* (1904).

Coomaraswamy, A.K., *Medieval Sinhalese Art* (Broad Campden, 1908).

Dalhousie Institute, Calcutta; report for the year ending 31 October 1888 (Calcutta, 1888).

Das, D., *Sketches of Hindoo Life* (1887).

Dass, Rev. I., *Domestic Manners and Customs of the Hindoos of Northern India or … North West Provinces of India* (Benares, 1866).

Davy, J., *An Account of the Interior of Ceylon* (1821).

Deighton, C., *Domestic Economy* (Madras, 1909).

Deschamps, J., *Scenery and Reminiscences of Ceylon* (1845).

Diver, M., *The Englishwoman in India* (Edinburgh and London, 1909).

Dodwell, H., *The Nabobs of Madras* (1926).

Doyley, C., *The European in India* (1813).

Duncan, S.J., *The Simple Adventures of a Memsahib* (1893).

Eastwick, E.B., *Handbook of the Madras Presidency* (1879).

Eastwick, E.B., *Handbook of the Punjab, Western Rajputana, Kashmir …* (1883).

Edis, R.W., *Decoration and Furniture of the Town House* (1881).

Emerson, R.W., 'English Traits', *Manchester Guardian* (9 February 1857).

The Englishwoman in India (1864).

The Englishwoman's Domestic Magazine (1852–77).

Ferguson, A.M., *Souvenirs of Ceylon* (1869).

Ferguson, J., *Ceylon in 1883* (Colombo, 1883).

Forster, E.M., *A Passage to India* (1924, reprinted 1987).

Garrett, E., *Morning Hours in India; practical hints on household management* … (1887).

Gordon Cumming, C.F., *Two Happy Years in Ceylon*, 2 vols (Edinburgh and London, 1892).

Goulding, H.R., *Old Lahore; reminiscences of a resident* (Lahore, 1924).

Graham, M., *Journal of a Residence in India* (Edinburgh, 1813).

Grant, C., *Anglo-Indian Domestic Life; a letter from an artist in India to his mother in England* (Calcutta, 1862).

A Guide to the City of Madras and its Suburbs (Madras, 1889).

A Handbook for Travellers in India, Burma and Ceylon (1909).

Hart, W.H., *Everyday Life in Bengal and Other Indian sketches* (1906).

Haweis, M.E., *Beautiful Houses* (1882).

Henderson, H.B., *The Bengalee; or sketches of society and manners in the East* (1829).

Home Chat (1895–1958).

Home Circle (1849–53).

Hull, E., *The European in India; or Anglo-Indian's Vade-Mecum* (1874).

Hutton-Taylor, G., *An Illustrated Guide to India and its Hotels* (Calcutta, 1899).

The Imperial Census of 1881; operations and results in the Presidency of Bombay, including Sind, vol. 1 (Bombay, 1882).

The International Album of Permanent Photographic Views of Calcutta (Calcutta, n.d., c. 1907).

Ivey, Lt. Col. J.G., *The Club Directory; a general guide or index to the London and county clubs and those of* … *British colonial possessions* (1879).

[J.A.D.], *Notes on an Outfit for India and Hints for the New Arrival* (1903).

Jennings, H.J., *Our Houses and How to Beautify Them* (1902).

Jones-Bateman, Mrs R., *An illustrated guide to the buried cities of Ceylon* (Frome and London, 1932).

Journal of the Indian Institute of Architects, vol. 3, no. 1 (July 1936); vol. 3, no. 2 (October 1936); vol. 4, no. 1 (July 1937); vol. 4, no. 2 (October 1937); vol. 4, no. 3 (January 1938).

Kaye, Sir J., *Peregrine Pulteney; or life in India*, 3 vols (1844).

Kerr, J., *The Domestic Life, Character and Customs of the Natives of India* (1865).

Kindersley, Mrs, *Letters from the Island of Teneriffe, Brazil, the Cape of Good Hope and the East Indies* (1777).

Leigh Hunt, Maj. S. and A. Kenny, *Tropical Trials; a handbook for women in the tropics* (1883).

Lewis, J.P., *Ceylon in Early British Times* (Colombo, 1913).

Liesching, L., *A Brief Account of Ceylon* (Jaffna, 1861).

Life in Bombay and the Neighbouring Out-Stations (1852).

Life in the Mofussil; or, The Civilian in Lower Bengal (1878).

Maclean, J., *A Guide to Bombay; historical, statistical and descriptive* (Bombay, 1876).

The Madras New Almanac for 1852 (Madras, 1852).

Madras Exhibition of 1855; catalogue raisonné (Madras, 1855).

Madras New Almanac … with general directory for Madras, Calcutta and Bombay, 1852–1855

(Madras, 1855).

The Magazine of Domestic Economy (1836–44).

Maitland, J.C., *Letters from Madras during the Years 1836–1839* (1846).

Manual of Indian Etiquette for the Use of European Officers Coming to India (Allahabad, 1910).

Map of Madras (Madras, 1911).

Moses, H., *Sketches of India; with notes on the seasons, scenery and society of Bombay, Elephanta and Salsette* (1850).

Nagpur; Nagpur Hunt Club (Nagpur, c. 1922).

The New Calcutta Directory for 1856 (Calcutta, 1856).

The New Calcutta Directory for the Town of Calcutta, Bengal and the North-West … for 1858 (Calcutta, 1858).

W. Newman and Co.'s Handbook to Calcutta; historical and descriptive with a plan of the city (Calcutta, 1892).

Padfield, Rev. J.E., *The Hindu at Home* (1896).

Pal, B.C., *Memories of my Life and Times* (Calcutta, 1973).

Pankridge, H.R., *A Short History of the Bengal Club (1827–1927)* (Calcutta, 1927).

Percival, R., *An Account of the Island of Ceylon* (1803).

Perrin, A., *The Anglo-Indians* (1912).

Pershad, B., *Law of Landlord and Tenant and of Hotel-keeper and Guest* (Lahore, 1902).

Platt, K., *The Home and Health in India and the Tropical Colonies* (1923).

Postans, Mrs M., *Western India in 1838* (1839).

Pridham, C., *An Historical, Political and Statistical Account of Ceylon* (1849).

Prinsep, J., *Benares Illustrated in a Series of Drawings* (Calcutta, 1830).

Reid, W.M., *The Culture and Manufacture of Indigo; with a description of a planter's life and resources* (Calcutta, 1887).

Report on the Census of Bengal, 1881 (Calcutta, 1883).

Reynolds, Mrs H., *At Home in India; or Taza-be-Taza* (1903).

Roberts, E., *Scenes and Characteristics of Hindoostan; with sketches of Anglo-Indian society* (1837).

Rules of the Club of Western India (Bombay, 1891).

Russell, W.H., *My Diary in India*, 2 vols (London, 1860).

Shadwell, Maj. L.J., *Notes on the Internal Economy of Chummery, Home, Mess and Club* (Bombay, 1904).

A Short Account of the Madras Presidency (Madras, 1861).

Sirr, H.C., *Ceylon and the Cingalese*, 2 vols (1850).

Staley, Dr J., *Handbook for Mothers and Wives in India* (Calcutta, 1908).

Steel, F.A. and G. Gardiner, *The Complete Indian Housekeeper and Cook* (1888, 11th edition 1921).

Sylvia's Home Journal (1878–91).

Tennent, Sir J.E., *Ceylon; an account of the island, physical, historical and topographical*, 2 vols (1859).

Thacker's Directory for Bengal, the North Western Provinces and the Punjab ... for 1865 (London, Allahabad and Bombay, 1865).

Thacker's Directory for Bengal, North West Provinces ... for 1867 (Calcutta, 1867).

Thacker's Directory for Bengal and the North West Provinces &c. for 1868 (Calcutta, 1868).

Thacker's Reduced Survey Map of India (Calcutta, 1914).

Valentia, Viscount, *Voyages and Travels to India, Ceylon, the Red Sea, Abyssinia and Egypt in the years 1802–1806* (1809).

A Visit to Madras; being a sketch of the local and characteristic peculiarities of the Presidency in the year 1811 (1821).

The Warrant of Precedence (Calcutta, 1921).

Wilson, Lady, *Letters from India [1889–1909]* (1984).

Winslow, Rev. M., *Memoir of Mrs Harriet L. Winslow; 13 years a member of the American mission in Ceylon* (New York, 1840).

Wright, A. (ed.), *Twentieth Century Impressions of Ceylon* (London, Durban and Colombo, 1907).

Yule, Col. H. and A.C. Burnell (eds), *Hobson-Jobson; a glossary of colloquial Anglo-Indian words and phrases, and of kindred terms, etymological, historical, geographical and discursive* (London, 1886, reprinted 1994).

Secondary sources

Abelson, E., *When Ladies Go A-Thieving: middle-class shoplifters in the Victorian department store* (New York and Oxford, 1989).

Aijazuddin, F.S., *Lahore Recollected: an album* (Lahore, 2004).

Aiken, S.R., 'Early Penang hill stations', *Geographical Review*, vol. 77, no. 4 (October 1987).

Alff, J., 'Temples of light: Bombay's Art Deco cinemas and the birth of modern myth', in P. Pal (ed.), *Bombay to Mumbai: changing perspectives* (Mumbai, 1997), pp. 250–7.

Allen, C. (ed.), *Plain Tales from the Raj: images of British India in the twentieth century* (1975).

Allen, C., *Raj: a scrapbook of British India, 1877–1947* (Oxford, 1977).

Alwis, L., *British Period Architecture in Sri Lanka* (Colombo, 1992).

Anderson, B., *Imagined Communities: reflections on the origin and spread of nationalism* (London and New York, 1994).

Archer, M., *Patna Painting* (1947).

Archer, M., C. Rowell and R. Skelton (eds), *Treasures from India: the Clive collection at Powis Castle* (1987).

Arnold, D., *Colonizing the Body: state medicine and epidemic disease in nineteenth- century India* (1993).

Attfield, J., *Wild Things: the material culture of everyday life* (Oxford and New York, 2000).

Bachelard, G., *The Poetics of Space* (Boston, 1994).

Ballantyne, A., 'The architectural uncanny: essays in the modern unhomely', *British Journal of Aesthetics*, vol. 34, no. 2 (April 1994), p. 193.

Ballantyne, T. and A. Burton (eds), *Bodies in Contact: re-thinking colonial encounters in world history* (Durham, NC and London, 2005).

Ballhatchet, K., *Race, Sex and Class under the Raj* (1980).

Ballhatchett, K. and J. Harrison (eds), *The City in South Asia: pre-modern and modern* (1980).

Bangalore Club: a club's world, ed. M. Bhaktavatsala (Bangalore, 1993).

Banks, J.D.N., *The History of the Hill Club* (Colombo, 1988).

Barker, F. et al. (eds), *The Politics of Theory* (Colchester, 1983).

Barr, P., *The Memsahibs* (1976).

Barr, P., *The Dust in the Balance: British women in India, 1905–1945* (1989).

Baucom, I., *Out of Place: Englishness, empire and the locations of identity* (Princeton, 1999).

Bayly, C.A., *Indian Society and the Making of the British Empire* (Cambridge, 1988).

Bayly, C.A. (ed.), *The Raj: India and the British, 1600–1947* (exhib. cat., 1990).

Bence-Jones, M., *Palaces of the Raj: magnificence and misery of the lord sahibs* (1973).

Bennett, T., *The Birth of the Museum: history, theory, politics* (1995).

Benton, C., T. Benton and G. Wood (eds), *Art Deco 1910–39* (exhib. cat., 2003).

Bhabha, H.K., 'The other question: difference, discrimination and the discourse of colonialism', in F. Barker et al. (eds), *The Politics of Theory* (Colchester, 1983), pp. 148–72.

Blazé, B.R., *The Life of Lorenz* (Colombo, 1948).

Blunt, A., 'Imperial geographies of home: British domesticity in India, 1886–1925', *Transactions of the Institute of British Geographers*, vol. 24, no. 4 (1999), pp. 421–40.

Bonner, S. (ed.), *Consuming Visions: accumulation and display of goods in America, 1880–1920* (New York, 1989).

Boswell, D. and J. Evans (eds), *Representing the Nation: histories, heritage and museums* (London and New York, 1999).

Bourdieu, P., *Outline of a Theory of Practice* (Cambridge, 1982).

Bourdieu, P., *The Logic of Practice* (Cambridge, 1990).

Bourdieu, P., *Distinction: a social critique of the judgement of taste* (1994).

Brawer, N., *British Campaign Furniture: elegance under canvas, 1740–1914* (New York, 2001).

Breckenridge, C., 'The aesthetics and politics of colonial collecting: India at World's Fairs', *Journal of Comparative Studies in History and Society*, 31 (1989), pp. 195–216.

The British in India (exhib. cat., Brighton, 1973).

Brohier, D., 'Who were the Burghers?', *Journal of the Royal Asiatic Society (Sri Lanka Branch)*, vol. 30 (1985–86), pp. 101–19.

Brohier, D., *Dr Alice de Boer and Some Pioneering Burgher Women Doctors* (Colombo, 1995).

Brohier, R.L., *Furniture of the Dutch Period in Ceylon* (Colombo, 1969).

Brohier, R.L., *Changing Face of Colombo* (Colombo, 1984).

Bryden, I. and J. Floyd (eds), *Domestic Space: reading the nineteenth-century interior* (Manchester, 1999).

Burke, P., *History and Social Theory* (Cambridge, 1992).

Bushman, R.L., *The Refinement of America: persons, houses, cities* (New York, 1992).

Carlton, C. and C. Carlton, 'Gardens of the Raj', *History Today* (July 1996) www.findarticles.com (accessed 6 January 2005).

Celik, Z., 'Framing the colony: houses of Algeria photographed', *Art History*, vol. 27, no. 4 (September 2004), pp. 616–26.

Chattopadhyay, S., 'A critical history of architecture in a post-colonial world: a view from Indian history', *Architronic: the electronic journal of architecture* (May 1997).

Chattopadhyay, S., 'Blurring boundaries: the limits of "white town" in colonial Calcutta', *Journal of the Society of Architectural Historians*, vol. 59, no. 2 (June 2000), pp. 154–79.

Chattopadhyay, S., 'Goods, chattels and sundry items: constructing 19th century Anglo-Indian domestic life', *Journal of Material Culture*, vol. 7, no. 3 (November 2002), pp. 243–71.

Cieraad, I. (ed.), *At Home: an anthropology of domestic space* (New York, 1999).

Cohn, B.S., *Colonialism and its Forms of Knowledge: the British in India* (Princeton, 1996).

Cohn, B.S., *An Anthropologist among the Historians and Other Essays* (New Delhi, 1998).

Collingham, E.M., *Imperial Bodies: the physical experience of the Raj, c. 1800–1947* (Cambridge, 2001).

Country House Lighting (exhib. cat., Leeds, 1992).

Davies, P., *The Penguin Guide to the Monuments of India* (1989), vol. 2.

Davies, P., 'Bombay: history and urban development: early history, before 1803', *Grove Dictionary of Art Online* (Oxford University Press) www.groveart.com (accessed 26 March 2005).

Davies, P., 'Calcutta: urban development, 1690–1845', *Grove Dictionary of Art Online* (Oxford University Press) www.groveart.com (accessed 19 March 2005).

Davies, P., 'Madras: history and urban development', *Grove Dictionary of Art Online* (Oxford University Press) www.groveart.com (accessed 19 March 2005).

De Alwis, M., 'Notes towards the discussion of female portraits as texts', *Pravada*, vol. 4, no. 5/6 (1996), pp. 16–21.

De Bruijn, M. and R. Raben (eds), *The World of Jan Brandes, 1743–1808: drawings of a Dutch traveller in Batavia, Ceylon and Southern Africa* (Zwolle and Amsterdam, 2004).

De Silva, K.M., *A History of Sri Lanka* (Chennai, 1981, 1997).

De Silva, K.M., 'Sir James Emerson Tennent: colonial administrator and historian', *Journal of the Royal Asiatic Society of Sri Lanka*, vol. 41 (1998), pp. 13–37.

De Silva, R.K., *19th Century Newspaper Engravings of Ceylon – Sri Lanka* (1998).

Dewing, D. (ed.), *Home and Garden: paintings and drawings of English middle class urban domestic spaces, 1675–1914* (2003).

Dirks, N.B. (ed.), *Colonialism and Culture* (Ann Arbor, 1992).

Douglas, M. and B. Isherwood, *The World of Goods: towards an anthropology of consumption* (London and New York, 1996).

Duncan, J., *The City as Text: the politics of landscape interpretation in the Kandyan kingdom* (Cambridge, 1990).

Duncan, J., 'The power of place in Kandy, Sri Lanka, 1780–1980', in J. Duncan and J. Agnew (eds), *The Power of Place: bringing together geographical and sociological imaginations* (Cambridge, 1989), pp. 185–201.

Dwivedi, S., 'Homes in the nineteenth century', in P. Pal (ed.), *Bombay to Mumbai: changing perspectives* (Mumbai, 1997), pp. 152–67.

Dwyer, R. and D. Patel, *Cinema India: the visual culture of Hindi film* (2002).

Eaton, N., 'Excess in the city: the consumption of imported prints in colonial Calcutta, 1780–95', *Journal of Material Culture*, vol. 8, no. 1 (2003), pp. 45–74.

Edwardes, M., *Glorious Sahibs: the romantic as empire-builder, 1799–1838* (1968).

Edwardes, M., *The Sahibs and the Lotus* (1988).

Eliens, T. (ed.), *Domestic Interiors at the Cape and in Batavia, 1602–1795* (The Hague, 2002).

Emmison, M. and P. Smith (eds), *Researching the Visual: images, objects, contexts and interactions in social and cultural inquiry* (London, Thousand Oaks and New Delhi, 2000).

Evans, R., 'Figures, doors, passages', *Architectural Design*, vol. 48, no. 4 (1978), pp. 267–78.

Falconer, J., *India: pioneering photographers, 1850–1900* (2001).

Fernandes, L., *India's Middle Class: democratic politics in an era of economic reform* (Minneapolis and London, 2006).

Foley, T.P. et al., *Gender and Colonialism* (Galway, 1996).

Fraser, H., S. Green and J. Johnston (eds), *Gender and the Victorian Periodical* (Cambridge, 2003).

Furedy, C., *British Tradesmen and Shopkeepers of Calcutta, 1830–1900* (Québec, Canadian Society for Asian Studies, 1976).

Furedy, C., 'Development of modern elite retailing in Calcutta, 1880–1920', *The Indian Economic and Social History Review*, vol. 16, no. 4 (1979), pp. 377–94.

Gell, A., *Art and Agency* (Oxford, 1998).

George, R.M., 'Homes in the empire, empires in the home', *Cultural Critique* (Winter 1993–94), pp. 95–127.

Gere, C., *Nineteenth Century Decoration: the art of the interior* (1989).

Gere, C., *An Album of Nineteenth Century Interiors* (New York, 1992).

Ghosh, S.C., *The Social Condition of the British Community in Bengal, 1757–1800* (Leiden, 1970).

Gilmour, D., *The Ruling Caste: imperial lives in the Victorian Raj* (2005).

Girouard, M., *Life in the English Country House: a social and architectural history* (1978).

Glover, W., '"A feeling of absence from Old England": the colonial bungalow', *Home Cultures*, vol. 1, no. 1 (2004), pp. 61–82.

Goffman, E., *The Presentation of Self in Everyday Life* (Harmondsworth, 1959).

Gore, A. and A. Gore, *The History of English Interiors* (Oxford, 1991).

Gray, R., *Cinemas in Britain: one hundred years of cinema architecture* (1996).

Grier, K.C., 'Imagining the parlor, 1830–1880', in G.W.R. Ward (ed.), *Perspectives on American Furniture* (New York, 1988), pp. 205–39.

Grier, K.C., *Culture and Comfort: parlor making and middle class identity, 1850–1930* (Washington, D.C. and London, 1997).

Guha, R. and G.C. Spivak (eds), *Selected Subaltern Studies* (Oxford, 1988).

Gutman, J.M., *Through Indian Eyes: 19th and early 20th century photography from India* (New York, 1982).

Guy, J. and D. Swallow, *Arts of India, 1500–1900* (1990).

Hall, C., *Civilising Subjects: metropole and colony in the English imagination, 1830–1867* (Cambridge, 2002).

Hall, C. (ed.), *Cultures of Empire: colonizers in Britain and the empire in the nineteenth and twentieth centuries* (Manchester, 2000).

Hall, S. (ed.), *Representation: cultural representations and signifying practices* (London, Thousand Oaks and New Delhi, 1997).

Hamlyn, R., 'Martin, John', *The Grove Dictionary of Art Online* (Oxford University Press) www.groveart.com (accessed 18 April 2006).

Hardy, A., *Indian Temple Architecture: form and transformation* (New Delhi, 1994).

Henning, M., *Museums, Media and Cultural Theory* (Maidenhead, 2006).

Hoffenberg, P.H., 'Photography and architecture at the Calcutta International Exhibition', in M.A. Pelizzari (ed.), *Traces of India: photography, architecture and the politics of representation, 1850–1900* (New Haven and London, 2003), pp. 176–92.

Holt, R., *Sport and the British: a modern history* (Oxford, 1989).

Jackson, A. and A. Jaffer (eds), *Encounters: the meeting of Asia and Europe, 1500–1800* (exhib. cat., 2004).

Jacobs, J., *Edge of Empire: post-colonialism and the city* (London and New York, 1996).

Jaffer, A., 'De quelques aspects des intérieures domestiques Anglo-Indiens de 1750 à 1830', in *La Route des Indes: les Indes et l'Europe, échanges artistiques et héritage communs, 1650–1850* (exhib. cat., Paris, 1998), pp. 69–79.

Jaffer, A., *Furniture from British India and Ceylon: a catalogue of the collections in the Victoria and Albert Museum and the Peabody Essex Museum* (2001).

Jaffer, A. and M. Schwabe, 'A group of sixteenth century ivory caskets from Ceylon', *Apollo*, vol. 149, no. 445 (March 1999), pp. 3–14.

Jayawardena, K., *Nobodies to Somebodies: the rise of the colonial bourgeoisie in Sri Lanka* (Colombo, 2000).

Jones, R.D., 'Hewavitarne Don Carolis: a case study of a nineteenth century Colombo furniture maker', *Regional Furniture*, vol. 14 (2000), pp. 74–86.

Jones, R.D., '"Furniture of plain but substantial kind" at the British governors' houses in Ceylon, *c.* 1830–60', *Studies in the Decorative Arts*, vol. 10, no. 1 (Fall/Winter 2002), pp. 2–34.

Jones, R.D., 'Furnished in English style: Anglicization of local elite domestic interiors in Ceylon (Sri Lanka), *c.* 1850–1910', *South Asian Studies*, vol. 20 (2004), pp. 45–56.

Jones, R.D., 'An Englishman Abroad: Sir James Emerson Tennent in Ceylon, 1845–50', *Apollo*, vol. 164, no. 537 (November 2006), pp. 36–43.

Kalpana, K. and F. Schiffer (eds), *Madras: the architectural heritage* (Chennai, 2003).

Karlekar, M., *Re-visioning the Past: early photography in Bengal, 1875–1915* (New Delhi, 2005).

Karunaratna, N., *From Governor's Pavilion to President's Pavilion* (Dehiwela, 1984).

Karve, I., *Kinship Organisation in India* (New Delhi, 1968).

Kennedy, D., 'Imperial history and post-colonial theory', *Journal of Imperial and Commonwealth History*, vol. 24, no. 3 (September 1996), pp. 345–63.

Kennedy, D., *The Magic Mountains: hill stations and the British Raj* (Berkeley, Los Angeles and London, 1996).

Kinchin, J., 'Interiors: nineteenth-century essays on the "masculine" and "feminine" room', in P. Kirkham (ed.), *The Gendered Object* (Manchester and New York, 1996), pp. 12–29.

King, A.D., *Colonial Urban Development: culture, social power and environment* (London and Boston, 1976).

King, A.D., *The Bungalow: the production of a global culture* (1984).

Kirkham, P. (ed.), *The Gendered Object* (Manchester and New York, 1996).

Kunzru, H., *The Impressionist* (2002).

Kwint, M., C. Breward and J. Aynsley (eds), *Material Memories: design and evocation* (Oxford and New York, 1999).

Laermans, R., 'Learning to consume: early department stores and the shaping of modern consumer culture, 1860–1914', *Theory, Culture and Society*, vol. 10, no. 4 (November 1993), pp. 79–102.

Lewcock, R., B. Sansoni and L. Senanayake (eds), *The Architecture of an Island: the living legacy of Sri Lanka* (Colombo, 1998).

Lewandowski, S., 'Urban growth and municipal development in the colonial city of Madras, 1860–1900', *Journal of Asian Studies*, vol. 34, no. 2 (1975), pp. 341–60.

Logan, T., *The Victorian Parlour: a cultural study* (Cambridge, 2001).

Losty, J.P., *Calcutta: city of palaces* (1990).

Losty, J.P., 'British settlements and trading centres', in A. Jackson and A. Jaffer (eds), *Encounters: the meeting of Asia and Europe, 1500–1800* (exhib. cat., 2004), pp. 142–53.

MacKenzie, J.M. (ed.), *Imperialism and Popular Culture* (Manchester, 1986).

MacKenzie, J.M., *Orientalism: history, theory and the arts* (Manchester and New York, 1995).

MacMillan, M., *Women of the Raj* (New York, 1988).

Maguire, H., 'The Victorian theatre as a home from home', *Journal of Design History*, vol. 13, no. 2 (2000), pp. 107–21.

Malan, A., 'Furniture at the Cape in the eighteenth century: an archaeological approach', in T. Eliens (ed.), *Domestic Interiors at the Cape and in Batavia, 1602–1795* (The Hague, 2002), pp. 139–59.

Mangan, J.A., *The Games Ethic and Imperialism: aspects of the diffusion of an ideal* (1998).

Marshall, P.J., 'The whites of British India, 1780–1830: a failed colonial society?', *International History Review*, vol. 12, no. 1 (February 1990), pp. 26–44.

Marshall, P.J., 'The white town of Calcutta under the rule of the East India Company', *Modern Asian Studies*, vol. 34, no. 2 (2000), pp. 307–31.

Marwick, A., 'The Great War, mass society and "modernity"', in C. Benton et al., *Art Deco 1910–39* (exhib. cat., 2003), pp. 29–36.

Massey, A., *Hollywood beyond the Screen: design and material culture* (Oxford and New York, 2000).

Maxwell, A., *Colonial Photography and Exhibitions: representations of the 'native' and the making of European identities* (London and New York, 1999).

McClintock, A., *Imperial Leather: race, gender and sexuality in the colonial conquest* (New York, 1995).

McCracken, G., *Culture and Consumption: new approaches to the symbolic character of consumer goods and activities* (Bloomington and Indianapolis, 1990).

Metcalf, T.R., *An Imperial Vision: Indian architecture and Britain's Raj* (London and Berkeley, 1989).

Metcalf, T.R., *Ideologies of the Raj* (Cambridge, 1995).

Michell, G., *The Islamic Heritage of Bengal* (Paris, 1984).

Miller, D., *Material Culture and Mass Consumption* (1987).

Miller, D. (ed.), *Home Possessions* (2000).

Mills, S., 'Gender and colonial space', *Gender, Place and Culture*, vol. 3 (1996), pp. 125–47.

Misra, B.B., *The Indian Middle Class: their growth in modern times* (London, New York and Bombay, 1961).

Morgan, H., 'Danby, Francis', *Grove Dictionary of Art Online* (Oxford University Press) www.groveart.com (accessed 18 April 2006).

Morris, J., *Stones of Empire: the buildings of the Raj* (Oxford, 1983, reprinted 2005).

Morrison, K.A., *English Shops and Shopping: an architectural history* (New Haven and London, reprinted 2003).

Mudiyanse, N., 'Art and architecture of the Kandy period (16th–18th centuries)', *Spolia Zeylanica*, vol. 35, no. 1/2 (1980), pp. 369–407.

Muthiah, S., 'From sandy strip to metropolis', in K. Kalpana and F. Schiffer (eds), *Madras: the architectural heritage* (Chennai, 2003), pp. 19–24.

Neild, S.M., 'Colonial urbanism: the development of Madras city in the eighteenth and nineteenth centuries', *Modern Asian Studies*, vol. 13, no. 2 (1979), pp. 217–46.

Neild-Basu, S., 'The Dubashes of Madras', *Modern Asian Studies*, vol. 18, no. 1 (1984), pp. 1–31.

Nilsson, S., *European Architecture in India, 1750–1850* (1968).

Nora, P., 'Between memory and history: les lieux de mémoire', *Representations*, vol. 26 (Spring 1989), pp. 7–25.

Orlin, L., 'Fictions of the early modern English probate inventory', in H.S. Turner (ed.), *The Culture of Capital: property, cities and knowledge in early modern England* (New York and London, 2002), pp. 51–83.

O'Shea, W.T., *The Social History of Lighting* (1958).

O'Sullivan, T., J. Hartley, D. Saunders, et al., *Key Concepts in Communication and Cultural Studies* (London and New York, 1994).

Pal, P. (ed.), *Bombay to Mumbai: changing perspectives* (Mumbai, 1997).

Pearce, S., *Museums, Objects and Collections* (Leicester and London, 1992).

Pearce, S., *On Collecting* (1999).

Peebles, P., *Social Change in Nineteenth Century Ceylon* (Colombo, 1995).

Pelizzari, M.A. (ed.), *Traces of India: photography, architecture and the politics of representation, 1850–1900* (New Haven, 2003).

Pinney, C., *Camera Indica: the social life of Indian photographs* (1997).

Ponsonby, M., 'Ideals, reality and meaning: homemaking in England in the first half of the nineteenth century', *Journal of Design History*, vol. 16, no. 3 (2003), pp. 201–14.

Postle, M., 'Cooper, Thomas Sidney', *Grove Dictionary of Art Online* (Oxford University Press) www.groveart.com (accessed 18 April 2006).

Pott, J., *Old Bungalows in Bangalore* (1977).

Prakash, G., 'Subaltern studies as postcolonial criticism', *American Historical Review*, vol. 99 (1994), pp. 1475–90.

Pramar, V.S., *A Social History of Indian Architecture* (New Delhi, 2005).

Prasad, S., 'A tale of two cities: house and town in India today', in G.H.R. Tillotson (ed.), *Paradigms of Indian Architecture: space and time in representation and design* (Richmond, 1998), pp. 176–98.

Pratt, M.L., *Imperial Eyes: studies in travel writing and imperialism* (1992).

Procida, M., *Married to the Empire: gender, politics and imperialism in India, 1883–1947* (Manchester and New York, 2002).

Raheem, I., 'Colombo', *Grove Dictionary of Art Online* (Oxford University Press) www.groveart.com (accessed 19 March 2005).

Raheem, I. and P. Colin Thomé, *Images of British Ceylon: nineteenth century photography of Sri Lanka* (Singapore, 2000).

Rappaport, E.D., *Shopping for Pleasure: women and the making of London's West End* (Princeton and Oxford, 2001).

Regeneration: a reappraisal of photography in Ceylon, 1850–1900 (exhib. cat., 2000).

Riggins, S.H., 'Fieldwork in the living room', in S.H. Riggins (ed.), *The Socialness of Things* (New York, 1994), pp. 101–48.

Roberts, M., *Caste Conflict and Elite Formation: the rise of the Karava elite in Sri Lanka, 1500–1951* (Cambridge, 1982 and reprinted New Delhi, 1995).

Roberts, M., I. Raheem and P. Colin Thomé, *People Inbetween: the Burghers and the middle class in the transformations within Sri Lanka, 1790s–1960s* (Ratmalana, 1989).

Rose, G., *Visual Methodologies: an introduction to the interpretation of visual materials* (London, Thousand Oaks and New Delhi, 2005).

Ross, R., *Status and Respectability in the Cape Colony, 1750–1870* (Cambridge, 1999).

Ryan, D., *The Ideal Home through the Twentieth Century* (1997).

Said, E., *Orientalism: western conceptions of the Orient* (1978).

Said, E., *Culture and Imperialism* (1993).

Saunders, N., 'You are what you own and inhabit', *Times Higher Education Supplement*, no. 3 (November 2000), p. 34.

Scott, P., *The Jewel in the Crown* (1973, reprinted 1983).

Senftleben, W., 'Some aspects of the Indian hill stations: a contribution towards a geography of tourist traffic', *Philippine Geographical Journal*, vol. 17, no. 1 (January–March, 1973), pp. 21–9.

Shah, A.M., *The Household Dimension of the Family in India* (1974).

A Shifting Focus: photography in India, 1850–1900 (exhib. cat., 1995).

Sinha, M., *Colonial Masculinity: the 'manly Englishman' and the 'effeminate Bengali' in the late nineteenth century* (Manchester, 1995).

Sinha, M., 'Britishness, clubbability and the colonial public sphere', in T. Ballantyne and A. Burton (eds), *Bodies in Contact: re-thinking colonial encounters in world history* (Durham and London, 2005), pp. 183–200.

Smith, J., *Osler's Crystal for Royalty and Rajahs* (London, 1991).

Spear, T.G.P., *The Nabobs: a study of the social life of the English in 18th century India* (1932, revised 1963).

Srivathsan, A., 'City and public life: history of public spaces in Chennai', in K. Kalpana and F. Schiffer (eds), *Madras: the architectural heritage* (Chennai, 2003).

Staley, E., *Monkey Tops: old buildings in Bangalore cantonment* (Bangalore, 1981).

Stamp, G., 'British architecture in India, 1857–1947', *Journal of the Royal Society of Arts*, vol. 129 (May 1981), pp. 357–79.

Stein, B., *A History of India* (Oxford, 1998).

Stoler, A.L., 'Rethinking colonial categories: European communities and the boundaries of colonial rule', *Comparative Studies in Society and History*, vol. 31, no. 1 (1989), pp. 134–61.

Stoler, A.L., *Race and the Education of Desire: Foucault's 'History of Sexuality' and the colonial order of things* (Durham, N.C., 1995).

Stoler, A.L., 'Cultivating bourgeois bodies and racial selves', in C. Hall (ed.), *Cultures of Empire: colonizers in Britain and the empire in the nineteenth and twentieth centuries* (Manchester, 2000), pp. 87–119.

Strobel, M., *European Women and the Second British Empire* (Bloomington, IN, 1991).

Taylor, B.B., *Geoffrey Bawa* (New York, 1995).

Thomas, N., *Colonialism's Culture: anthropology, travel and government* (Cambridge, 1994).

Thornton, P., *Authentic Décor: the domestic interior, 1620–1920* (1984).

Tillotson, G.H.R., *The Rajput Palaces: the development of an architectural style* (New Haven and London, 1987).

Tillotson, G.H.R., *The Tradition of Indian Architecture: continuity, controversy and change since 1850* (New Haven and London, 1989).

Tillotson, G.H.R. (ed.), *Paradigms of Indian Architecture: space and time in representation and design* (Richmond, 1998).

Tindall, G., *City of Gold: the biography of Bombay* (1982).

Tosh, J., 'Imperial masculinity and the flight from domesticity in Britain 1880–1914', in T.P. Foley et al., *Gender and Colonialism* (Galway, 1996), pp. 72–85.

Tosh, J., *A Man's Place: masculinity and the middle class home in Victorian England* (New Haven and London, 1999).

Turner, H.S. (ed.), *The Culture of Capital: property, cities and knowledge in early modern England* (New York and London, 2002).

Veenendaal, J., *Furniture from Indonesia, Sri Lanka and India during the Dutch Period* (Delft, 1985).

Vickery, A., 'Golden age to separate spheres? A review of the categories and chronology of English women's history', *Historical Journal*, vol. 36, no. 2 (1993), pp. 383–414.

Vickery, A., *The Gentleman's Daughter: women's lives in Georgian England* (New Haven and London, 1998).

Vidler, A., *The Architectural Uncanny: essays in the modern unhomely* (Cambridge, MA, 1992).

Ward, G.W.R. (ed.), *Perspectives on American Furniture* (New York, 1988).

Weatherill, L., *Consumer Behaviour and Material Culture in Britain, 1660–1760* (1996).

Webster, J., 'Resisting traditions: ceramics, identity and consumer choice in the Outer Hebrides from 1800 to the present', *International Journal of Historical Archaeology*, vol. 3, no. 1 (1999), pp. 53–73.

Wheeler, K., 'Interior decoration at the Cape, 1815–1835', *Bulletin of the South African Cultural Museum*, vol. 6 (1985), pp. 5–15.

Wilk, C., 'The healthy body culture', in C. Wilk (ed.), *Modernism: designing a new world,*

1914–39 (exhib. cat., 2006).

Williams, J., *Cricket and Race* (Oxford and New York, 2001).

Woodward, C., 'From multi-purpose parlour to drawing room: the development of the principal *voorkamer* in the fashionable Cape house, 1670–1820', *Bulletin of the South African Cultural Museum*, vol. 4 (1983), pp. 5–19.

Films and television programmes

Ivory, J. and I. Merchant, *Heat and Dust* (1982).

Morahan, C. and J. O'Brien, *The Jewel in the Crown* (1984).

Unpublished dissertations

Poulson, M., 'The Glass Furniture of F. & C. Osler: an investigation of the firm's international marketing and consumption of its products within the Indian Subcontinent, *c.* 1875–1900', MA dissertation, Southampton Institute, 2003.

Index

Note: 'n' after a page number indicates the number of a note on that page.
Numbers in italics refer to illustrations